# ALTERNATIVE
# TO ARMAGEDDON

"Marshal Tran Hung Dao, the Vietnamese general who defeated the Mongols almost seven hundred years ago, described his successful strategy: 'The enemy must fight his battles far from home for a long time. . . . We must weaken him by drawing him into protected campaigns. Once his initial dash is broken, it will be easier to destroy him. . . . When the enemy is away from home for a long time and produces no victories and families learn of their dead, then the enemy population at home becomes dissatisfied and considers it a Mandate from Heaven that the armies be recalled. Time is always in our favor. Our climate, mountains, and jungles discourage the enemy; but for us they offer both sanctuary and a place from which to attack.' "

# ALTERNATIVE TO ARMAGEDDON,

The Peace Potential of Lightning War

COLONEL WESLEY W. YALE,
*U.S. Army (Ret.)*

GENERAL I. D. WHITE
*U.S. Army (Ret.)*

GENERAL HASSO E. VON MANTEUFFEL
*German Army (Ret.)*

RUTGERS UNIVERSITY PRESS
New Brunswick, New Jersey

# Contents

# Foreword

It is curious that in all military history, and in fact all literary history, so few books have attempted to cover the command methods used by famous captains. Particularly, there is a void, with the exception of the works of Liddell Hart, where the practitioners of lightning war (now known as blitzkrieg) are concerned.

The senior tactical level, that is, the level of the division and the corps, marks the point where campaigns are won or lost. Napoleon once said, in effect, that God was on the side of the best battalion. Today, in an era when electronic control and close integration of sophisticated weapons are vital, the expression may be more suited to the division.

Interest in command methods of blitzkrieg should no longer be confined to the military. War, great or small, is a matter of direct concern to all citizens of the Free World. And although any war is to be deplored, the realities of the world are such that too often not only the possibility but the actuality of war must be faced. Indeed, the less clearly we face and prepare for the possibility, the more probably we will have to face the actuality.

Regarding the conduct of military operations, the past quarter of a century has seen the evolution of a widespread misconception that there is only one military alternative to nuclear holocaust. That alternative is held to be a campaign in which military objectives and the methods of seeking them are sharply restricted and the military forces are politically shackled. In application, this approach has been marked by steady and protracted attrition, to no end except qualified success at best—paid for in wasted blood and treasure. It has forced us to fight on the enemy's terms, not ours; it has represented ineffective and inefficient use of our capabilities; and in the poverty of its results compared with the cost, it has degraded our world stature, encouraged our antagonists and disheartened our people.

The fact remains that we must be able to deal successfully with the military challenges confronting us. Clearly a requirement exists for an acceptable means of meeting and overcoming these challenges—a means lying between the two extremes of the devastation of nuclear war and the sterility of excessively limited and restricted operations. As we have seen in the great decisive, rapid, and cheap victories of the Israeli against the Arab States, lightning war fits this requirement. It is "limited" because it is quickly finished. It does not surrender the initiative to the enemy as does a war of gradualism or attrition. In addition, lightning war requires the vital fundamentals of forces maintained in a high state of readiness, superbly trained and equipped with the very best modern weapons and equipment to insure the high degree of command and control and shock action so essential to the accomplishment of decisive results. But it demands a degree of mobility and a degree of command excellence not ordinarily encountered. This is the type of warfare that best fits the Free World temperament and best utilizes a generation of soldiers tempered in battle in Korea and Southeast Asia, possibly the best in history.

It would be difficult to find three authors more qualified to discuss the history and methods of lightning war. All have been intimately associated with its modern development and its practice. All have been identified with military research through the years since leaving the active services and have thus kept fully abreast of projected concepts.

Isaac D. White has had a long career in Cavalry and Armor, serving as a commander in every echelon, through his final post as Commander-in-Chief, U.S. Army Forces, Pacific. In a moving eulogy at the time of his retirement, ARMOR magazine referred to him as "Mr. Armor." He participated in eight major campaigns with the famous 2d Armored (Hell on Wheels) Division, serving in every grade from major to major general and succeeding to its command at the close of the great Bulge action. He then successively commanded the Cavalry School, the crack U.S. Constabulary in Europe and the Armored Center at Fort Knox. During hostilities in Korea General White commanded the X Corps and was commended by President Rhee for his brilliant coordination of Eighth Army and Republic of Korea forces, where a disorderly retreat was forced on the enemy.

After Korea, General White served as Fourth Army commander and as Commander, Army Forces in the Far East and the Eighth Army, finally heading all Army elements in the Pacific, as related.

General I. D. White is an outstanding mobile leader, a brilliant tactician of tank warfare and a commander invariably beloved of his troops. A most unusual combination. But, even more, his ability as a soldier-statesman has earned him the respect of political leaders in both Europe and Asia.

Hasso von Manteuffel, as well as General White, unquestionably deserves to be included as one of the "masters" of the blitz who are discussed in the text. Von Manteuffel began his career in the Cavalry, but fought with dismounted troops in the great Somme battle of 1916, where he was severely wounded. In the years between the wars, he continued his association with mobile arms and transferred to tanks in 1937 when he became identified with the Supreme Command-Inspection element of the Ober-Kommando Wehrmacht (OKW) in Berlin.

With the outbreak of World War II, von Manteuffel successively commanded a battalion, regiment and brigade in the 7th Armored Division in Russia, where he led the assault over the Volga-Moscow Canal within 40 kilometers of Moscow. He was then shifted to Africa and given command of the "Division von Manteuffel" in Tunisia in 1942–43. In the fall of 1943 he was returned to Russia where he assumed command of his old 7th Armored Division. After a brief tour in command of the Panzer-Grenadier Division Gross-Deutschland he was moved to the western front in time to lead the Fifth Panzer Army in the great Ardennes offensive which came so close to success.

General von Manteuffel is a true disciple of the great Guderian and undoubtedly ranks with Rommel as a Panzer-leader. His is a quiet and unassuming character, far from the image of the Prussian militarist that exists in the Anglo-Saxon mind. He is a "general's general." As a wearer of the Iron Cross, with oak leaves, swords and diamonds, and rated as the "twenty-fourth soldier of the Wehrmacht," his qualifications to contribute to a book on mobile war are beyond question.

General von Manteuffel served postwar Germany as a member of the Deutscher Bundestag from 1953 to 1957 and now lives quietly in Diessen am Ammersee at the foot of the Bavarian Alps.

Wesley W. Yale, while not attaining the rank of his distinguished colleagues, nevertheless served with great distinction as a cavalryman and tank commander. He assisted in writing much of the cavalry doctrine and his was the leading command of Patton's Third Army from the Bulge to the end of combat at Linz, Austria, in World War II. Of him one of his commanders wrote:

". . . he was given the troops and responsibilities of a general officer during the entire period of combat—he was invariably entrusted with the major effort of the Division and displayed outstanding skill in combining air and artillery action with that of armored elements— his combat leadership was the most adept, clever, aggressive and productive of rapid and successful results I ever witnessed in any of the armored Divisions I served with. . . ."

Yale followed his active service with over ten years in military operations research, becoming senior analyst with one of the major research organizations of the country. His research work has continued to date and has involved participation in or leadership of projects devoted to command and control of all echelons from the small unit to the global. He is considered an expert on nuclear strike control, particularly in the NATO environment. He assisted the German Army in the establishment of a research center and has pioneered in studies of Middle East air defense.

The combination of these three authors brings an array of talent before the public which is unique to military literature. Theirs is a knowledge of tactics, strategy, techniques, weapons, and vehicles that extends from the "dogface" through the "top brass" and into the area of the statesman. Their contribution to thinking along the lines of mobile, decisive and potentially nuclear warfare comes at a time when the nation badly needs a respite from seemingly unending conflicts of attrition.

L. L. LEMNITZER
*General, U.S. Army (Ret.)*

# Preface

Where two or more individuals are engaged in a joint enterprise, it is a general custom, one not confined to the military, for the junior member to write up the proceedings. Hence, it is my lot to explain the motivation for, and the development of a book which, it is reasonable to say, is unusual in military and political terms.

General White and I, friends of nearly fifty years' standing, spent most of our active careers in positions relating either to tactical command or to combat training and its supervision. Retirement was followed by several years in the so-called military-industrial complex where, free of military responsibilities, we had an unusual opportunity to further our special interest in command problems, through the analysis of tactical and strategic communication systems, nuclear strike control operations in the United States and in Europe, large- and small-scale maneuvers and air-defense problems of the Strike Command in the Middle East. While we may have viewed the military-industrial complex with mixed emotions, the association in some ways provided the most interesting phase of our respective careers.

By 1966 we had begun to realize that publicized military thought was drifting away from the concepts of mobility that had not only won World War II, but had proved decisive in every conflict in which they had been applied. Looking back, it seemed over the years that the military school system, splendid as it was, had perhaps necessarily emphasized staff practices at the expense of command techniques, or methodology. And the training and maneuver restrictions attending military life in crowded civilian environments were making it increasingly difficult to develop young leaders through realistic and challenging experience.

Certain senior officers in the Pentagon shared our concern that mobile war concepts were going down the drain at a time when the possibility of a major confrontation between powers would demand their use. In consequence, in 1966, we found ourselves conducting a survey of command methods in the senior echelons of the Seventh Army in Europe. Some months prior, through another agency, the opportunity had been offered of conferring on similar subjects with the major headquarters of the Bundeswehr.

This proved a refreshing experience in the light of the high quality of personnel exercising command and staff duties. Everywhere, it seemed, there was support for concepts of high mobility in spite of the fact that the same old inhibitions to leadership development remained. The senior grades, all veterans of World War II combat, were disappearing, while just about everyone was fully occupied with the rendition of bale upon bale of the periodic reports required by Washington and Bonn.

Winding up the survey, we had arranged to meet General von Manteuffel in Garmisch-Partenkirchen, just as the first snows were beckoning skiers up the road from München. As a matter of interest we wanted to exchange views on the Battle of the Bulge in which we had all participated. Professionally, we wanted to determine whether command and control problems of the mobile arms were purely American, or whether they were more than national in scope.

General von Manteuffel, in our view, had an unusually wide reputation as a blitz commander, with a background fully as impressive as that of Marshal Rommel; he had grown up with Guderian, had kept abreast of recent developments and had served in the postwar Bundestag.

The visit proved to be the highlight of the European trip. General von Manteuffel confirmed our impression that mobile war problems were common to both Europe and America. We further agreed that the subject of command methodology, and, in fact, a realistic history of lightning war, had never been adequately covered in literature, in spite of the fact that the *principles* by which new weapons are applied do not change with the years.

Yet the idea of doing a book to fill these needs did not occur until later, after a lively exchange of correspondence took place.

By then the American involvement in Southeast Asia, a true war of attrition, was dragging on inconclusively. Both Americans and Europeans were becoming alienated more because of the indecisive nature of the conflict and the failure to apply, at top level, the lessons of history, than because of the obscure objectives.

Then in 1967 the stunning sweep of the Israeli air and armor through the Sinai showed that the blitz was not dead, at least among those who had profited by experience and training.

In 1967, also, Liddell Hart repeated in his book, *Strategy,* his previously expressed views that the great nuclear "deterrent" had failed to accomplish its purpose and was unlikely to be effective in the future because of the evident unwillingness of the United States to invoke the threat. We had discussed this aspect of geopolitics at Garmisch and had agreed that use of a nuclear threat, especially if it were considered an empty one by adversaries, was unsuitable to the Western character. An alternative of some sort was manifestly urgently needed; training men to prowl around the jungles of far-off lands, playing the enemy's game, was certainly not the answer.

Inasmuch as the Israeli had for over twenty years, except for a matter of days, deterred an overwhelmingly superior Arab coalition solely by the possession of a blitz-oriented and highly trained corps of tactical commanders, the answer seemed obvious.

Western nations need to have the capability of responding immediately and decisively to any act of foreign aggression that can be shown *to the satisfaction of the peoples and their elected representatives* as being critical to the interests of freedom and the national economy. A common policy of launching a lightning war by air and ground mobility to protect those interests should prove reassuring to a public weary of indecisive, attritive, protracted, and expensive wars.

It is recognized that lightning war requires the aforesaid high quality of leadership at all levels. Fortunately, this kind of leadership is inspiring to those serving within the military structure, is responsive to civilian controls, and can be applied to conflicts where high mobility may not always be practicable. At the moment, development of required leadership standards is subject to some very serious obstacles.

Thus the thinking that might have led to a book on the history and methodology of lightning war was altered. Instead it was decided to undertake a book that would bring out not only those aspects but would point to the fact that a blitz-type military posture for Western nations is an essential in the modern world. The chapters that follow elaborate on this theme and, in a general way, suggest means of overcoming the obstacles.

There is nothing new in blitz methodology; in fact, it is its very sameness over the centuries that makes it an interesting subject. But we may take comfort from Liddell Hart's *Strategy,* where he says,—

Looking back on the steps by which fresh ideas gained acceptance, it can be seen that the process was eased when they could be presented not as something radically new, but as the revival *in modern terms* of a time-honored principle or practice that had been forgotten.

This book has other motives, to be sure. A voice is raised in defense of the professional military; there is a view-with-alarm at the military-industrial complex, a phrase with misdirected emphasis; the reader is invited to share the terrible impact of nuclear war on the battlefield commander. All these are important, but of course are only incidental to the main theme of developing a strategic deterrent through blitz-oriented field commanders, leading blitz-adept forces.

W. W. Y.

# Acknowledgments

The authors are deeply indebted to Dr. Robin Higham, Professor of History at Kansas State University and noted author and editor of *Military Affairs,* for detailed advice on format and content. There are others, too, including but not confined to:

Creighton W. Abrams, General, U.S. Army
Dr. R. A. Baker, former Senior Staff Scientist, the Armor School
Charles H. Bonesteel III, General, U.S. Army (Ret.)
Command and General Staff College, U.S. Army
Alfred Gause, Lt. General, German Army (Ret.)
S. L. A. Marshall, Brig. General, U.S.A.R. (Ret.)
Luther Nichols, Doubleday and Company, San Francisco
James Root, Colonel, U.S. Army
Harold Silverstein, Office, Chief, Communications-Electronics, U.S. Army
Hans Speidel, General, German Army (Ret.)
Siegfried Westphal, General, German Army (Ret.)
Avraham Yoffe, Major General, Israeli Army (Ret.)

# ALTERNATIVE
# TO ARMAGEDDON

# 1  A New Deterrent

"The Deterrent is everything. We cannot wait until the shooting starts to determine what we must do."—Dean Rusk, former Secretary of State, on ABC "Issues and Answers," July 27, 1969

In the closing months of 1969 discerning observers saw the first political ripples from the United States' disengagement in Vietnam. West Germany was making unprecedented overtures to East Germany and the USSR; the Philippine contingent in Southeast Asia was withdrawn in spite of the millions alleged to have been spent on subsidizing it; Wheelus Air Force base on the Mediterranean was about to be evacuated; Turkey was restless, and Japan sought new guarantees for Okinawa. In short, geopolitical realignments were being explored.

In the *U.S. News and World Report* of September 13, 1965, President Eisenhower is reported to have said in 1963, "If the United States sent the flag and its own military establishment into the Indo-China war, then the prestige of the U.S. would be engaged to the point where we would want to have a success. We could not afford to engage its prestige and suffer a defeat which would have worldwide repercussions."

Time was to show whether gradual disengagement would improve on the policy of gradual escalation begun in 1961.

In 1953, according to the same issue of *U.S. News and World Report,* Eisenhower had sent word to Peiping through India's Prime Minister that unless the Korean truce talks showed satisfactory progress, the U.S. intended to "move decisively without

3

inhibition in our use of weapons, and would no longer be responsible for confining hostilities to the Korean Peninsula."

This was the last time that nuclear arms, following the policy of massive retaliation, were invoked as a credible threat. "Incidents" occurred all over the world—Lebanon, Quemoy-Matsu, Central Africa and Dominica, with the United States responding in varying military and political degrees. The western use of the nuclear deterrent has apparently lost its credibility. Many major American politicians have loudly proclaimed that the threat of nuclear retaliation, for an act not in itself related to nuclear arms, will never be resorted to. It is entirely possible that the reluctance of the United States to employ full military power in Southeast Asia is due wholly or in part to the credibility of the Soviet nuclear threat, either actual or implied.

If the nuclear deterrent is not to be used, then a credible and effective deterrent must replace it, specifically an alternative to Armageddon. Logically, the most practical deterrent to foreign aggressive probes aimed at testing the will of western powers to defend either homeland, or global points demonstrably affecting national interests, is a capability to wage immediate, decisive and highly mobile, or "lightning" warfare. Inherent in this capability is the basic ingredient of mobile war—a trained corps of tactical leaders at all levels, adept in the techniques of this sort of combat.

Since the foregoing premise implies a redirection of the objectives of national military policies, there are several factors which affect and are affected by it, quite aside from that of the unsuitability of the nuclear deterrent. These factors warrant a brief analysis to establish the validity of the premise and include:

(1) The current public attitude of antimilitarism.
(2) The difficulty of assuring public assessment of the gravity of the composite threat to national security.
(3) The successful application of the principles of the premise by the Israeli.

In the present antimilitary mood prevalent in the western world, it is questionable whether any announced military policy would find immediate favor, much less one pointing the central effort to the conduct of a blitz, with all its World War II aggressive connotations.

But what really is blitzkrieg? The dictionary defines it as "a conflict conducted with lightning speed and force . . . a violent surprise offensive by massed air and ground forces in close coordination, and designed to achieve victory in a minimum of time."

Although the word "offensive" is used, it does not necessarily follow that the action must be politically aggressive in character. In fact, the true meaning is summed up in President Kennedy's budget message to Congress in 1961, when he said, "We shall never threaten, provoke or initiate aggression, but if aggression comes our response will be swift and effective."

Two things are important to note. First, the blitz is historically far older than Hitler's decimation of the Polish armies in 1939. Second, the blitz is really limited in scope. While it may have strategic aspects, it is primarily a tactical battle or series of related battles, fought at the level of the division or the corps (15,000–60,000 men), and having characteristics that might add up to a "lightning war." This follows the Clausewitz notion that "we have only one means in war, the battle."

Advocacy of a lightning-war capability does not mean that a more static style of combat might not be forced upon a government by a given set of circumstances. It does imply that a capability to wage highly mobile war will increase the capability to undertake other forms of combat.

It would be foolish to deny that a war phobia exists among the nations of the West, and equally foolish to believe that this phobia extends to nations under Russian and Chinese influence. Public disaffection has followed naturally in the wake of many years of frustrating conflicts in which grass roots support was whipped up through highlighting incidents like the sinking of the *Lusitania* or the bombing of Pearl Harbor. But the world has not been made safe for democracy nor was World War II the war to end wars.

It is significant that in pursuing the Southeast Asian adventure, the United States government failed to capitalize on incidents like the Tonkin Gulf or the *Pueblo* to generate voter support of its policies. In the early stages of the Vietnam conflict, polls showed adequate home support. It is therefore reasonable to assume that the subsequent loss of support stemmed from public exasperation with an indecisive, protracted, and costly operation, basically politically oriented. It also seems reasonable that national policies aimed at blitz objectives in the event of emergencies, promising rapid success at the outset, would overcome most, if not all, of the antimilitarism of thoughtful people. Provided grave interests were shown to be at stake, and provided that military action was retaliatory rather than provocative, such policies would promise the public backing so essential for field operations.

Unfortunately, the basis of public support is in large degree dependent upon an appreciation of geopolitical factors and of the present-day composite threat to national security. An ignorance of geopolitical implications surrenders the initiative to the forces of aggression, who rest their constant tests of western will on the principles of geopolitics. They are keenly aware of the influence of internal and geographic factors, both physical and economic. They weigh the international distribution of social groups, while they exploit the existence of hunger and poverty. They improve on the one-time world domination concepts of Britannia by substituting the entire Mediterranean for Gibraltar, and all of Southeast Asia for Singapore. Potential trouble spots are carefully cultivated—Korea and the Middle East, for example—where Russia urged on Britain the creation of the State of Israel, only to arm the enemies of the new state after it came into being. The Berlin corridor can be heated up at any time. Even the *Pueblo* incident was contrived, according to the testimony of a defecting Soviet general.

Disposition to ignore or dismiss the very real threats to the existence of the free world contributes indirectly to antiwar sentiment and is equally inhibiting to the adoption of reasonable national defense measures. There are frequent press references to different aspects of the threat, some nuclear and some conventional, but there is little documentation for public consumption that synthesizes the subject into its proper dimension as a cause for real alarm. The emotional refuse to acknowledge it, and the practical are termed warmongers.

One cannot ignore the expansion of their spheres of influence

made by Chinese and Russian interests. There is the development
by the Chinese of nuclear weapons in the megaton range, the
enormous Soviet submarine fleet, many times the size of Hitler's,
its incursion into the Mediterranean, and the assurance by every
Soviet head of state in the last fifty years that the USSR aims at
world domination. General Lyman Lemnitzer, retiring Supreme
Allied Commander, Europe (SACEUR), whose views reflected those
of NATO has stated in an interview in *U.S. News and World Report*
on May 12, 1969, that the threat is greater today than at any time
in the past 20 years because of the steady buildup of the Soviet
military potential.

Soviet military philosophy has been expressed authoritatively
by the Communist Party writer, L. P. Prusanov, in an article titled
"Increased Organization and Directive Influence of the Party in
the Armed Forces" which appeared in *Problems of the History of
the Communist Party*, published in Moscow in 1965. Because
Prusanov wrote the official party line, his message was reprinted
by the respected American Security Council in a study undertaken
for the House Armed Services Committee (*The Changing Strategic
Military Balance, USA vs USSR*):

The essence of Soviet military doctrine is this, if a future war is
unleashed by the imperialists, then it will be a decisive collision between two social orders and nuclear rockets will inevitably be used.
All this presupposes an extremely dynamic and violent character of the
conflict—high maneuverability of combat operations, the absence of
continuous fronts and well marked boundaries between front and rear,
the appearance of possibilities for striking sudden blows of great force,
both against the troops and the homelands of the warring nations. In
connection with this, great attention is devoted to the initial period
of the war.

Prusanov's description of the environment of any major future
confrontation is generally agreed with by the NATO professional
military. But the stress on the inevitability of nuclear release is
Prusanov's and clearly indicates a Soviet resolution to use atomics
when they consider it necessary.

In sum, all aspects of the threat are real and are only too evident
in all corners of the globe. The threat warns the West to be on

guard to prevent probings of the will to resist in remote yet critical areas where genuine western interests are affected, to fend off more significant attempts to encroach on Allied territory and, finally, to insure that the homeland is safe in a era when strategic deployments by air, under cover of nuclear rockets, or the threat thereof, are becoming daily more feasible.

This triple threat demands a viable deterrent, but one preferably short of nuclear war. Probings, the Prusanov environment, and the speed of present day political developments suggest likewise that the deterrent should be a known and effective capability to wage immediate retaliation aimed at cutting off the threat before it escalates into a major conflict, in other words, a blitz capability.

It is perhaps unjust to reproach the public for failure to appreciate geopolitical factors and the composite threat when eyes and ears are daily assailed by outpourings from the news media aimed at appeasement. As Allen Drury wrote in *Capable of Honor:* The gospel comes down to the basic arguments that have been offered ever since the end of the second World War, endlessly repeated through every means of communication:

America is declining in influence and therefore is unable to meet her problems with firmness and integrity.

Communism is gaining in strength and therefore had best be accommodated, because its advances aren't really very important anyway, and it might be dangerous to try to stop them. . . .

And a blind fear of atomic war, offered as the final, obliterating answer to all who dare to suggest that if America will only stand for the great principles upon which she was founded, she can achieve . . . an honorable and lasting peace.

All this alienation of the public from the legitimate needs of national defense is unquestionably a formidable obstacle to the creation of a viable and acceptable deterrent. But there is another factor as well, one even affecting the professional military. This is the inclination to regard guerrilla warfare as the wave of the future in accordance with the writings of Che Guevara and Chairman Mao, based on several years of preoccupation with unconventional warfare in Asia. Many military professionals have subscribed to the doctrine without considering that the prosecution of land wars, far from home, against populations of millions, is precisely the kind of conflict that the nation as a whole must and wishes to avoid. Conversely, the guerrilla wars of liberation invariably serve the Kremlin without the commitment of a single Russian soldier.

Whether a redirection of effort is inhibited by present commitments to jungle warfare, by the public antiwar sentiment, or by the failure to appreciate the nature of the threats facing the free world is immaterial. It is certain that little can be accomplished by hewing to the same line of attritive wars and that almost any redirection would be beneficial. But the entire concept of developing a blitz capability as a deterrent is aptly illustrated by the military policy of the State of Israel, and its implementation in the 1956 and 1967 campaign against the Arab nations.

Israel early chose the adoption of a blitz capability as a primary objective of national defense planning. And how impressive the results in comparison with the drawn out, inconclusive, and staggeringly costly American adventures in Korea and Vietnam!

In the years following the formation of Israel, the threat was evident almost daily, what with active raids by guerrilla bands, incidents, and published diatribes against the nation by various Arab chiefs. The effect was to solidify the national will behind a national defense program—the first step. The nearness of the Arab states was naturally a major factor in developing this national will; other contributing influences were the common religious attitude and its opposition to Islam, and the determination of arriving immigrants to achieve success and stability in the new land.

Both planning and execution were facilitated by the ready availability of World War II surplus arms and equipment stocks, and by the eagerness of British, French, and American arms agencies to sell newly developed weapons systems.

To developing the national will and providing the necessary arms was added a third element, the training of the military forces and especially the training of tactical leaders. Israel dipped into its treasure trove of officers who had demonstrated their aptitudes in the mobile wars of the western deserts. Results show plainly that this was the most rewarding and, therefore, the most important step of all. Finally, the area of expected operations lent itself admirably to this form of conflict, in the air and on the ground. While such points may appear obvious, the fact that a nation formed in the democratic tradition was able to implement them is historically unusual.

In any event, the smashing victories that ensued astonished the world and to some extent the Israeli themselves. If the critics and analysts had known the true conditions within the respective armed forces, the defeat of a theoretically superior Arab enemy should have been expected. The Israeli tactical commanders understood lightning-war techniques and, most important, could apply them, but the Arabs were bound up in command doctrines which were the very antithesis of the blitz.

The Negev wars should not be dismissed as runaways against an incredibly inept enemy. When lightning-war methods are properly applied, the victims always look inept. But the successes were impressive, even when viewed solely as triumphs over the open but forbidding terrain of the Sinai.

Between 1948 and 1969 in an atmosphere of almost constant tension and threats, coupled with frequent transfers of war matériel from Soviet sources to the Arab world there were only two weeks of actual hostilities. Yet Israel's Prime Minister has indicated that the nation can still deter its enemies without assistance or interference from outside agencies, other than the purchase of modern arms. Which of the western powers can say the same?

An analogy between the adoption of a lightning-war capability by Israel and the desirability of duplicating it in western nations may seem far-fetched in view of the disparity in national size and responsibilities. However, it is not the objective itself that is important but the principles by which it is attained. If war must be considered at all, a capacity to wage lightning war against a recognized threat is a part of the most appropriate defense for western nations. To a public tired of inconclusive wars of attrition it holds the promise of sudden though comparatively limited force in crisis situations, the resolution of which is demonstrably in the national interest, it offers rapid and decisive results, and it avoids nuclear confrontation. Its relevance to major confrontations in the environment forecast by Comrade Prusanov should give the concept additional broad acceptance. And, as demonstrated by the success of both motor and air mobility in some of the critical actions in Southeast Asia, lightning war may be the most suitable tactic for future jungle fighting, should such an unfortunate commitment again be made.

In the Israeli formula of the shaping of public opinion, the procurement of weapons, and the development of leaders only the last factor is subject to military control. Public opinion, as already pointed out, is a matter of press and government; weapons procurement is now the subject of innumerable programs, though the weaponry for blitzkrieg is the least complicated and least expensive in the massive defense inventory. There remains the greatest contribution that can be made by the professional military, the development of the corps of tactical commanders, adept in the art of controlling mobile troops.

There are too many thoughtful analysts of the international scene who feel that World War III is already well advanced. A known capability for settling budding conflicts or crises in a matter of days cannot fail to halt further deterioration, giving pause to potential aggressors and reassurance to a worried public.

The requirements for blitz leadership are not easy to explain. Many will insist that both the leaders and the programs for developing them already exist. This is true in part, made so by the incomparable professional school systems of the U.S. military services. But a new kind of leader is needed to cope with new kinds of problems. He is describable only by examining the long history of lightning-war battles, by relating the stories of the colorful commanders who have all too infrequently appeared to conduct lightning-war campaigns, and by forecasting the leadership requirements of the air and nuclear ages.

# 2 Characteristics, Research Objectives

The rather loose definition of lightning war reads, a war "conducted with lightning speed and force—a violent, surprise offensive by massed air and ground forces in close coordination—a conquest in a minimum of time." This is too inexact for strict analysis. If the development of the blitz had not been accompanied by popular and even professional misconception through the years, it would be simple enough to state briefly what seem to be its obvious principles, yet almost every famous exponent of the mobile art has had to overcome strenuous opposition. Within the last generation, such eminent analysts as J. F. C. Fuller, Guderian, Liddell Hart, and Chaffee were virtually ignored until their precepts proved correct in battle.

By its dictionary definition, lightning war is generally characterized by extreme violence in the application of mobility, firepower, and close control. While these elements apply to any military action, they must be emphasized if a lightning-war battle is to succeed.

Mobility is an example of a problem in semantics. It means many things to many men under a variety of circumstances. It does not imply a jump from an ox to an aircraft, but, for purposes of analysis, implies the speed of movement of platoons, companies, and larger tactical elements over the varying terrain of the battlefield. Thus, the motor and air-borne vehicles of today do not necessarily represent a speed change from two to 600 miles per hour but rather the speed with which a movement can be

12

controlled by a leader, limited by physical obstacles and vulnerability to enemy fire. Technology aims at freeing combat formations from such inhibitions to mobility by, for instance, the use of helicopters and air-cushion vehicles.

An example of mobility can be seen in the colorful spectacle of the American Plains Indian tribes, immortalized in the paintings of Remington, Russell, and Schreyvogel. The strong, lean faces of Crazy Horse and Gall of the Ogallala Sioux typify the leadership of what some have termed the greatest cavalry of all time. Yet the Indian was an individualist. He carried a rifle, but the rifle was for his personal use in face-to-face engagements. Rarely if ever did one group of Indians fire their weapons in support of their swift-mounted brothers. They indeed had mobility, but of the kind that demonstrates that mobility alone is not enough.

They had guns, but they did not have firepower, a most important blitz characteristic that grows more important as the years blend into the nuclear age. Firepower is more accurately termed "destructive force," since weapons other than projectiles may conceivably be used, or weapons activated by other than explosive force. Rommel, for example, said that victory goes to him who first plasters the enemy with fire—a principle that covers everything from a shower of arrows to artillery concentrations, biologicals, and nuclear rockets.

Close control over maneuver and weaponry by a single leader is a special mark of lightning war, with effectiveness generally dependent upon the tempo of the action. In modern times, increased mobility and firepower tend to complicate the control problem, a condition that may be offset by improved communications, staff assistance, and electronic data processing. The opposing nature of these factors makes up the heart of the tactical challenge to the future commander, who must contend as well with a mounting load of administrative and logistical worries.

And, indeed, the "single leader" aspect must be emphasized. Blitz battles of history have almost without exception been resolved by the brilliance of one man—a Gustavus Adolphus, a Napoleon, or a Rommel. Colorful and in many cases flamboyant, these men invariably moved analysts to comment that here was a new kind of warfare. One of the objectives of this book is to show that, on the contrary, each of these leaders moved in a similar pattern.

The basis of successful control lies in what may be called integration of effort, or the ability to coordinate weapons effects with the maneuver of assault troops. In this sense firepower serves as much for its suppressive effect (silencing the defenders' weapons) as it does for its lethality. The U.S. Artillery and Missiles School at Fort Sill, Oklahoma, has estimated that suppressive fire missions run as high as 70 percent of all those fired, though where nuclear weapons are used another figure is probably warranted.

A simple illustration of integration of effort is played out interminably in western films. The hero is shown moving around to the rear of the cabin while he is covered by the pistol fire of a deputy. His flushing out of the villains is indeed a simple task compared to the integration, by split-second timing, of the efforts of thousands of men and weapons, spread out over an area of many square miles. Napoleon referred to timing in his classic statement about defeating the Austrians because they did not know the value of two minutes; in the air age two minutes is a long time.

Integration of effort also includes the idea of mass (which may be applied either by fire effects or by assault troops, singly or in combination), a cardinal principle of war. The massing of force with violence today tends to emphasize destructive force rather than the casualty-courting shock assault of men or vehicles.

Certain other blitz qualities are worth noting, or recalling in brief:

(1) The blitz must be kept in mind as a battle, or a series of battles, rather than a campaign or an entire war.

(2) Study of Creasy-Mitchell's *Twenty Decisive Battles of the World* discloses that none were of the lightning-war type. "Decisive," in the Creasy sense apparently refers to political and long-term strategic effects rather than to tactical decisions.

(3) The scope of lightning-war battles with respect to the span of control of the commander, usually involves the modern division, consisting of some 16,000 men, or its "equivalent," since at that level control facilities are at their most effective. Equiv-

alence is necessary in considering the history of blitzkrieg, because disparities in the size of forces are more apparent than real. The tightly packed formations of the Napoleonic era, for example, enabled a single leader to control many times the number of men in the average divisional area today. Today's powerful weapons require wide dispersal and the men handling them cannot be so conveniently supervised. However, the selection of the division as an analytical tool is arbitrary. With modern electronic control devices, it is theoretically possible for a corps of two or three divisions to be directly controlled by its commander. Smaller units, too (as in the case of the Israeli), often manifest the degree of integration of arms ordinarily found in the division.

In discussing mobile integration of effort, it is tempting to include the many examples of the blitz in naval warfare. For speed in response, an incident in the Solomons campaign of 1943 reported in *U.S. Navy in World War II* comes to mind. In a melee with Japanese ships Commander Lampman's flag destroyer found itself in the line with a salvo from Captain Arleigh (31-Knot) Burke's fast-shooting division; over the TBS (Talk Between Ships) he shouted, ". . . hope you are not shooting at us!" Back came Burke's reply, "Sorry . . . excuse the next four salvos; they are already on their way!"

Or one may consider amphibious operations, handled through the elaborate communications and control facilities of Amphibious Control Vessels (ACVs) which offer almost ideal illustrations of coordination and timing of dissimilar forces.

Then there is Douglas MacArthur's great western Pacific campaign closing out the war in the Pacific or the Inchon landing of the Korean War (1950–1953). But it would only confuse a discussion of ground-air war and the problem of creating an army of blitz-trained leaders, to introduce examples of blitz amphibious or naval engagements, magnificent as they have been.

Lightning-war objectives ordinarily involve effecting a swift and locally powerful thrust through a suspected weak point in the enemy defenses to destroy control or logistical facilities in the rear. It is the tactic Liddell Hart calls the "indirect approach." Where this is done by maneuver, it sets the blitz apart as the most humane form of warfare; thousands may be cut off from further effective participation in the conflict, rather than swelling the casualty lists. Dayan's *Diary* states that "it was clear that we had no intent to destroy enemy forces (as is customary) . . . and it is better that as little blood be shed as possible. I therefore used the formula 'to confound the organization of the Egyptian forces and bring about their collapse.' In other words, we seized key positions and agencies which gave us control of the area."

Clausewitz expressed the same idea in another way: "The object of combat is not always the destruction of the enemy's forces. . . . The object can often be attained without combat taking place at all." And in Dayan's quote, the parenthetical "as is customary" points to a common and basic error of tactics, that of hitting the enemy just because he is there.

General George S. "Old Blood and Guts" Patton expressed the idea of integration of effort, with its corollary characteristics of mobility, firepower, and control, when he repeated most eloquently and pungently his doctrine, sometimes to the rawest recruit, "Grab him by the nose and kick him in the ass!"

The figurative grasp by the nose symbolizes the delivery of firepower to hold the enemy in place, while the swift kick to the posterior illustrates the maneuver to the seat of the hostile organizational structure (deep objective). Recruits, and indeed everyone else, never forgot the meat of "Georgie's" expressive principle.

Blitz characteristics are portrayed graphically in the accompanying sketch. It shows integration of effort as the central theme. A moment's reflection will demonstrate that most of the contributing elements are interdependent. That is, mobility is a function of firepower and both are functions of control.

The mobile, decisive battle is in many respects like the long-range scoring play in American football. On the gridiron, the far-flung forward pass for a score at a critical point in the game (the "bomb" in the sports writers' idiom) is always a marvel of exquisite timing, of placing violent force at key points, and of the thorough coordination of every player on the team. Football teams train long and carefully so that when the opportunity for the "bomb" comes, they are prepared to execute it successfully. They and their coaches are fortunate that it is the same personnel fighting "wars" over an extended series of gridiron battles, with

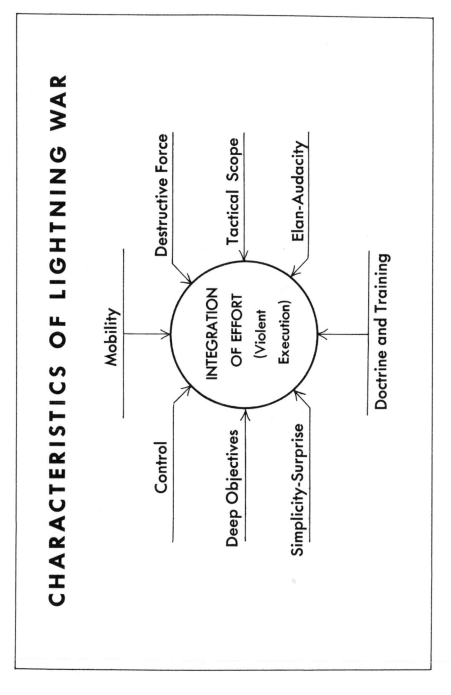

CHARACTERISTICS OF LIGHTNING WAR

the consequent steady improvement in team play. Military teams
enjoy no such advantage, but it is nonetheless logical that the
entire national military posture should aim at the capability of
capitalizing on opportune moments.

There is a disquieting contemporary disposition to downgrade
military historical research. The reasons given center on the idea
that today's total-destruction weapons and the marvels of electronics have created such a wholly different environment that com-
parisons of past and present are not possible. Or preoccupation
with guerrilla warfare as the wave of the future obscures all other
considerations.

One may hope that the tendency is not widespread. For those
who disparage study by overemphasizing field experience, there is
a pertinent story quoted by Field Marshal Montgomery of Alamein in his *History of Warfare,* attributed to Frederick the Great.
Frederick rebuked a young officer who derided book study, "I
have two mules with the army who have accompanied me on more
than 40 campaigns," he said, "and they are still mules."

Guerrilla warfare has its own history. The Che Guevara-Mao
concepts were practiced by American Colonial "irregulars" in
campaigns fought in the backwoods against British redcoats who
cried foul when fired upon from behind trees. The Peninsular
Campaigns (1808–1814) featured an effective use of Spanish guerrillas by Wellington which had a significant effect on Napoleon's
ultimate downfall by constantly threatening the French line of
communications. This kind of warfare supported Abd El Krim in
North Africa in 1924 and sustained Castro in Cuba (1956–1959),
giving Guevara his ideas.

The guerrilla types have recognized the value of terrain, of
popular local support, either genuine or induced by terrorism,
and of time. The guerrilla fights an enemy who must operate far
from supporting bases, an enemy usually ill-equipped for fast
movement over local ground. It is only necessary to fight and run
away, re-form and again retreat. In time the invading enemy tires
and, as he tires, the guerrilla bands become better equipped with
captured matériel and ultimately are capable of winning in a
"conventional" and decisive manner. The impatient American,

especially on the home front, falls a ready victim to the Maos and the Hos.

Nevertheless, the guerrilla cannot cope with a force more mobile than himself. The helicopter has now conquered terrain that once was the haven of the guerrilla. Coupled with the destruction of his sources of arms and subsistence, he can be pursued until superior mobility defeats him decisively.

There are few American military, for example, who do not believe that Vietnam could have been won early in the game by the ruthless application of all-out, coordinated effort in local areas to gain the limited objectives sought. Perhaps in some instances it might have been a case of killing a fly with a pile driver, yet using a pile driver for immediate success spells cheap victory, plus cumulative effects. In any case Vietnam was by no means a test, either of the efficacy of guerrilla warfare or of the inadequacy of conventional means to check that kind of warfare.

It is therefore the more conventional type of mobile war that furnishes history's most valuable lessons for the future, lessons in which brilliant and flexible commanders apply a common set of principles in various creative ways. A study of their techniques should provide food for thought for the blitz commander of 1990, even as they did for Napoleon in 1790.

There are special objectives to be kept in mind in undertaking lightning-war historical research. These are important if the average student of history is not to be misled. It is not a case of studying tactics or the planning of campaigns. In searching for battles typifying the blitz through the ages, the action described must follow the lightning-war characteristics of maximized mobility, integrated force, violence, and close control.

The commanders chosen to illustrate the manner of conducting lightning war cannot be selected solely on the basis of the fact that they have won great battles or campaigns. There were many able generals operating during the Hundred Years War (1337–1453) and many aside from Gustavus Adolphus in the Thirty Years War (1618–1648). One may admire Grant for "fighting it out on this line if it takes all summer," or Jackson, who "stood there like a stone wall." But one may hope that the future will develop great leaders who can resolve a conflict in thirty days, or at most a hundred days, rather than passing the baton from one generation to another.

One may assume that in a battle resulting in a great victory, the commander conducted the action from a position which afforded him the best control. Where was this position? Was he in the van, in the thick of the fighting, or did he anticipate an IBM 360 computer by retiring to a safe cave, with a crystal ball and accompanying necromancers?

His use, or nonuse of a staff is critical, to include planning assistance as well as conduct of the battle. Most important is the method by which integration of effort was achieved, especially that between different kinds of maneuvering troops and different kinds of weapons. Some kind of communication system had to be employed, not only to set matters in motion but to provide the all-important adjustments when plans went astray, as they usually did and usually do.

These are all included in "techniques" or methodology and do far more to explain why battles are won or lost than the study of brilliant plans of campaign.

The following battle accounts and character sketches have been chosen to illustrate lightning wars in the years before the Napoleonic era. They bring out the thinking that led up to the stunning combinations of tanks, infantry, mobile artillery, and engineers that Guderian loosed in 1939, and they presage even more exotic combinations of rocketry, airmobile "cavalry," and computerized control in the future.

Only those factors bearing on command methodology, or highlighting one or more essential blitz characteristics are discussed. Many exciting engagements and many worthy commanders have been omitted. But the sample is sufficient to show that a blitz battle pattern and a blitz command pattern have existed for many centuries.

Much of the methodology for the years prior to 1800 is unrecorded. Yet most of the great generals who are mentioned evolved and operated by the correct concepts of lightning war. Their methodology may, for the moment, be assumed or deduced for later comparison with better data accruing in the post nineteenth century period.

There have not been a great many lightning-war battles, even allowing for the probability that a good number have gone unrecorded. True blitz leaders have been rare. If this form of warfare is to be an effective war deterrent as opposed to either the war of attrition of nuclear warfare, it is clear that the careful and intensive training of competent leaders is essential.

# 3　From Antiquity to Napoleon

As far back as the fourteenth century B.C. mobility and shock action concepts can be identified in the military organization effected by Rameses I of Egypt. His troops were highly controlled and disciplined. Striking power was provided by chariots, numbering in the thousands, in both heavy and light categories. These were manned by archers, thus presenting the counterpart of modern tank gunners. Coordination, that vital adjunct of the blitz, was achieved by drum and trumpet signals.

Both the Persians and the Assyrians had similar resources. The Greeks, too, advanced the art by creating phalanxes of eight files and eight ranks, utilized in a shock role. Philip of Macedon (382–336 B.C.) increased the phalanx to a 16 x 16-man pattern and used it in conjunction with the shock of horse cavalry, timed for a critical moment.

Countermeasures designed to drive deep into hostile battle positions were developed along the lines of the modern blitz through the techniques of Epaminondas of Thebes (371 B.C.) who broke up phalanxes by using a wedge formation.

Alexander the Great (356–323 B.C.) employed the same tactic and as a result foresaw a need for increasing the size of his own phalanxes, which were usually supported by cavalry.

Alexander, son of Philip of Macedon and conqueror of the known world of his day, considered mobility the governing tactical element; the battlefield existed only as a prelude to pursuit and annihilation of the beaten foe. His keen sense of timing was reflected in the organization of light infantry battalions of about

22

1000 men each to fill the gaps between the assault of cavalry forces and the final shock of the phalanx.

The casualty count of the battle of Arbela (331 B.C.) in which Alexander defeated the Persians under Darius was phenomenal; the historian Arrian claims 300,000 Persians slain as against 100 men and 1000 horses lost by Alexander. Although this is probably an exaggeration, the figures given by Diodorus are impressive enough—90,000 Persians compared to 500 Macedonians—a true blitz in results, regardless of the methodology employed to plan and direct it.

Hannibal (247–183 B.C.), son of the ruler of Carthage, in 216 B.C. scored one of the world's decisive victories by routing the Romans under Tarentus Varro and Amelius Paulus. After crossing the Alps and winning a series of minor engagements he faced the Romans at Cannae. Here he made history by planning and executing its most famous double envelopment, ruthlessly decimating his adversaries.

The double envelopment is a difficult and risky maneuver, making extraordinary demands on timing. As performed by Hannibal, it has ever drawn historians' comments that no army in recorded time was ever more magnificently "handled," a word that suggests that information was transmitted rapidly and accurately concerning both friend and foe. The movement of the wings had to be perfectly timed. Hannibal had to know at every moment where everyone was and what he was doing. This meant the exertion of close control over the action by Hannibal in person.

The tactic at Cannae was typical of many similar stratagems of the ancients in that a formation of wings and a center was so managed as to allow the center to fall back when pressed by the enemy, only to have the wings converge and surround the entrapped foe. It is not uniformly successful.

Hannibal was rated as being quick-witted, demonstrating both reckless courage and cool judgment under stress. Polybius cited his ability to adapt his actions quickly to changing circumstances, a mark of later great blitz commanders. But his defeat at Zama (202 B.C.), triggered by the stampede of his own war elephants, and their stampede of the cavalry in turn, suggests that his control system was not up to the problem of bringing order out of unexpected confusion.

Firepower, or its equivalent, appeared in the ancient world in the Parthian Empire of Mithradates I (160 B.C.) who organized a force of mounted archers; under him General Surenas assured a capability for sustained action by supporting the archers with 1000 arrow-carrying camels for each 10,000 archers. Catapults entered the picture in the armies of the Caesars when each legion (about 3000–7000 men) was supported by sixty carriages of small-missile launchers, which could be fired over the heads of the draft animals, plus ten large catapults. Evidence is lacking that there was any standard method of coordinating these heavy support weapons with maneuvering troops. A large percentage of combat at the time involved the reduction of fortified towns and the "artillery" was primarily if not exclusively designed for this function.

Theodore A. Dodge compares the leadership of Pompey with that of Julius Caesar (*circa* 100–44 B.C.). Whereas the army of Pompey suffered from the lack of a single guiding head, Caesar *was* his army. "The whole body was imbued with his purpose, all, from low to high, working on his own methods. . . . [Caesar] controlled its every mood and act."

Caesar in his *Civil War* cites an occasion when Pompey's forces began to surround his exposed flank. Caesar, in close observation "gave the signal to his 4th line . . . which advanced to attack Pompey's cavalry in such fury that they fled to the hills. With the same onslaught, the cohorts surrounded the left wing and attacked the rear—simultaneously Caesar launched his reserves."

An action of this description certainly suggests correct employment of lightning war control techniques. It is unfortunate that accounts do not detail how the action was regulated.

Appian's account of the battle of Philippi in 42 B.C., where Brutus and Cassius were arrayed against Antony and Octavian, describes how "Antony continued his charge on the run, advancing under a shower of missiles until he struck Cassius' troops, which were amazed at the unexpected audacity." But the inability to maintain an effective level of control soon manifested itself. Appian continues, "the victory was complete and alike on either side, Brutus defeating the enemy left wing while Antony overcame Cassius"; but they were ignorant of each other's fate with the result that a blitz ending was not achieved.

Belisarius, a general under Justinian the Great, attempted to crush revolting forces of Vandals in Carthage (533) under Gelimer. As if to demonstrate the perils of highly coordinated action where the means of coordination were lacking, Gelimer attempted a three-pronged attack aimed at a simultaneous strike. But timing, which was the prerequisite of success, was faulty. A piecemeal effort resulted. Even then, Procopius wrote, Gelimer might have triumphed had he pressed home at least one of the prongs. But he was unaware of the course of events and, after falling back, suffered the rout of his command.

The importance of inspirational leadership, concurrent with being at a critical point at a critical time, was demonstrated by William the Conqueror at the Battle of Hastings, probably the most decisive encounter in English history. Panic swept the ranks when William was unhorsed. But he remounted and, shouting encouragement, restored order—an important development, for in medieval warfare loss of the commander in chief usually led to wholesale and immediate disaster.

William, according to another William (of Poitiers) was always very much in personal charge, dominating his battles. This permitted him to employ a favorite tactic, feigning retreat to invite pursuit, then suddenly wheeling to the counterattack. This device was twice successful at Hastings.

Coordination was present in principle when the Byzantine forces under Romanus fought the Turks at Manzikert (1071). The Byzantines had artillery of a sort in the form of catapults, ballistae, and trebuckets. In concept, hostile troops were first disrupted by a cavalry charge and then an assault by heavy infantry was made while a barrage of arrows was fired over the heads of the moving infantry. In practice, however, execution must have been frequently faulty for, at Manzikert, Romanus suffered a Cannae-like defeat.

No chronicle of mobile war would be complete without mention of Genghis Khan (1162–1227), called the "Scourge of God," who, though not of the western world and its comparatively precise records, ranks as one of the great exponents of the art. Leading a lean and hard-eyed horde of Mongols, fresh from the conquest of Cathay, the Khan swept out of the East, overran most of Europe, and then was gone like the mist under a hot morning sun.

He created an empire seemingly out of thin air, evolved a code of conduct in a culture where the written word was essentially unknown, and ended with his columns ranging on tough and tireless mounts over a full quarter of the globe.

The Khan undoubtedly influenced Napoleon to exercise great care in the selection and consequent quality of his marshals. Columns under Chepe Noyon and Subotai operated through the Indus, the Caspian area, and as far west as Kiev and Cracow. In two months three great European armies and twelve smaller ones were defeated by the flying nomads whose commanders, like Subotai, did not think it unreasonable, when summoned home by the messenger of the Khan, to take a pony ride of some 2000 miles. Subotai had once marched a division 190 miles in three days, a time-distance feat that not many gasoline-powered units of similar size could emulate today.

The exploits of the Mongols were described by hostile writers of the day (they had no writers of their own) as dealing in "a new form of warfare," the common phrase used from one century to another when a new blitz appeared. But it was nothing more than the characteristic coupling of very fast maneuver with the "firepower" of heavy bowmen. Certainly the Mongols were far from the disorganized mob that defined the Huns of an earlier day. Their forces numbered between 200,000 and a quarter of a million, divided into Center, Wings, Imperial Guard, and like contingents. Divisions and corps performed as tactical units and were given fixed and distant objectives that required them to follow coordinating directives. Intelligence was well organized; surprise and deception were emphasized.

The logistic achievements of Genghis Khan were fantastic, considering the era, and the size of a force literally living off the country, ranging through ninety degrees of longitude, altogether a most fitting exponent of lightning war.

By the fourteenth and fifteenth centuries, gunpowder had had predictable effects. Only a hundred years previously the Second Lateran Council of the Church had outlawed the use of the crossbow as un-Christian, thus tending to restore knighthood to flower. But all this was shattered with the development of "pots de fer," primitive multibarreled "machine guns," hand guns, and matchlocks. The medieval social orders were broken and warfare democratized.

Gibbon cites Sultan Mahomet II (1451–1481), conqueror of Constantinople and founder of the Ottoman Empire, as the supreme artillerist of his day—the first really great siege gunner of history. Mahomet always commanded in person, made his own decisions, brooked no interference, and demanded strict discipline. His forces were especially adept at reconnaissance and forced marches ending in surprise assaults. They were flexible, being employed according to the circumstances, were divided into tactical groupings, and were supposed to assault strategic positions in concert, at the sounding of huge drums. In spite of these manifestations of lightning war principles, however, Mahomet's artillery was apparently used only in sieges.

In contrast, Oman describes Charles VIII of France, who amazed Italy in 1494 by crossing the Alps with "a long train" of cannon of varying sizes which kept up with the columns and thus could be classed among the earliest examples of field artillery. In the account of the Battle of Marignano he attributes the victory to "cavalry charges and overwhelming artillery fire where neither would have succeeded without the other," surely an indication of some means of coordination.

The rise of Napoleon Bonaparte has been arbitrarily chosen as the beginning of the era of premodern and modern blitzkrieg because of the availability of data on mobile command, and particularly on mobile staff methodology. But between the early seventeenth century and the Napoleonic period three great generals not only made their mark on lightning-war development, but significantly influenced those who were to follow them, Bonaparte especially. These were Gustavus Adolphus, the Duke of Marlborough, and Frederick the Great.

Gustavus Adolphus (1594–1632), King of Sweden, is equated to Alexander the Great by Gindely and is described as athletic, imaginative, restless, adventurous, quick-tempered and compassionate. He, too, was a keen student of military history, Napoleon crediting him with being animated with the principles of Alexander the Great, Hannibal, and Caesar. In war he was an audacious innovator. He preached that mobility is based upon discipline and that discipline rests upon competent leadership. He apparently had little confidence in elderly generals and accordingly showed great skill in the selection of young and active subordinates.

He based his success on artillery firepower, supporting by shot and smoke cavalry charges made at the gallop. (The custom had been to advance at the trot.) He recognized the separate arms and combined their tactics, while keeping close control over logistical matters. Chemnitz says, "No one could divine enemy intentions, or take advantage of the chances of war more ably. He took in at a glance the whole position . . . and drew up his forces so as to profit by every opportunity." Fuller believes that no one, except perhaps Philip of Macedon, excelled him as a military organizer.

The beginning of the eighteenth century marked the advent of the Duke of Marlborough as the heir of Gustavus Adolphus and, with Frederick the Great, the forerunner of Napoleon. His character is of special interest to the student of the blitz, for he strongly advocated the offense in a day when defensive tactics were standard, a condition not unlike that of the 1920s. Indeed he proved that a vigorous offense is actually the strongest defense. He stressed the coordination of musket fires at short ranges of thirty to fifty paces, covering a bayonet assault (which may be said to have signaled the beginning of modern war). Like others cited, he made personal reconnaissances and took personal charge of the conduct of the battle.

En route to and during the great and decisive battle of Blenheim, which materially affected the future political alignments of Europe, he displayed characteristic audacity that was duplicated in many other encounters; at Schellenburg (1704) he perceived the critical moment of assault and was thus able to launch thirty-five squadrons in pursuit of the enemy for the decisive victory.

Montgomery's *History of Warfare* shows an engraving of Marlborough overseeing, from a high hill, the full panoply of fighting battalions at the Battle of Malplaquet, and in the act of giving orders to an aide. This would signify the probable use of trusted aides in the Napoleonic manner.

Frederick the Great was in all probability the most offensive-minded of all the great captains, even in the presence of superior forces. He always struck first. Napoleon cited him as "great in the critical moments." He based his tactics on mobility and on fire superiority and was the real creator of mobile horse artillery, the antecedent of the self-propelled guns of World War II. He promoted *esprit* by severe drills, teaching soldiers to treble their fire by reloading quickly while on the move. However, he never succumbed to the idea that rigid drill was a substitute for flexibility in maneuver, a lesson lost on many a military "expert" who followed Frederick.

Frederick would have delighted in having George S. Patton as one of his marshals, for he held to the belief that soldiers should be more afraid of their officers than of the enemy and the dangers of battle.

Napoleon considered Frederick's Battle of Leuthen (1757) a masterpiece of maneuver and resolution. He advanced, concentrated by surprise and struck with stunning force; cooperation was perfect and so were the dispositions of the three arms, all inspired by the confidence which Frederick's brilliance instilled in the troops.

As to audacity, Napoleon said, "He carried out things I would never have dared. He abandoned his line of operations and often acted as though he had no knowledge of the art of war."

Although specific evidence is lacking as to the methodology employed by the leaders in the great battles just chronicled, in terms of blitz characteristics, it seems none the less certain that some kind of system for initiating and (more important) maintaining control must have been present in nearly every case.

It is plain that from the dawn of organized warfare, the successful commanders habitually gave all possible personal direction to the planning and conduct of the action. They were strong and ruthless characters; yet it is interesting to note that in a day of comparative savagery, there were many evidences of kindness and compassion. Apparently they operated from either front line positions or from posts from which the course of action could be readily observed. All would, of course, have gloried in the use of a command helicopter.

There was unquestionably appreciation of the need for integrating the crude firepower of the time with the movement of attacking foot and horse troops. Drums and other signals are mentioned as means of setting plans into motion. From the numbers of disasters, or failures to capitalize on success that have been noted, however, it is logical to conclude that the foot or horse messengers of the day, or the visual signals, were inadequate to transmit command ideas in time to effect corrective action when plans went awry.

Polybius mentioned Hannibal's "ability to adapt to changing circumstances" which, in the long run, is the ultimate test of a command and control system. But, if he had a system, it was not equal to the disaster at Zama.

Commanders were nearly all dedicated to a policy of calculated risk, judging from the frequent mention of audacity. Risk implies the existence of options calling for a decision in the face of uncertainty or doubt. Where a risk is accepted it suggests faith in a control system adequate to effect a timely alteration in plans; but the systems unfortunately do not form part of historical narratives.

For the Napoleonic era and beyond, where better data prevail, though not to the degree desired, selected great leaders are given the title of "master" of lightning war. The foregoing account serves, nevertheless, to show that in the pre-1800 period great thinkers and great commanders provided a basis for applying new technology to time-honored principles.

# 4  Selection of Masters: Criteria

It is idle to speculate whether an old time boxing champion such as James J. Corbett in his prime could have defeated a Jack Dempsey or a Joe Louis in his prime. Where size, speed, agility, and professional competence appear to have remained constant factors, only strength of character remains, offering scant means of exercising judgment. On the other hand, there is little doubt that a football team of today would make short work of the best that 1910 had to offer. The size, strength, and speed of the players are vastly improved. Better equipment enables players to operate with greater confidence. But, most of all, the game itself moves at a faster tempo and involves complexities of timing and co-ordination unknown to the older generation. And so it is with war: the principles remain while demands on leadership multiply.

This is not to intimate that a Gustavus Adolphus, stepping in to command a modern division after a period of familiarization, could not defeat a run-of-the-mill general in battle. The great leaders of bygone days not only devoted themselves assiduously to mastering the lessons of history and the techniques of the day, but were innovators in the application of destructive force and mobility. They were men of execution as well as men of thought.

It seems probable, therefore, that although the game is indeed different, the great captains had basic personality traits that would serve them well in adapting the latest weapons, vehicles and communications facilities to the fundamental principles of command and control that they appeared to have in common.

They would find fertile fields for their talents in the potentially nuclear environment described by Comrade Prusanov: the fluid, dynamic collisions, the high maneuverability, lack of continuous front and opportunity to strike sudden blows of great force.

General William C. Westmoreland, Chief of Staff, United States Army, goes further. In an address to the Association of the United States Army, October 14, 1969, he foresees a capability of locating enemy forces accurately by aerial surveillance systems, unattended ground sensors and radars. He visualizes the concentration of firepower without the massing of troops, raining destruction anywhere within a matter of minutes; he forecasts fixing enemy formations by locating, tracking and targeting, almost instantaneously, through the use of data links, computer-assisted intelligence evaluation and automated fire control system. In this environment, where first-round hit probabilities approach certainty, and with surveillance devices continually following the movements of hostile battalions, the need for large forces to contain enemy formations physically will, he feels, be lessened. However, highly mobile units must continue to force canalization or the maneuvering of enemy groups so as to present the most profitable target.

Such farsightedness, based on scientific developments, is unquestionably reasonable. However, in the past, prophecies of the invincibility of one weapons system or another have invariably run afoul of practical problems once the gadgetry falls into the hands of the average American GI who, one must hasten to add, is usually much more adaptable than his adversaries.

Still, if a potential enemy can be credited with only a part of such capabilities, it is plain that the great captains would have much to learn, and much to contend with, in coping with the demands of today and tomorrow.

One may imagine Frederick the Great fighting a battle where all the electronic gadgetry is present. He has now forsaken the high hill from which he dominated the action at Malplaquet; he is disturbed at the thought that his Catholic foes may have made effective use of sensors; he hopes that wide dispersal of his own forces may have left few targets for the devastating long-range rockets that have already begun to take their toll. From his command helicopter he is confident that his dispersed troops may quickly concentrate, strike and again disperse; he can scarcely credit his senses with what he sees on his computer display, a picture of a large concentration of enemy troops at Point XY. Now is the time to place massive fires on XY and either destroy the grouping or contain it while he masses his brigades to strike at Z, reported to be the heart of General Wallenstein's control system. Orders flash over data links, facsimile, and computer display equipment.

But as the magic wand waves the picture of XY begins to move, then fades. Enemy electronic countermeasures are blocking out his surveillance and control devices. What has become of the force at XY? Why hasn't the Second Brigade acknowledged receipt of radio orders? Why . . . ?

Now Frederick must fall back on the techniques that won at Leuthen. If one system fails he must be ready with another. It is not illogical to assume that with one ultramodern device offsetting another, the tactical situation may well reduce itself to one involving only the crude weapons and control facilities of Leuthen, or even Arbela.

Now, the tempo of the action is perhaps twenty times that of Leuthen. Is he equal to it, or, for that matter, is anyone? Mobility is a wonderful attribute, but it is a sad fact that when bad decisions and poor control are the handmaidens of mobility, disaster strikes that much faster.

A summary of the characteristics that must be associated with command in the complicated environment of tomorrow serves several purposes. First, it will collate the traits and skills exhibited by the generals of pre-Napoleonic days; next, it will provide a basis of measurement for the "masters" of modern mobile warfare. Finally, it will establish a set of leadership criteria for a coming generation who must apply principles within the framework of a new technology.

General Dwight D. Eisenhower epitomized the lightning war leader in a television interview (Issues and Answers, American Broadcasting Company, July 31, 1967), answering a question concerning General Patton. "There are many good generals," he said, "but only a few capable of conducting a pursuit." And a pursuit is of course the decisive phase of a blitz battle, a phase even the great Napoleon neglected at Austerlitz.

It is obvious that he was differentiating between those leaders who are capable of planning and providing administrative support for great enterprises, and those who are capable of executing critical tactical requirements swiftly and surely. It is a reasonable authority on which to base an assertion that blitz leaders must have special qualities.

Factually, however, just as the characteristics of lightning-war battle should ideally describe any battle, the personality traits of blitz commanders should ideally apply to all leadership. The point is that as battle characteristics are emphasized or maximized if decisive results are to ensue with the desired rapidity, so must command characteristics be stressed.

The most important of the command characteristics, though not necessarily listed in order of their importance are

> Professional competence, or "knowing the job"
> Force
> Moral Courage and Integrity
> Initiative, or Audacity
> Creativity
> Flamboyance, or Color
> Inspirational appeal
> Physical stamina

Of these the first five deserve special comment.

*Professional competence* relates particularly to the ability to control men and arms physically. Many studious military men have absorbed all that books have to offer on the principles of war, but if they do not have practical field experience in command they are in the position of a football quarterback whose accomplishments have never gone outside the library. And the reverse is also true.

It is noteworthy that the professional competence of outstanding military figures developed in general from widely varying military backgrounds. The years of specialization in infantry, cavalry, tanks, or artillery have not prevented the rise of leaders versed in the techniques of all, suggesting that appreciation of the roles of all branches and the ability to blend them into a cohesive whole are the most important marks of lightning-war professional competence.

Professional competence is the source of much of the inspirational appeal of the outstanding commander. Inspirational talks or orders, or appearances on the battlefield at critical times have their place in firing up the will to win of a combat organization. But day-to-day morale is built on the confidence which the rank and file have that they are being led by an expert.

*Force* refers to the ability to dominate a command without being overbearing or taking on the character of a martinet. Quiet but positive force is especially associated with interface between the commander and his staff; the leader directs to a degree much greater than that exhibited in high-level planning headquarters such as the Eisenhower D-Day operation (OVERLORD). The blitz commander and his staff both actively supervise battle developments.

*Moral Courage* is demanded by rapidly changing conditions on a fluid battlefield.

Nearly every situation is rife with imponderables wherein information of enemy strength and dispositions, weather, terrain, and other factors intervene and, more often than not, intervene suddenly to produce the well-known "fog of war."

Matters rarely proceed as planned. Firepower can be delivered in the wrong place or at the wrong time; maneuvering troops lose their way or are otherwise delayed; timing may be misjudged; communications problems arise. Time presses constantly and there are few opportunities to refer matters to the staff or to weigh alternatives at length.

All such potential catastrophes must be anticipated and avoided. It requires an inordinate degree of moral courage to make critical decisions rapidly in the face of all these unknowns and threats of imminent disaster, and to accept responsibility for them cheerfully. President Truman's desk once carried the sign, "The Buck Stops Here." But for the tactical commander, there are way stations at many levels of command.

*Initiative* is vital as an accompaniment to moral courage, as is *audacity* in the face of the imponderables. One must be careful to distinguish between audacity and rashness, for it has been said that audacity marks the taking of a chance that succeeds, while rashness describes the same risk that fails. It is plain, however, that while most of the great commanders were audacious to a fault, they did not take chances without carefully weighing the factors connected with the decision. It was pointed out by General Hans Speidel, Rommel's Chief of Staff in the West, that Rommel, credited with great audacity, time and again insisted that he was never rash.

*Creativity* is a trait that describes the ideal modern leader, according to Mrazek in *The Art of Winning Wars*. The "masters" of antiquity, as well as those yet to be considered, have all been innovators. But their creativity was significantly founded on their professional competence. The U.S. Patent Office, for example, is filled with the products of creative thinkers that have no practical value. Similarly, creativity must be accompanied by the force necessary to "sell" the idea and the moral courage to persist in the face of initial reverses.

Taken together, these factors have prompted many analysts, among them the magazine *Armor* (May–June, 1967), to consider highly mobile leadership as primarily a state of mind and not a matter of matériel or dogma. History is full of instances where blitz and other battles were won almost solely by the morale of the commander and troops, and conversely lost when the state of mind of the commander, particularly, drifted into doubt, irresolution, and confusion. Napoleon's rating of the moral over the physical as three to one is well known.

Undoubtedly, the infrequency of lightning-war battles in history is due to the fact that a general with the necessary skills has been a rare bird indeed. The number of characteristics that have been cited, and the ease with which such attributes as timing can be upset, make it improbable that all can be combined at the opportune moment. Otherwise a Napoleon or a Rommel would never have met defeat.

Infrequency, too, has caused contemporary writers to greet each manifestation of lightning war as a new kind of warfare when in fact it is the same product in a different package. It is worth repeating that it matters little whether firepower consists of Genghis Khan's archers, Napoleon's cannon or Patton's Nineteenth Tactical Air Force; or whether mobility is provided by the horse, the jeep, or the helicopter. The same high degree of generalship is needed to integrate them.

But as time goes on and the speed potential increases, it seems obvious that timing and coordination become more difficult. Napoleon's premise that he defeated the Austrians because they did not know the value of two minutes, might reduce to fifteen seconds in the airmobile battles of today. Two minutes is a very long time. So, as standards continue to rise, it is probable that more commanders must have unusual training if the standards are to be met.

It will be found that the individuals selected as outstanding leaders of modern blitz history, and therefore as models, are strikingly similar personalities. It is most significant that their systems of command are parallel, bearing out the premise that technical developments in weapons, transport and the electronic fields do not alter the basic principles of lightning-war leadership.

A list cautiously chosen of great commanders whose careers represent the modern historical evolution of lightning war would include:

> Napoleon Bonaparte
> Nathan Bedford Forrest
> Erwin Rommel
> George S. Patton
> Ernest Harmon
> The Israeli Composite

With the possible exception of Harmon and the Israeli Composite, these names are well known. Harmon was the most colorful of the World War II American armored division commanders and may be said to symbolize many of his able colleagues, rather than standing alone.

Similarly, the Israeli Composite is simply a device for summarizing the characteristics of several outstanding command personalities into a single living and typical individual. To select any one Israeli as preeminent in carrying out either the 1956 or 1967 compaigns would be most unjust to others equally qualified. And to equate a leader of a campaign of a few days' duration, waged against a somewhat ineffectual enemy, with men of the stature of Napoleon or Patton would be unjust to veterans of many difficult campaigns involving formidable adversaries. Yet, it is precisely the fact that the Negev campaigns were of a few days' duration that makes them so suitable for modern geopolitical analyses. The men who conducted them cannot be lightly dismissed.

Pure generalship is not the only area in which personalities have influenced blitz history. Some of the most important influences have been exerted by the great analysts, or "architects" of present-day lightning war. These men, also keen students of military history, conducted in the 1930s running and frustrating arguments with the general staffs of their respective countries to overcome traditional hidebound military resistance to what seemed to be revolutionary ideas, however much of the ideas were actually based on time-worn principles.

The major architects were

> Major-General J. F. C. Fuller, Great Britain
> Sir Basil H. Liddell Hart, D.Litt., Great Britain
> Heinz Guderian, Germany
> Adna R. Chaffee, United States

There are no other military anaylsts who can compare in stature with these men.

The list of "masters," however, is troubling, which explains why it is presented cautiously. There are seemingly too many names of historical greats missing. Why reject Wellington, the conqueror of Napoleon? Or Montgomery, the victor over Rommel? Then there is Allenby, whose World War I campaign in Palestine was a veritable masterpiece of mobile war, and Jeb Stuart, the famous American Civil War cavalryman. And what about Grant and Lee, Douglas MacArthur and many German, American, or Russian corps and division commanders of World War II?

Reluctant rejection is based almost wholly on the aforementioned paucity of data to support a close analysis of their command system. For example, even considering the libraries of books on Napoleon, only one sets forth his system of command and control (dePhilip's *Étude sur le Service d'État-Major Pendant les Guerres du Premier Empire*). The art of Forrest is touched on in but a few biographies. Then, as we approach modern times, references become more numerous on Rommel and Patton, or, as in the case of Harmon, there are living persons, including the authors, with intimate knowledge of their careers. And the wars in the Negev were well documented.

But the careers of most candidates cannot be effectively researched for lack of data, or else they cannot be classed as truly mobile commanders. Finally, a list of six is sufficient to provide an idea of what the blitz type is like.

Wellington's campaigns were not featured by battles of mobility, according to Brett-James in *Wellington at War,* but there is reason to believe that he might have taken his place among the best had the opportunity offered. This, in spite of his own description of the Peninsular Campaign: "I (considering the risk) have determined to persevere in my cautious system."

He was always personally mobile, however, kept his staff very small, slept only in cat naps and, as a youthful commander in his forties was surrounded by even younger command and staff personnel. He was a most positive character and said (to support this premise) that he never offered battle without having his generals beg him not to. He was impatient with bureaucracy and railed at what is now known as public relations.

"The licentiousness of the press," he wrote," and the presumption of newspaper editors have gone far to stultify the people of England . . . it makes one sick to hear the statements of supposed facts . . . which have the effect of keeping the minds of the people in a state of alarm and anxiety." It is well that he is not alive today to command an American effort in Asia. It is well, also, that at Waterloo he was not faced with a Napoleon whose lightning-fast control system was still managed by the great Chief of Staff, Berthier. The Wellingtonian mobility would not have been up to it.

Montgomery defeated Rommel at El Alamein, but it was a Rommel broken in health, whose troops were starved for petrol and whose miracles in the North African desert could not long continue in the face of vast Allied air superiority.

Then again it was Montgomery in command of all Allied troops north of the Bulge salient in late 1944 who counseled a defensive attitude at the critical strategic moment. Had it not been for the initiative and drive of Generals J. Lawton Collins and Ernest Harmon, the German thrust to the Meuse might have gained the depots and supplies that would have sustained the effort still further. Montgomery's preoccupation with a policy of slowly building up those supplies kept an impatient and highly caustic Patton cooling his motors for lack of fuel. Montgomery of Alamein, unquestionably a leader, trainer and able general, with all the flamboyance of the blitz commander, still cannot be classed as one.

Douglas MacArthur's campaigns in the Western Pacific in 1944–45 and his Inchon landing in Korea have many of the elements of lightning warfare. Islands were by-passed to secure deep and more important objectives; there was swift and strategic movement together with wondrous integration of effort among Army, Navy, and Air Force in the many amphibious landings. But the scope of the action is outside the tactical limitations of lightning war; mobility was essentially strategic.

These examples offer a clue to the reasons for rejection of many famous commanders, other than those arising from lack of data as to their command systems.

But if any name not mentioned is cause for misgiving it is that of Major General John S. Wood, termed by Sir Basil H. Liddell Hart the "American Rommel." General Wood was a life-long student of history, like the others, and an especially keen analyst of mobile control methods. An artilleryman by specialty, he nevertheless fully appreciated the necessity for the careful coordination of all arms in the attainment of blitz results. Consultations with him leading to the preparation of this book were cut short by his untimely death.

As the trainer and commander of the famous 4th Armored Division, he made the decisive breakthrough at Avranches, France, in 1944 and continued its breakneck pace until ill health caught up with him. His case is especially illustrative of the difficulty of selecting any individual of modern times as a "master." He was indeed a master during the short months in which he displayed his talents. But against this limited period, Ernest Harmon demonstrated his right to the title all through North Africa, Italy, France, and Germany. In other words, all through World War II.

To extend the comment concerning the diverse professional backgrounds of great captains, it is noteworthy that names on the selected list bear out the assertion. There is no preponderance of infantrymen or artillerymen as opposed to cavalrymen or engineers. Napoleon was primarily an artillery officer; Forrest, Patton, Harmon and Chaffee were cavalrymen, and make up much of the list, but they did not revere the horse as a cult and they eagerly sought new solutions to the problems of the day. Fuller was one of the original tankers, if not *the* original. Rommel and Liddell Hart had initial experience with infantry while Guderian served in infantry, signal and transport elements. Wood began as a coast artilleryman and the Israeli Composite represent widely differing backgrounds.

As a final note, however, it is natural to ask why no Russian candidates have been selected or suggested as meriting the title of "master." It is a reasonable question, for the Russian cavalry has, through history, formed a significant proportion of Russian armed forces. Officered (as in most countries) by aristocrats, its tradition was one of charging mounted at the slightest provocation. When Napoleon met the Russian forces at Eylau, his own light cavalry, supported in a timely manner by artillery, defeated a vastly superior mass of Russian dragoons. Such disdain of integrated action seems to have persisted through World War I, and to have extended well into World War II, largely due to the impression that the vast Russian plains, susceptible to miring in bad weather, and with limited road networks, were suitable only for animal transport. British Major-General Sir Alfred Knox wrote two volumes dealing *With the Russian Army in 1914–17,* mentioning many mobile actions, while General Golovine of the Russian Army wrote several articles on small unit Cavalry action for the (U.S.) *Cavalry Journal* in the early 1920s; these writings bear out the lack of integration of firepower and maneuver, while lamenting the tendency to resort to massed charges rather than to rely on maneuverability.

However, Russian professionals were quick to see the value of mechanized warfare. Later chapters on the development of mechanization bring out Russian acceptance of the tank suspension system engineered by the American, Walter Christie, and their appreciation of the teachings of the analysts, Liddell Hart and Fuller. In the engineering sense, they enjoyed tank parity, if not superiority, and have maintained it to the present day.

Nevertheless, research into Russian leadership methods and mobile tactical principles is even more difficult than inquiry into matters of western generalship. Typical is *Marshal Zhukov's Greatest Battles,* a book dealing entirely with the strategic aspects of the 1941–1945 campaigns, albeit the strategy of a very mobile-minded commander.

During and after World War II the authors had the opportunity not only of opposing Russian units on the battlefield but of discussing command methods with the leaders of occupation forces.

At the risk of having the victors analyzed by the defeated, it is nonetheless evident that most German leaders ascribe Russian triumphs to overwhelming numbers, great stores of American-furnished equipment and fierce tenacity—triumphs that might well have been achieved earlier by better command methods. Moreover, in talking with commanders of occupation troops in 1945, and watching troop movements in the Russian zones, it was plain that at the time there was little Russian appreciation of blitz techniques. March discipline was lax; tank crews were observed holding up an entire column while they stopped to relieve themselves, or even to pick wild flowers, all without comment from officers; conversely, on one occasion a simple, drunken soldier was shot summarily by his captain.

A small sample size, to be sure! Yet these were rated as crack divisions. One guards division commander stated that he would not consider an attack without having at least 300 pieces of artillery in support, and was obviously scornful when his American questioner admitted that less than half that number would be highly unusual within his own formations.

There was no sign that artillery was employed in a flexible manner. The ability to shift concentrations rapidly at will appeared to be an unknown art, foregone by the simpler method of lining up guns hub to hub and blasting away.

There are indications in numerous journals and reports that the Russians have long since recognized these deficiencies and have done something about the situation. Meanwhile, however, it is risky to assume, in the absence of supporting data, that the Zhukovs, the Budënnys and the Konevs were true blitz-oriented commanders, able and mobile-minded though they might otherwise be. It is equally risky to assume that there were none, or that none have been developed. But that must await another book.

# 5 The Nineteenth Century

The Napoleonic era initiated a period of enormous significance in the annals of lightning war, for the Little Corporal was to develop a command system that remains essentially unparalleled, even considering today's sophisticated command environment of satellites, electronic displays, and digital computers.

A half century later the American Civil war brought forth a natural soldier, a natural general, really, in the person of Nathan Bedford Forrest who, without seeming to do so consciously, used the Napoleonic command and control system with devastating effect.

These "masters" are the first of the selected group to be discussed. A personal vignette, and a battle typical of the methods of each, lay the groundwork for demonstrating the similarities of personality and technique that extend to their counterparts in the twentieth century, when World War II burst forth with new weapons and transport without changing the fundamental principles of Bonaparte.

Since the center of interest lies in the command systems, the character sketches are generally limited in scope to those qualities and actions directly affecting the command function. The battle descriptions, too, aim at treating only those aspects of the conflict having a bearing on command and staff principles and techniques that relate to the character of blitz action.

## NAPOLEON BONAPARTE

Illustrations of the Napoleonic generation show the Emperor as physically unimpressive, small in stature and sallow of complexion. Some caught the flashing eyes and the imperial attitude, but usually one had to look twice to see what must have been a most compelling character.

He was to create and manipulate twenty-six Marshals of France, some of the greatest soldiers of all time. These were to serve him with devotion, tempered in the end with displays of self-interest.

When in 1796 the Paris politicians gave him command of the Army in Italy, mainly to get him out of the country, he met with his division commanders-to-be at Nice. Generals Sérurier, Augereau, and Masséna, as future Marshals and past experienced battle leaders, greeted the new and relatively green commander with ill-concealed contempt and rudeness. But Bonaparte stared them down, while quickly laying out his plans in a most incisive manner. When he emerged, Masséna, probably the ablest of the future twenty-six, muttered to his companions, "That little man frightened me!"

Apparently his commanding personality was not at its best when out of the military environment. He had little success with women, suffered himself to be unmercifully cuckolded, and was frequently disagreeable in ordinary social contacts. No man, however, could impose his will on the Massénas, the Neys and the Davouts, all outstanding fighters, without having forceful habits and extraordinary professional competence.

Bonaparte was an avid student of military history. He was a natural-born master of organization and management. His aptitude in the selection of subordinates was remarkable, for who today could be expected to choose top-flight generals from men who, a short period back, were bakers, barbers, smugglers, drapers, and followers of other equally unlikely professions and trades?

One of his outstanding traits was a capability for total recall of tremendous amounts of detail, coupled with a rare talent for mental marshaling of facts to be translated into concise directives, plans, and orders. He backed up this capability with an organized clerical staff trained to maintain files of pertinent information, which could be later sifted for essential details of immediate problems.

His sense of battle timing was acute and his overall appreciation of the value of time, always a precious commodity to the mobile commander, was often expressed in writing and in speech.

Incident to planning the political coup that put him in power in 1799 he faced the "Council of 500" in the Orangerie. His speech was received with catcalls and insults and he left the hall half fainting; but this lapse is wholly obscured by the many examples of physical and moral courage that featured his campaigns. His cool habit of making personal reconnaissances near or even within the enemy lines, and his seizure of the flag at the Battle of Arcola, November 15, 1796, to lead the advance, were typical battlefield performances. These were apparently calculated risks; he broadcast to the troops before Austerlitz that this was an out-of-the-ordinary situation that required his presence in the rear. But he did not remain there long; front line action was normal to him. He was able to inspire troops without getting into positions that would compromise tactical control.

He was a born gambler, either in combat or at games; he philosophically accepted risks inherent in unfavorable battle odds. He never hesitated to cheat at cards, considering this practice to be one way of showing contempt for the rules of both the table and the battlefield. Again he probably calculated battle odds carefully, always depending upon his magnificent control system to get him out of trouble.

Initiative was the mark of La Grande Armée. The Emperor, as well as most of the Marshals, was a natural experimenter. At the Nice meeting comments were made about Sérurier, the "copybook soldier," by the other Marshals-to-be, thus displaying their dedication to new ideas. Perhaps they thought their concepts of mobile war to be new, but they could not have been new to Napoleon, the keen student of lightning wars of the past. Initiative, extending all through the ranks, was very probably the true cause of the reputation for color and flamboyance which was gained by La Grande Armée.

Napoleon himself could not have been considered "colorful" in view of his unprepossessing appearance, save for the brilliant uniforms affected by him and the entire generation of new leaders; his own showiness was manifested in the speed and dash of galloping horses amid the smokes and hazes of the battlefields. He certainly was not affected in speech or manner; in combat at least he was all business.

In his physical activities Bonaparte was indefatigable. He constantly visited troops and installations, where he expected to be informed of the status of personnel and supplies; he frequently complained that a given troop movement had not been adequately supervised (except by himself). He slept only at intervals, mainly from about 1800 or 1900 hours to about 0100, after which he studied dispatches. A nap of one or two hours was sufficient to restore his energy. Travel of seventy-five miles a day was not unusual, using saddle horse or coach; in the battle area he was always at the gallop. He had a sharp sense of the limitations of his subordinates in the physical sense and worked them to the limit.

In an era not distinguished for concern for social welfare, the solicitude for the well-being of the common soldier was unusual and permeated all ranks of the Napoleonic Army. It was axiomatic that care of men and animals was a command responsibility, accounting in no small measure for the devotion of the men, not only to Napoleon but to all of the Marshals. As for morale, Desaix wrote of Bonaparte that there was not a single brigade that had not been personally persuaded by the Emperor that it was the very best in La Grande Armée.

It may have been the mores of the period that neither the Emperor nor the Marshals would rate high in personal integrity or loyalty. True, they cared for their troops, which is certainly evidence of loyalty both from the command standpoint and from the devotion it inspired in the ranks. However, Napoleon and the Marshals as persons were something else. Most of the latter became kings, princes, dukes and men of wealth. Perhaps concern for their own riches dulled their loyalty to the Little Corporal, for sooner or later almost all defected. But then, they could remember how the Emperor deserted the Army after Aboukir, running the British blockade to reach Paris and assume political control. On that occasion Kléber said, "There goes the little scoundrel; he's no bigger than my boot!" Again, he left La Grande Armée freezing after the Russian disaster, when he simply rode away. And again, after Waterloo, he turned his horse toward Paris without a word and melted away in solitary despair. Loyalty is a two-edged sword. The Marshals, as they fell away, had memories to ease their consciences.

The genius of the Emperor for evolving and practicing a matchless system of battlefield control, however, stands out above all. A later analysis of this system will demonstrate how closely methods of nearly 200 years ago are suited to the apparently over complex problems of today.

The political background of Austerlitz is of no consequence in an examination of command methods. Suffice to say that the victory was the turning point of Napoleonic history, finally establishing him as the undisputed Emperor of the French.

The battle was fought on December 1–2, 1805, in Moravia, near the confluence of the two branches of the Goldbach, a small stream running southward, and just west of the town of Austerlitz, which itself was never the scene of action. Well below the stream junction, forming a large Y, are the hamlets of Telnitz and Moenitz. Immediately east of the junction is a hill mass called Stahre Vinobrad, capped by the tiny village of Prätzen. To the north lie the Moravian mountains, terrain too rough for maneuver.

Into this area the planning genius of Napoleon mobilized the bulk of La Grande Armée. Illustrative of the way the Emperor could dominate a staff by explicitly outlining the general plan campaign, he dictated the entire concept directly to his "Intendant-General," Count Daru. In this manner the deployment of the entire French army from western Europe to the Rhine, and then the Danube, was visualized in detail: the marches, the location of the bivouacs, the routes and the timing for their use, the bridges and the plan for ultimate assembly. The Intendant-General thus operated as a chief of administrative services. Marshal Berthier, the actual Chief of Staff, would work out the remaining details and would see to the supervision of their execution.

Yet, it was not genius at work. Napoleon maintained a veritable library of notebooks, posted by a group of clerks, from which he could extract every fact connected with his corps, his divisions and his regiments, to include traits of personality and the combat records of leaders. So, though his dictation of a mobilization order may have been a marvel of lucid thinking, his facts were always at his elbow.

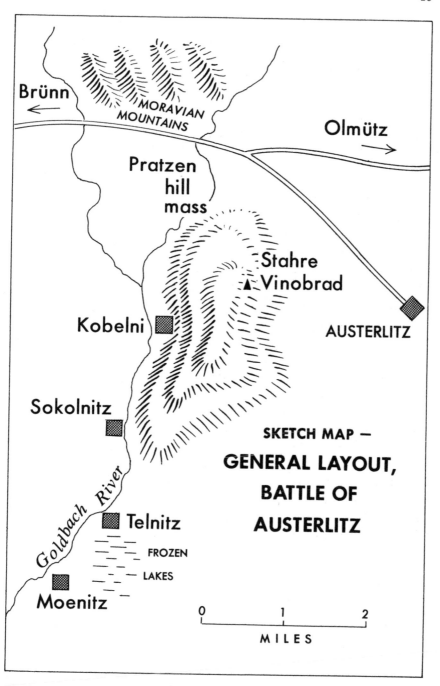

Brünn

MORAVIAN MOUNTAINS

Olmütz

Pratzen hill mass

Stahre
▲Vinobrad

Kobelni

AUSTERLITZ

Sokolnitz

*Goldbach River*

SKETCH MAP —

**GENERAL LAYOUT,
BATTLE OF
AUSTERLITZ**

Telnitz

FROZEN

LAKES

Moenitz

0          1          2

MILES

Austerlitz brought the full flower of La Grande Armée into action. Here was Napoleon, at thirty-five, solidifying his power; here were his best marshals, generals, and aides, Davout, Murat, Soult, Lannes, Bernadotte, Bessières; Berthier, the indefatigable Chief of Staff was fifty-five, but all others were under forty except for Bernadotte at forty-one; all but three had attained the rank of general officer within the past ten years. It was, in truth, the "first team."

The "Allies," a coalition of Austrians under the Emperor Francis, and Russians under the young Czar Alexander I, were able to muster nearly 90,000 men and 278 artillery pieces for the effort to destroy Napoleon after his conquest of Vienna. Their forces were concentrated while the French were still en route to assembly areas. By the end of November, 1805, it was clear that the French (in Allied eyes) were moving into a trap where they could be decimated by the superior forces after a classic envelopment. Plans to accomplish this were drawn up by the Austrian General Weirother, though the plans were by no means acclaimed as brilliant by numerous critics, the foremost being the Russian General Kutuzov, a canny and experienced field general. Picturing the French forces as assembled in the area just west of the Goldbach River fork, Weirother planned to encircle the French south flank near Telnitz at daylight with three columns. By combining this strike with an attack due west from the Prätzen hills across the Goldbach, the French would be routed, while cavalry tightened the noose on both south and north flanks.

Napoleon considered his strength of 60,000 men and 139 guns, though numerically inferior by a wide margin, quite sufficient for victory. If he seemed to be risking both France and his career, his lack of consideration for possible withdrawal routes did not indicate it. On December 1 Davout's Corps had yet to arrive in the area. But the Emperor indulged himself in pseudo-efforts to talk peace with the Allies, seeking to give the impression of weakness and fear. Meanwhile he had not only divined the enemy plans but had arranged to counter the enemy trap by creating one of his own.

In any event his peace feelers bore fruit. Weirother became convinced that Napoleon was about to withdraw without a fight.

Davout finally arrived with his Corps, after covering ninety miles in two days, with his exhausted men expected to bear the brunt of the probable enemy attempt to encircle the French south flank. While Murat and Lannes held the north wing, just below the Moravian mountains, the French spearhead was to be aimed at the enemy center, against the high ground of Stahre Vinobrad and Prätzen. The reduced Allied forces in the center were to be overwhelmed and the attack carried through to strike the flanks of the Allied columns attempting to move around the French south; Soult's Corps was charged with making this main effort.

Personal reconnaissance was a fetish with Napoleon. On December 1 he made a preliminary exploration that tended to confirm his prediction of the forthcoming Allied course of action. Another at 0200 hours the next morning, on which he was so close to the enemy lines that he was nearly hit by Russian gunfire, produced two results. First, the furor over his safe return, manifested by torchlights and cheering in the French camp and seen and heard by the Allies, cemented the opinion of the latter that the French were about to withdraw. Second, he adjudged it necessary to change his plans to some degree. The spearhead of the attack on the Allied center was shifted slightly to the south.

The important point is that the Napoleonic control system was capable of deciding on a change in plan at 0300 hours and disseminating it through the entire army by 0700. It showed the mutual confidence between the leader and the led. In contrast, a single Russian order, issued by Kutuzov, required three hours for dispatch over a distance of four miles from Allied headquarters to the southern flanking force.

The Emperor had cannily formed his troops, once assembled, in a tightly massed group in the geographical center of the area. Coupled with the mistaken Allied idea that he was withdrawing, this added inducement for the enemy to undertake the encirclement of the south flank. Now the trapper was to be trapped!

As a matter of hindsight, had the Allies held the high ground, the issue might well have been resolved in their favor. This was the element of risk in the Emperor's plan, one he recognized.

The advance command post layout favored by Napoleon was readied for displacement to the high ground near Prätzen as soon as its capture was assured. But, preliminary to the action, all major commanders save Davout were assembled for final instructions. Napoleon was awaiting last-minute evidence that enemy moves would validate his timing. By 0800 the rising sun silhouetted the southward-bound Allied encircling columns, even though the light fog simultaneously and obligingly screened the French formations poised to strike the flanks. Then the Emperor's signal! Away galloped the generals and marshals to launch their own forces; but Napoleon stayed the impatient Soult, "Wait another quarter hour," he said, "then it will be time."

The battle did not, however, proceed exactly according to his predictions. Russian cavalry, screening the southern envelopment, lost their way and delayed matters to the point where the Prätzen hill mass, the initial French objective, still held troops that should have been well on their way. In consequence, Soult's attack, once launched, encountered unexpected numbers.

Moreover, the action to the south took on a savage, see-saw aspect. Fortunately, Davout's tired troops regained their élan and strength once the sound of battle reached their ears. In spite of being badly outmanned and outgunned they held on with a magnificent display of courage and tenacity.

Nevertheless, Soult's drive had surprised the Allied center on the Prätzen hill mass which had planned an attack of its own. However difficult the storming of the heights, the objective of Vandamme's division of Soult's corps was gained within an hour. And, on his right, St. Hilaire's division succeeded in their thrust in only twenty minutes of approach and assault. The lucky break of low-hung camp fire smoke and fog had indeed cloaked the initiation of the attack, unexpected as well because of the success of Napoleon's deceptive measures of the past twelve hours.

By now the Emperor and his party were on the heights of Stahre Vinobrad and in touch with the center and the south; to the north, Lannes' corps and Murat's cavalry were silent; actually they were slowly driving back the Allied right wing. Meanwhile, Napoleon's right hand, the tireless Berthier, and his staff assistants had provided Bonaparte with an updated situation map reflecting the latest developments. There was still cause for worry in the south, though Davout was holding against odds of over seven to one; accordingly, reserves were readied to bolster either the right wing or the center, as might be necessary.

Compared with this tight control of forces, the Allied attack in the south was essentially leaderless. General Buxhöuden, the senior commander, was hopelessly drunk throughout; in consequence he was never able to comprehend how, in the end, Davout and his men, inspired even after their ninety mile hike, not only held but finally turned and broke the Allied "envelopment." Miloradovitch, the Russian general commanding the center, galloped wildly to and fro between his troops and the enemy, making a most heroic spectacle but too occupied with his heroism to give any orders whatever to his men; where the drunken Buxhouden in the south was covered to some extent by able subordinates, Miloradovitch unfortunately postured alone.

Napoleon was now sensing the possible impact of the risks which his plan had accepted so calmly. In the center, both Vandamme's and St. Hilaire's divisions were assailed by vicious counterattacks, one by the Imperial Russian Guard. Another, in fact, almost succeeded in persuading St. Hilaire to withdraw from the heights, a move that might well have lost everything. When St. Hilaire suggested retreat to Thiébault, one of his brigade commanders, Colonel Pouzet, in command of the 10th Light, broke in to urge not retreat but a bayonet charge. This was made with such verve that the Allied counterattack was checked long enough for Soult rapidly to bring up the corps artillery which, at point blank ranges, restored the situation.

Prompt artillery displacement also featured the action under Lannes and Murat in the north. Here the Allied wing under General Bagration fell back, as much from the failure to receive coordinating instructions from Allied Headquarters as from the pressure of Lannes and Murat. This action was likewise touch and go for some time, and was charged with the same drama that characterized the main battle. Bagration had tried to encircle Lannes from the north, even as the Supreme Command had hoped to encircle Napoleon from the south. But the response of Lannes was identical to that of his Emperor's; he drove directly at Bagration's center and left, causing Suchet to compliment him later for "the precision and rapidity with which the maneuver was effected." Had Bagration not immediately sensed his peril and withdrawn his own enveloping force, the Russian army might have been destroyed.

Murat, charged with exploiting the breakthrough in the center in true blitzkrieg style, failed to act energetically. By the time Napoleon assessed the situation it was too late to prevent the escape of a significant portion of the enemy force.

The evidence points to a rather indifferent attitude on the part of Bonaparte regarding the situation in the north. Not long after noon he was convinced that the day was won. His attention became centered on shifting his effort to the south in order to crush the bulk of the Allied enveloping force between Soult and Davout. In this he was eminently successful, and this was the measure of his victory. But by the time orders for pursuit of all elements of the enemy were disseminated, Bagration had eluded entrapment and started back for Russia. This development appears to have been the only lapse from close control on the part of the French command and staff.

Before and during the battle Napoleon made frequent use of his personal staff and security forces to supplement the usual chain of command that was so effectively managed by the great Chief of Staff, Berthier. An aide, Savary, had set the stage for the battle by a straight-faced delivery of the message that deluded the Allies into the belief that Napoleon feared defeat and was preparing to withdraw from the area.

When the situation during the eve of battle was obscure, the Emperor turned to Lebrun and directed him to verify personally the initiation of the Allied move to the south; and it was Lebrun, too, who after the battle, was charged with riding posthaste to Paris carrying the news of victory.

At a critical moment, while the Allies were counterattacking to high ground, Napoleon summoned Marshal Bessières, directing him to launch the Imperial Guard into the fray. But when Bessières responded with less force than was warranted, Bonaparte called to his aide-de-camp, Colonel Rapp. The dashing colonel thereupon headed two squadrons of chasseurs into the thick of the fight. He would have been taken prisoner but for the nick-of-time charge by a troup to effect his release. But he accomplished his objective.

The use of the aides is an important aspect of the Napoleonic system of control, and will be given great emphasis in succeeding chapters because of its bearing on modern lightning war. At Austerlitz the system showed its effectiveness by bringing Bonaparte information he was not receiving fully from his regular chain of command (though one of the best of all time) and by allowing him to deal a critical blow at a critical moment.

In defeating a force half again the size of his own, with the latter exhausted by long marches to assembly areas from the ends of Europe, what were Napoleon's essential ingredients for success? Planning brilliance? Fighting spirit? Deception?

It is true that the Allied plan of attack discounted the very move that Napoleon ultimately made, in spite of the warnings given Weirother by other Allied generals. It is true that French élan overcame fatigue and it is true that deception played a significant part in the surprise of the Allies. But it is inescapable that at every turn the French were far more responsive to orders and that their orders emanated from a single commander who was forcefully aware of every development, barring the lost chance for pursuit of Bagration. The French were kept in hand in a central location while the enemy dissipated his forces around the perimeter. Napoleon was personally active, and used his personal staff actively to supplement Berthier's staff organization. Troops were astonishingly mobile, as witness Davout's timely arrival from a march that was long by the standards of today; artillery displacement was rapid and timely and was the critical factor on at least two occasions; generally, communications were excellent and in stark contrast to those of the enemy. In short, all the characteristics associated with the 1940–67 blitzes were present, though in lesser degree according to the technology of the day.

A very basic principle was again emphasized, in addition, as it will undoubtedly be emphasized innumerable times in the future, namely, that mobile war is normally a state of confusion as well as a state of mind. Victory depends upon how quickly and how effectively order can be periodically brought out of this confusion by cool and resourceful commanders.

Many of the same leaders were present at Waterloo. What happened, then, to bring on disaster?

Among the absentees, the principal emphasis must be laid on the great Chief of Staff, Alexandre Berthier, the man closest to Napoleon throughout the years of the First Empire, and a Marshal of France. But now Napoleon had returned from Elba. The day of reckoning was approaching and Berthier was gone from the entourage. He was to be sadly missed.

Berthier may well deserve the rating as the greatest chief of staff in history. But he was never noted for being decisive, at least in his own behalf. His detractors, of whom there were naturally many, maintained that he simply repeated what the Emperor had said and never did anything himself to add to it. They failed to give him credit, however, for being the mainspring of Supreme Headquarters in the matter of complete and timely information exchange. Most important, Berthier provided the impulsion insuring that urgent or crucial messages were brought to Napoleon's attention without delay.

It was quite in keeping with Berthier's character that, after accompanying the new French King and his court, fleeing from the advance of the recently exiled Bonaparte, he quitted the Bourbon retinue and went home to Bamberg. There, after two months of soul searching over his defection from his old commander, he went upstairs to a window from which he watched the passing of a column of soldiers en route to join Napoleon's army. Whether an accident or a suicide, he inexplicably fell to his death in the street below. This tragic event was world-shaking in its implications, for what might have been the results of Ligny, Quatre Bras, and Waterloo had not the brilliant Chief of Staff, for the first time, been absent from Bonaparte's side? And what of the history of Europe had these battles been won by the French?

In *Campaigns of Napoleon,* David Chandler quotes Napoleon's saying that "Loss of time is irreparable in war. . . . I may lose a battle but I shall never lose a minute."

The Emperor's misfortunes of the fateful days of June 15–18, 1815, may be summed up in the complete negation of this principle. Beginning with the opening engagements nearly everything that took place on the French side went contrary to what would have been expected such a short time previously when Masséna, Davout, and Suchet, among the other great Marshals, formed the "first team." Now, Ney, Soult, the aging Kellermann, and the newly-created Marshal Grouchy took over. They performed with incredible ineptitude, considering the reputations of all but Grouchy.

The basic French objective was simply one of defeating the Allies, under the British Wellington and the German Blücher, singly and in succession, while preventing them from joining forces. Pursuing this aim, preliminary battles, which many have mistaken for skirmishes ushering in Waterloo, took place just south thereof at Quatre Bras and Ligny. They were indeed battles in which the collapse of Napoleon's once-great command system was plainly evident, even before Waterloo itself was fought.

Chandler charges Wellington with a complete misapprehension of Napoleon's scheme of operations. Wellington, believing that Bonaparte would envelop the west flank to get at Brussels, not only shifted the weight of his forces in that direction but did so in a most dilatory and careless manner. The English center of gravity was moved away from a juncture with Blücher's troops on the east, a maneuver that should have played directly into Napoleon's hands; this because of Bonaparte's concept of attacking with Ney and Grouchy abreast, with the weight of the effort placed on Grouchy's effort to crush Blücher.

Yet this was a new, or rather a different Napoleon, who had grown stout and sluggish, perhaps, at Elba, or possibly he was ill and not up to the demands of the day. Still, he was in the saddle some fifteen hours during June 16, proving that he was physically active, though his mental alertness may have been affected.

He had chosen most unwisely in the matter of major subordinates for his one-hundred-day effort to return to power. Soult was now Chief of Staff and was about to demonstrate his unfitness for staff work, whatever his one-time brilliance as a field commander. Grouchy, a cavalryman, was selected to work in the unfamiliar environment of the infantry. Ney, whom some credited with "battle fatigue" as a result of the Russian campaign, was given unprecedented freedom of action, only to illustrate that courage, without battle control, is not enough.

Murat, one of the great cavalry leaders of all time, and Suchet and Davout, both able Marshals, were passed over for good or for ill.

Detailed battle accounts of the momentous three days, with appropriate map references, serve no purpose here. Tabulation of a few incidents will amply illustrate how far the command-control system had deteriorated since the days when a gentle but firm rein had been exercised over a group of clever and aggressive Marshals.

On June 15, 1815, when Ney was headed towards Quatre Bras and Grouchy, on the right, moved on Ligny and Blücher, orders were five hours late. Even then, the Allies were surprised by the appearance of the French. A morally courageous British officer took it upon himself to countermand Wellington's orders to displace West, thus assuring the defense of Quatre Bras and probably saving the battle for Wellington.

Napoleon rode in person to Grouchy's headquarters to spur on a lethargic Grouchy, arriving back at his own command post at 2100 hours. This ended his fifteen-hour day in the saddle, which should not have been overtaxing for a man of forty-six.

Napoleon's scheme of operations envisaged holding the Imperial Guard under his control as a reserve, in the classic triangular battle organization. Whether the idea of making the initial main effort was known to Ney or not is problematical, but by 1100 hours on the morning of the 16th Ney had not moved at all in the direction of Quatre Bras. For its part, Supreme headquarters issued orders at 0830, in stark contrast to the old habit of dissemination at 0200, with receipt by the troops no later than 0700 or 0800.

Ney apparently had been under the impression that the I Corps, under d'Erlon, would reinforce his efforts. But this Corps suffered the most incredible treatment of any unit in the history of La Grande Armée. With Grouchy battling hard for Ligny, Soult, as Chief of Staff, dispatched a note to Ney directing him to envelop Blücher's west wing. At the time, Ney was heavily engaged, so

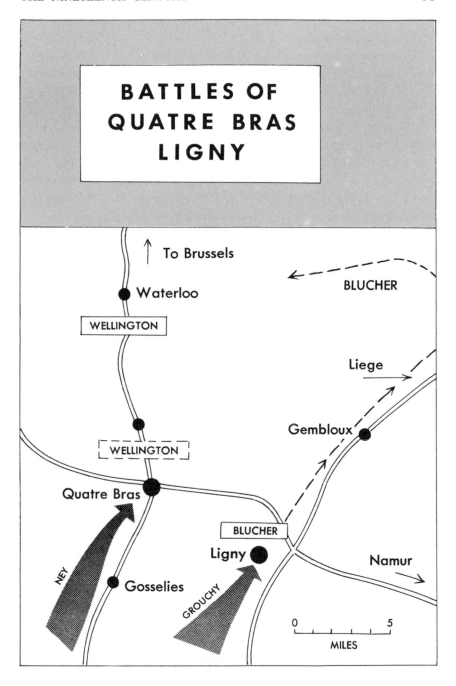

BATTLES OF
QUATRE BRAS
LIGNY

To Brussels

Waterloo

WELLINGTON

BLUCHER

Liege

WELLINGTON

Gembloux

Quatre Bras

BLUCHER

Ligny

NEY

Gosselies

GROUCHY

Namur

0          5
MILES

d'Erlon was ordered to move toward Ligny. This move seems to have infuriated Ney.

Napoleon in the meantime had sensed that the critical moment was at hand for the launching of the Imperial Guard to finish off Blücher; but then word came that enemy forces were closing in from the west. Accordingly the orders to the Guard were countermanded. It then developed that the reported enemy forces were actually the troops of d'Erlon, moving towards Grouchy. For some reason an aide of the Emperor turned the I Corps back toward Ney so that not only did d'Erlon see no action whatever, but a force of 10,000 uncommitted troops were "overlooked" by Bonaparte. These could certainly have eased Grouchy's problems, for he suffered severe losses before beating back the Prussian troops as night fell on the 16th.

Both Napoleon and Grouchy failed to exploit the victory at Ligny. The action at Quatre Bras could have been termed a draw, with Ney heaping criticism on d'Erlon for the futile shuttling back and forth between the columns. The curtain of charity was apparently drawn over Soult's management of headquarters control procedures.

Napoleon felt relief that the morning of the 17th found Wellington's troops still at Quatre Bras; he held to the opinion that he could now turn on the English. Grouchy had been sent in pursuit of Blücher, a pursuit in name only, for dilatory command action soon lost contact with the Prussians. But any French assumption that Blücher was defeated was sadly in error, for the German had no other idea than to circle and join forces with Wellington.

On the 17th Ney did nothing whatever, wasting five hours of precious time. Napoleon arrived at Ney's headquarters at 1400 hours and was enraged at the lack of aggressiveness. By this time, however, Wellington had concluded that Blücher was badly beaten and that his own recourse must be withdrawal. He began the move to what next day became Waterloo, and Bonaparte, sensing the retreat, charged d'Erlon's Corps with conducting a belated pursuit. But a violent rainstorm came up, making the whole battlefie'd a sea of mud.

As an interesting measure of latter-day Napoleonic communications effectiveness, the Emperor received a message from Grouchy at 0400 hours on the 18th that had been written at 2200 the previous night and had lain untouched in someone's "in basket" since 0200.

In spite of the fact that Grouchy had indicated that Blücher had eluded him and that linkage with Wellington would be possible, Napoleon took no action until 1000 hours on the 18th when, due to Grouchy's slowness, it became a matter of too little, too late. It is debatable whether positive action by the Emperor could have forced Grouchy to move out at least a division at full speed, and perhaps delay Blücher until the battle with Wellington was resolved.

In view of all these uncharacteristic mistakes, Waterloo itself was inevitable.

On the day of destiny Jerome Bonaparte, who had been directed to make a feint against the Allied center, permitted over-enthusiasm to turn the feint into a major effort that failed with heavy losses. Could not the same aide-de-camp system that served so brilliantly at Austerlitz have prevented this useless blow?

Controversy arose over the use of the French artillery, involving the desirability of waiting until the ground dried so that ricochet effects would improve, all at a period when time favored the Allies.

Marshal Ney initiated a cavalry charge in the wrong direction without attempting to coordinate it in any way with support artillery. The failure of this charge on such grounds seems inexplicable in view of a subsequent charge which was properly coordinated and locally successful. But time was running out.

Napoleon, according to Chandler, sensed impending defeat and attempted to buoy up the spirits of his troops by spreading the rumor that Grouchy was coming immediately to their aid. But when the Imperial Guard was thrown in, and, of all things, repulsed, panic spread more quickly than if sent over the Napoleonic communications system of June 18, 1815. Finally, when troops turned to find Blücher on their heels, rather than the expected Grouchy (who never arrived), rout was complete.

For research in the influence of command and control on the outcome of battle, the series of engagements that culminated at Waterloo offers a remarkable study in contrasts. Commanders noted for audacity and mobility displayed only rashness and lethargy. Those who had worshipped at the shrine of exquisite timing threw timing into the Belgian mud. An army steeped in the principles of blitzkrieg ignored the urgency of rapid information exchange.

Evidence indicates that Bonaparte tried to continue his habits of personal mobility and that he was shocked at the lack of aggressiveness he might have expected from Grouchy and from Ney. But his ability to inspire at critical battle moments had been left behind at Elba.

The striking feature, however, was unquestionably the collapse of headquarters control procedures, once the province of Alexandre Berthier. Even a Napoleon cannot be expected to be everywhere at once, and the spark that should have prodded Ney while Bonaparte was with Grouchy, and vice versa, was not there. Soult was but a pale imitation of the Great Clerk. Indeed one may suspect that a large portion of the spirit of Napoleon Bonaparte went out the second story window at Bamberg.

There are many curious parallels between the breakdown of the French blitz capability at Waterloo and the German failure in the Ardennes in World War II.

Finally, as an observation on span of control statistics in comparing battles of the Napoleonic era with modern and future war, 140,000 troops were deployed within an area of some three square miles in the Waterloo area, though the accepted tactics of the day visualized about 20,000 men per mile of front. This space would accommodate at most two or three battalions today and perhaps even less for the nuclear age.

It is unfortunate that the source material on General Nathan Bedford Forrest's command techniques is not so extensive as might be desirable. The biographies by John A. Wyeth and Robert S. Henry are excellent as biographies but require careful extrapolation of a sentence here and a paragraph there to shed light on methodology. Much more material of the word-of-mouth variety came to the authors via Major General J. Franklin Bell, U.S.A. (1856–1919), known as the father of the U.S. Army Command and General Staff College, who was a devotee of Forrest and a young contemporary of officers who had once served with the great Confederate leader. Bell imparted his store of knowledge to Hamilton S. Hawkins, who served briefly as his aide, and who as a brigadier general was termed the "Mr. Cavalry" of the 1920s and 1930s. Before his death in 1950 Hawkins had passed on much of the data that follow. These are adequate, though not as voluminous as the data relating to Napoleon and others, so that the comparative treatment may appear uneven.

Forrest is an excellent example of the selection process by which "masters" were chosen from among many contemporaries of renown, such as R. E. Lee, Jackson, Grant, and Sherman. His choice reflects the need of a model suitable for the highly mobile and violent environment of the 1970s and 1980s, an environment in which Grant cannot compete with Forrest, however secure his place in history.

Like many of Napoleon's Marshals, Forrest was of humble origin. The son of a blacksmith, he entered the Confederate Army as a private in 1861 and emerged in 1865 as the most famous cavalry general of the American Civil War.

Unlike Bonaparte, Forrest was a man of commanding presence. Six feet two inches in height, broad-shouldered and robust at over 180 pounds, and black-bearded according to the custom of the times, he awed friend and foe alike as he moved into the front line with pistol or saber thrust point blank into the face of the enemy.

He was a man of opposites. He flew into towering rages, especially when any evidence of cowardice cropped up in battle; on more than one occasion he wrought swift justice by personally dealing with the culprit on the spot. On the other hand, he was a thorough gentleman in the best traditions of the South; he was good-humored at social gatherings, swift at repartee and appreciative of a joke, even on himself.

Legend has it that Forrest was essentially ignorant because of his lowly upbringing. It is true that he was relatively uneducated; his writing was especially primitive because of basic spelling errors. The story is told of a subordinate officer who had been denied a leave of absence, but who chose to ask for a reconsideration. Back came his letter with Forrest's penciled scrawl, "I tole you twicet godamit no!"

At the same time, he was a voracious reader. He appeared to have an inherent appreciation of mathematics, solving problems through algebra and trigonometry when given only the barest essentials.

He had a passion for neatness, cleanliness, and soldierly appearance, taking drastic action against those who could not or would not conform to his standards. In general, one must agree with the Confederate leader Beauregard, who said of Forrest, "His capacity for war was limited only by his opportunities for displaying it." Forrest's rating by such authorities as British Field Marshal Haig fixed his reputation among European professionals.

The forceful and personal direction of battle that characterized the Brice's Crossroads fight was typical of Forrest's entire period of service. He may well have been the epitome of the front-line general. Twenty-nine horses were killed under him while his own wounds were miraculously light. Any intimation that he might be a "creature of his staff" would be laughable, for he ran a battle as a drill sergeant might run a parade. Certainly, he listened avidly to advice from his staff, but battle concepts, plans, and orders were all Forrest.

His professional competence was manifested in countless ways, intuitive though most of it might have been. His sense of timing was extraordinary. Of the Battle of Okolona, which was fought in the open with opposing troop dispositions visible to both sides, Forrest said, "I saw Grierson make a bad move and I rode right over him!" At Oxford, his command swept entirely around a Federal army in a night march, completely cutting off all enemy control facilities.

Forrest's dedication was to deep objectives, gained through wide envelopments piercing the hostile rear as a matter of standard procedure. Concurrent with this doctrine was his (then) unorthodox habit of operating artillery in the very van of attack, simplifying the coordination of fire and maneuver, and depending upon the elements of mobility and surprise to keep the guns out of enemy hands.

He emphasized ruthless and tireless pursuit of a beaten enemy as the best assurance of a decisive victory; in these operations he continually demonstrated his ability to sense just how far troops can be pushed without really exhausting them.

His penchant for personal combat has been regarded as a fault, but, he weighed the situation and got into the fight only when relatively small numbers of combatants were involved. In larger engagements he realized that the size of his force demanded that he control from a position further, but not too far, to the rear.

He employed his aides-de-camp in the Napoleonic manner, calling them "gallopers." These trusted aides, carefully selected by Forrest for their dash tempered with cool judgment, moved rapidly over the battlefield and kept Forrest apprised of the most recent developments. Similarly, he kept abreast of logistical requirements, hostile as well as friendly, for Forrest's raids on Federal supply centers delivered some of the most telling blows of the war.

Forrest's conduct could not help but inspire his entire command to the extra effort that usually spelled victory against odds. He exhorted his men, he "rode the line" and he spurred on every effort. True, his command was small compared to those of most mobile war commanders, except for the brigades of the Israeli campaigns. But, whatever the span of control, his efforts have never been excelled. The sight of their commander rising in his stirrups, or striding purposefully ahead, pistol or saber in hand, eyes flashing and beard flying in the wind, must have put heart into the occasional fearful soldier, of whom there were apparently but few.

Moral courage was of course a watchword. Forrest always attacked whatever the odds and whatever the circumstances. But this was the opposite of rashness. Forrest's reasoned decisions were based on throwing the enemy off balance and deceiving him into the belief that Forrest enjoyed a superiority that he in fact did not have. Forrest considered the attack actually a measure of safety.

If all this does not speak of creativity, his efforts to stage elaborate "shows" to conceal his own weakness testify both to creativity and initiative. He adopted a drill, triggered by a bugle signal, whereby columns would move at a gallop into the sight of the enemy, and then disappear around a hill, only to circle and join the tail of the column thereby giving the illusion of thousands of reinforcements streaming into the battle. His instructions to the cavalry at Brice's Crossroads, to stage "demonstrations" on the flanks of the hostile army form part of the battle description that follows.

Forrest's robust constitution allowed him to keep up with long marches, plan, participate in, and control battles, and then shrug off the fatigue that to some men results from responsibility alone.

In contrast to some colorful mobile leaders, Forrest was a hidebound moralist, wreaking his ire against any subordinate caught in compromising situations with women. True, it was a convention of time and place, but one doubtless honored more in the breach than in the observance. Forrest was wholly abstemious, being neither a smoker nor a drinker, and conducting his headquarters life along austere lines. Such traits may accompany bold leadership, but unhappily are rarely the cause of it.

Brice's Crossroads, in Lee County, Mississippi, was the scene of one of Forrest's most incredible battles. On June 10, 1864, Forrest with about 4700 cavalry (who customarily rode to action and fought on foot) and a dozen artillery pieces, opposed a Union force under General S. D. Sturgis with 4500 infantry, 3200 cavalry and twenty-two pieces of artillery. The battle followed unusually heavy rains, complicated by suffocating June heat.

Sturgis prepared carefully. Union forces had been drawn up in battle array in a terrain featured by thick brush. But Forrest had banked on the cover to confuse the enemy as to the number of attacking Confederates as well as to play on the average soldier's apprehension of the unknown. To repeat, attack was the only form of combat that Forrest ever employed. Here it was most suitable in view of his reasoning that the Union cavalry would precede their infantry by some three hours, and that the former could be "whipped in that time." Then, when the infantry, exhausted by the heat and mud, came forward to reinforce their cavalry "we would ride right over them, with everything moving as fast as possible."

Forrest's command had to march twenty-five miles over the

same heavy roads to reach the scene of action. The artillery had an eighteen-mile march before contact could be made. But, in spite of the fact that his forces were arriving piecemeal, or perhaps because of it, Forrest ordered the lead elements to attack as a show of force, even in the face of formidable odds. When fresh troops arrived they were immediately thrown in. After about an hour of probing, the Confederates retired temporarily into the thick cover.

At this point Forrest rode the length of the line encouraging all men to hit hard on the next attempt, which this time would not be a feint. Against approximately double their own numbers, troops made the assault with such fierceness that hand-to-hand fighting ensued. Even with two additional regiments thrown in by the Union commanders, the southerners carried the day.

Forrest now directed his artillery, under Captain Morton, to come forward at the gallop. Simultaneously he ordered his small screening cavalry detachments to strike the hostile flanks and rear, a classic and favorite maneuver. The "superior" Union cavalry was beaten and in disorder; it remained to deal with the oncoming 4500 infantry.

Forrest had calculated correctly. The Union infantry arrived exhausted, but when added to the defeated cavalry added up to some 8000 men. The half-hour lull had restored the Confederate strength and part of the command had been on duty as horse holders, so the advance was resumed.

It was hard going in the heat and undergrowth and a strong counterattack was launched by the Union forces. But Forrest in person dismounted and, with drawn pistol, rallied the men, checked the counterattack and again took up the pressure.

At this critical point Forrest was informed of a deceptive attack made by his cavalry on the right wing. By rushing to and fro, firing and creating every possible noise, this force succeeded in representing itself in double or triple strength. In fact, General Sturgis' after-action reports were to credit Forrest with a strength of 15,000 to 20,000 men.

Forrest then ordered Captain Morton's artillery to advance with the leading lines when the attack was resumed. In effect it was a mobile assault by artillery, with guns alternately firing and displacing, coordinated by an agreed signal of firing from the right of the line, to which Forrest at once repaired.

In spite of their own fatigue, the southerners, exhorted by Forrest, were able to charge all along the line, while cavalry stabbed at the flanks of the enemy. Soon all gave way.

The pursuit was relentless. Both Federal and Confederate elements became confused, and at one point Morton's guns were trained on friendly pursuing companies. Forrest exchanged battle-tired men for fresh horse holders and the latter took up the chase. In the end, Morton's artillerymen, having started with an eighteen-mile march to the combat area, and fighting with mobile guns for five hours, followed the foe until well into the night. Then, resting some hours, the pursuit was resumed, keeping pace with Forrest's advance guard elements and, finally winding up with a drive of sixty-one miles in thirty-eight hours, excluding the five hours of combat. Bell's Brigade made eighty miles in forty hours, excluding combat time. An ideal example of mobility exercised at the period when it would best pay off.

Brice's Crossroads was a battle dominated by a single personality, where personality acted to imbue the command with confidence and fighting spirit in the face of highly unfavorable odds. Forrest correctly assessed the debilitating effect of mud, heat, and heavy cover on his enemy. And his control system based on his own presence at the critical point, and upon his highly mobile staff, allowed him to encircle the flanks and adopt deceptive measures to hide his own inferiority. His flair for close integration of artillery and maneuvering troops, even on a small scale, was a major factor in the Union rout. But of all the characteristics of blitzkrieg that were clearly exemplified, personal and forceful leadership, acting to inspire the command, was the dominant one. It was the triumph of an almost uniquely mobile state of mind.

# 6 The Birth of Modern Blitzkrieg

The modern era of lightning war begins in the period between World Wars I and II. It was then that the architects or analysts who forecast the blitz initiated their frustrating efforts to convince reluctant general staffs that the doctrines of trench warfare were both suicidal and outmoded. The period continues through World War II, when the actual blitz, as now defined, was presented by the great German plunge through Poland. The end is not marked by any specific date, for the modern blitz lives on. But for historical purposes it enters a period of transition effective with the Israeli wars in the Sinai. At this point it melds into an age of promise, when sonic and rotary-wing aircraft combine with electronic control devices to free warfare from terrain restrictions and speed coordination.

Certain developments in and following World War I, however, had a significant bearing on the development of lightning war. In the twenty years preceding the emergence of the great analysts, the Western world lived through a generation in which interest unfortunately centered on trench warfare. The effect on the history of mobile combat was wholly negative. Not only did ponderous staff procedures become popular, but many superficial thinkers deduced that new weaponry would make offensive combat so costly as to be unthinkable. To proponents of open warfare it was a lost generation.

There were few publicized exceptions. Winston Churchill wrote a book which received scant attention and which was aptly titled *The Unknown War*. In it he outlined the gigantic contortions of armies of millions of men, under the Germans Hindenburg and Ludendorff, and the Russians Samsanov and Rennenkampf, grappling in terrain unfamiliar today to the bulk of Western minds. Tannenberg and the Masurian Lakes saw the destruction of an entire Russian army, but few realized that the German corps commander, von François, was most directly responsible. He, by recognizing the critical moment, took the chance of acting counter to Ludendorff's specific orders. As Churchill says, von François, "operating with that rare combination of prudence and audacity that characterizes true soldierly genius," made the encirclement that prevented the Russian escape. It is one of many instances that should dispel the myth that German militarism is marked by inflexible adherence to orders. Under a doctrine of this kind the blitz would never have been born. In fact, German tactical principles have ever extolled the energetic assumption of the initiative. As proof, the photograph of the principals in the Tannenberg action at the tenth anniversary of the battle shows von Francois in the place of honor. The example of initiative undoubtedly helped gain General Staff acceptance of the Guderian concepts of mobile war which followed a decade later.

In the Middle East, General Allenby, Lawrence of Arabia, and their associates staged mobile and highly dramatic warfare over the Palestine deserts (1917–18), foreshadowing the Israeli strikes of 1956 and 1967. But Allenby never captured the attention of the general public and the top brass. Their interest was wholly on the just-finished war of attrition in France, with its appalling personnel losses measured in the millions at Sedan alone.

The effect of this misplaced interest on military instruction extended world-wide. With little or no movement to be considered, battle planning gave free rein to the bureaucratic ideas of the less imaginative generals, who formed a solid phalanx to resist intrusion by the adherents of mechanization. Intelligence gathering became subject to infinite detail, logistical requirements were of unprecedented complexity, and the staggering losses gave rise to personnel management problems never before encountered.

No general at the senior combat levels in 1918 had dared make decisions without extensive and tedious staff conferences.

The staff practices in many cases developed to the point where the commander became a figurehead. An attack or defense posture might be assumed, but this was as far as command went; the staff did the rest. It was a situation ideally suited to the avoidance of responsibility. When things went wrong, as they usually did, the blame could ordinarily be shifted around until it was lost in the maze of staff sections and subsections.

The momentous result of these conditions, however, was that in the postwar era, the staff conference system and its attendant procedures lent themselves perfectly to academic instruction in military professional schools. The closer procedures came to making war a science, the further instruction departed from the art of command. The latter was de-emphasized in favor of a curriculum that could be programmed, while experts in intelligence, personnel management and logistics sprang up like weeds.

Few generals could keep up with the dizzying developments in the "schools" and many were afraid to display ignorance in the presence of recent graduates of the War Colleges. It was not uncommon for one staff officer to remark, upon the arrival of a new commander, "Now we'll have to start all over and break in a new general."

The Spanish Civil War (1936–39), which Germany and Russia used as a proving ground through the medium of military aid, might have suggested something to the pundits who were convinced that attack was gone from military language because of the defensive power of new weapons. Actually, considerable success was achieved by Franco's horse cavalry, proving that mobility and leadership were just where Allenby had left them. However, the Civil War was shrugged off by the experts while the French finished the Maginot Line and succumbed to the pseudosecurity that it appeared to offer.

Instruction in the art of the static defense and the cumbersome staff methods associated with it has its place; the American military school system is without a peer. That a mutual affinity should develop is not surprising. But mobile command and staff methods cannot be taught in a classroom from books and maps; as in the case of football "skull practice," there is no substitute for getting out onto the field. Admittedly, without the superior instruction in high-level staff work provided by the schools in this era, the great strategic campaigns of World War II would never have got off the ground. But mobile warfare is not conducted at these high levels and the environment of 1918–38 was not conducive to its development.

In the 1920s, beginning with the construction of the Maginot Line, a young French general named de Gaulle protested against the state of mind it typified, and vainly tried to interest the French General Staff in the concept of using tanks in mass. But he did not make a business of it. The four who did were Major-General J. F. C. Fuller and Captain Sir Basil H. Liddell Hart in Britain, General Heinz Guderian in Germany, and General Adna Chaffee in the United States. Guderian owed much to Fuller and Liddell Hart, having made a thorough study of their writings. Chaffee worked independently. All owed a great deal to history and all ultimately overcame major obstacles in their efforts to implant the doctrine of lightning war and to urge the creation of the necessary mechanization with which to wage it.

J. F. C. Fuller was born in 1878. A soldier, analyst, and historian, he had the usual military duties until appointed Chief of Staff of the newly formed Tank Corps in 1916. He possessed a lively imagination and constantly sought new applications of modern arms. He planned the initial tank attack at Cambrai in 1917, involving 381 tanks, and was in charge of all planning for the 1918 operations. Failure to appreciate the role of the tank on the part of the high command was unquestionably the cause of the tactical blunder whereby the Cambrai operation was not exploited and a major success assured.

In 1922 Fuller became chief instructor at the Staff College and thus had a ready-made forum for his advanced thinking; in 1926 he was appointed Military Assistant to the new Chief of the General Staff and was made a major-general in 1930, an advancement inadequate for his talents, though perhaps surprising in view of his unorthodoxy, for he was without doubt a controversialist. His critics regarded him as an extremist and a visionary. He chose retirement in 1933 to devote himself to writing, in the belief that he could do more to advance the interests of the Army if he were not on active status.

His lectures on field regulations in 1932 were adopted for study by the German, Russian, and Czech armies, even while his concepts of armored warfare brought him into conflict with the establishment of the day on the home front. For example, his prediction that the Maginot Line would be France's tombstone aroused the proponents of defensive tactics. In consequence he exercised greater influence abroad than at home, for his influence on German and Russian tactical thought, along with that of Liddell Hart, was translated into action in World War II.

General Fuller was the author of more than thirty books. It was said of him that no other analyst of the twentieth century had such effect on the military thought of his day; however, Fuller advocated a separate tank arm and thereby differed from his fellow countryman, Liddell Hart, who correctly foresaw that an integrated force of combined mobile arms would be the answer to the coming era of mechanization. For this reason General Fuller does not carry quite the weight as an analyst that his distinguished contemporaries enjoy. Nevertheless, no one excelled him in advocating and hastening the putting of the armed forces on wheels.

Captain Sir Basil H. Liddell Hart, D.Litt., was born in England in 1895, attended St. Paul's and Cambridge and received an early commission in World War I. He participated in the first Somme campaign and, after a spell of illness, was moved to the Ypres area where he was wounded. He returned to France for the next Somme offensive (1916), was gassed and thereafter given light duty. In many ways this proved to be a blow that in the end resulted beneficially for the British armed forces, since it gave free rein to one of the outstanding military minds of modern times.

Liddell Hart's contributions may be somewhat wryly summed up in a recent quote by A. J. P. Taylor in the *London Observer*, "Capt. Liddell Hart has been asking innocent questions about military affairs for the best part of half a century and has never wearied of providing rational answers. The Germans learnt from him, the Russians learnt from him and the Americans learnt from him. Only the British generals lagged behind."

Yet the statement that a prophet is never without honor save in his own country is far from true in this case, at least. His analyses of tactics were recognized early by the most distinguished of the London newspapers and he went on to publish a host of books dealing with history, with mechanization, and with the requirements for future war. His knighthood and his D.Litt. were perhaps long in coming, but they came.

In his memoirs he stated that one of his earliest efforts was concerned with a study of the requirements of football goal kicking and of cricket bowling. He acquired special though wholly unorthodox skills in these departments. But then appeared a certain headmaster who frowned severely on the unorthodox. Thus the budding analyst was awakened to the British national tendency to cherish such disasters as Balaclava far more than to rejoice in victory.

His coinages and his innovations were many. He developed the concept of the "expanding spearhead," a basic tactic of lightning war, from Sun Tzu's 2000-year-old studies. He actually originated the term "lightning war" from his investigations of the American Civil War, a conflict slighted by many foreign military scholars. His book on the American General Sherman was widely admired, especially by Adna Chaffee. He coined the idea of a "combat unit" as far back as 1918, suggesting a combination of tank and infantry forces, and recommending further development of the concept.

Fuller and Liddell Hart espoused generally the same cause, mechanization; still, the latter's visualization of a balanced force put him more in tune with Guderian and Chaffee, though there was no joint work project.

Sir Basil and General Fuller had their admirers and their detractors. It is ironic that the fruits of their efforts were garnered by the Germans and Russians, with the former being the first to implement the lessons learned.

Heinz Guderian in his early career performed the usual duties of a professional officer, but quickly sensed the impact of the motor age. A diligent student, he voraciously absorbed works on mobile war, including those of Fuller and of Liddell Hart.

Guderian came on the scene at the time when the restrictions imposed by the Versailles Treaty were severely limiting the development of modern German military forces. The situation was galling, especially so when Hitler's rise was accompanied by nationalistic resurgence. How to achieve armed might without outward manisfestations of it became the burning question.

The brain behind the conceptual development of the German war machine was that of Heinz Guderian. Concepts were actuated by a host of brilliant field commanders, Erwin Rommel, Hasso von Manteuffel, and others.

Yet the initial task was a formidable one. In addition to the problem of creating new engines of war, forbidden by the Treaty, there was the opposition of the German General Staff, still wedded to what it considered the correct and orthodox methods of 1918, even against obstacles of the Maginot Line type.

But Hitler was urging the expansion of arms regardless of obstacles and Hitler was in command. His imagination was fired by Guderian's ideas and his power assured their implementation. So gradually the armored force took shape.

There was no basic disagreement with the Liddell Hart doctrine: the tank, used in mass according to the old heavy horse cavalry concept, was the central core around which a balanced force of infantry, artillery, engineers and other auxiliary troops was built, operating in close conjunction with support aircraft.

As far back as 1927 wooden and canvas mock-ups had been used for training. Now, pushing these crude imitations ahead of them, troops learned basic lessons from a 1929 study published by Guderian. Gunnery was simulated by firing flares through holes in the canvas mock-ups.

As the German effort progressed, Britain and France either refused to believe what was going on or were unable to muster the will and the means to stop further development. The American Military attaché in Berlin gave out a series of factual reports on the German evolutionary program. These produced no reaction whatever.

At the outbreak of the war in 1939 Guderian was given command of the XIX Corps in Poland and also led troops during the blitz of France. Afterward he was undermined by Hitler's sycophants; his advice was ignored and he was relieved of his command. But he had all the qualities of the great captains including that of humility, which he displayed when he uncomplainingly discharged his duties after being recalled to duty after his initial relief. He displayed a high degree of mental mobility as well in the crucible of the battlefield. Von Manteuffel stresses the point that Guderian's concepts, when tried out in combat, required no changes whatever.

Heinz Guderian should be remembered as the "father of German armor." As a field commander he undoubtedly ranks with the "masters," but his primary contribution to the saga of blitzkrieg rested in the fields of analysis and pedagogy.

As Guderian was the father of German armor, so Adna Chaffee was the father of American armor and of the doctrine under which it was ultimately employed.

There were other voices heard, however, during the years of Chaffee's battles with the General Staff, though it cannot be said that they contributed much to their final resolution.

According to his memoirs, General Dwight D. Eisenhower, then a field officer, and the then Colonel George S. Patton had many an informal conference on the probabilities of and the requirements for mobile war. Eisenhower relates the difficulty of finding any sympathetic reception for their views, either in the Army or in Congress; additionally, he wrote to a friend in 1967, "In 1920 and 1921 George Patton and I publicly and earnestly expounded [these ideas] in the service journals of the day. The doctrine was so revolutionary, as compared with World War I practice, that we were threatened with court-martial. [Our basic principles] were anathema to the high military officials of the time."

In 1935 a break in the pattern of antiquated thinking occurred with the publication of the annual report of the Chief of Staff, Douglas MacArthur. The report called for a study of the great potential of new defensive weapons, but stressed that only through mobility and surprise could success be hoped for. Tactical doctrine was foreseen as a combination of mobile mechanized forces, together with aircraft, directed against the flanks of hostile formations and aimed at deep objectives in their rear. The document went on to recommend study of the campaigns of Genghis Khan and was, all in all, a reflection of the views of Liddell Hart and Guderian, though quite independent thereof.

In spite of the report's origin in the Office of the Chief of Staff, the essence of its content was unpopular and had been for years. In consequence, its injunctions were conveniently forgotten except by Chaffee and his adherents.

For example, the Chief of Infantry had expressed himself as opposed to "the tendency to set up another branch of the service with the tank as its nucleus. . . . It is as unsound as was the attempt by the Air Corps to separate itself from the rest of Army. The tank is a weapon and as such it is an auxiliary to the Infantryman, as is every other arm or weapon that exists."

So it was in this frustrating environment that Adna Chaffee was compelled to labor. As early as 1927 he began his campaign for mechanization as a member of the General Staff in Washington. Shortly afterward, General Summerall, then Chief of Staff, issued a directive for the organization of a mechanized force based on concepts furnished by Chaffee, who also contributed to a written report of the War Department Mechanization Board, of which he was a member.

This latter paper was noteworthy in that it outlined for the first time a plan for creating a mobile force over a four-year period, beginning with a self-contained mobile regiment. This unit would serve as a testing laboratory for similar new fighting units, all to be part of a separate branch of the service, with a general officer serving as its organizer and commander. July 1, 1930, was set as the time for activation.

Although conceived independently, the new force might well have served as the blueprint for what ultimately developed under Guderian in Germany. Its tactical role was based on its characteristics of speed, armor, and operating radius and included the seizure of distant crucial points, turning and enveloping movements, counterattacks, advance, flank and rear guard actions, and exploitation of a breakthrough.

"If tanks can operate in this manner," declared Chaffee, "we may greatly aid in restoring mobility to warfare."

But in the depression years Congress was in no mood to appropriate funds to support any such activity. Moreover, the limitations on appropriations in general spurred on the jealousies of service branch chiefs who saw their very existence threatened. The result was ten years of bickering and political infighting which told heavily on Chaffee's health.

He prepared a lecture, "Mechanization of the Army," which he delivered at all the service schools and finally before the students and the president of the Army War College. He concluded the talk with the remark, "The main point is that we, as soldiers, must recognize the tremendous strides our automotive industry has made since the last war. If we neglect to study every possible use of this great asset in the next war, we would not only be stupid, but incompetent."

"I then had the honor," said Chaffee, "of being told by the President of the War College that my lecture was visionary and crazy."

Through Chaffee's recommendation, Colonel Daniel Van Voorhis was selected to command the experimental mechanized force that was assembled at Fort Eustis, Virginia, in 1930. It became a political prize, fought over by branch chiefs to determine whether the force should become part of the infantry, the cavalry or what-not. While Van Voorhis favored a separate arm of integrated troops, similar to Liddell Hart's recommendations in England, Chaffee teamed up with the Chief of Cavalry to persuade MacArthur to assign the force to the cavalry, while keeping the concept of a force of integrated and mechanized arms. But MacArthur dallied and in the meantime a new Chief of Cavalry damned the mechanized force with thinly disguised intolerance.

Adna Chaffee was the product of the old American Indian frontier Army and was steeped in its traditions. His father had been Chief of Staff, but the son needed no family help to climb the military ladder. He was an early graduate of the famous French Cavalry School at Saumur and then as a major won an assignment as Assistant Chief of Staff for Operations (G-3) of the great 1st Cavalry Division; his concepts for mobile command and control were implanted in the division and served it well during the amazing record it earned in the Pacific Theater in World War II, in Korea, and in its transition to the Army's first airmobile division.

Chaffee's realization that the motor had replaced the horse came as a shock to many service friends. In the United States, as in Britain, the tradition of the horse died hard.

But he persisted and went on to succeed Van Voorhis in command of the mechanized regiment, now termed the 1st Cavalry (Mechanized) as a result of the break-up of the horse regiment of the same numerical designation. He led the regiment on its first extensive training maneuver and, as the expansion of mechanization continued, succeeded to the command of the 7th Cavalry Brigade (Mechanized). His brain child was growing.

When the Armored Force was finally formed, with Chaffee in command it might have been said that he had gained his objectives. But the years of frustration had taken their toll. Broken in health, he died in 1941 at the age of fifty-six, after a recommendation for his promotion to the grade of lieutenant general had been made, and just as the German panzers were demonstrating the soundness of Guderian's doctrine, so much like his own. It is curious that the two owed nothing to each other.

Chaffee, of course, had help. Bruce Palmer, Charles L. Scott, and Willis D. Crittenberger all pioneered in the development of the nucleus of the American lightning-war capability, all except Palmer going on to brilliant field or school commands. Then too, there were unsung young lieutenants, Withers, Heiberg, Sears, and many others of like grade who evolved the tactics of the smaller units and kept their cranky and unreliable vehicles in operation through sheer determination; many even purchased gasoline from their own limited funds, an unchallengeable sign of personal interest. Mildred Gillie, in her fine study, *Forging the Thunderbolt,* recounts the details of these formative years.

One of the great prophets of blitzkrieg, in the field of automotive design, and one without honor in his own country was J. Walter Christie. As an engineer Christie developed a new and critically important suspension system for tracked vehicles. But for reasons most combat-experienced officers have never been able to fathom, the Christie system was never acknowledged by the U.S. Ordnance Department. Yet the concept was welcomed abroad, especially in Russia, where tanks began to be mass produced in 1936, using the Christie design. In this year the United States ceased to give Christie further consideration. Ultimately, the Russian T-34 tank, then the best in its field, emerged not only with his suspension system but with his ideas on sloping armor as well.

All in all, one must conclude that the development of a modern blitz capability, although not peculiarly American, owes little to foreign sources. It seems undeniable that the germ of the idea was nurtured by Liddell Hart, to whom Guderian turned before finally implementing what became the first true blitz. But to Chaffee, more than to any one man or group of men, belongs the credit for the organization and the tactical philosophy that translated itself into the smashing successes of American armor through France and Germany in 1944–45.

On the other hand, the more or less simultaneous development of the same doctrine in three different countries is significant in that in every case it was based on historical research to determine principles that were independent of technology. What had held in ancient times and had been adapted by the great commanders of the nineteenth century was now ready for use in the age of wheeled and tracked motor vehicles.

# 7 World War II: Personalities and Engagements

By the end of World War II in Europe it could be reasonably said that the machinery for establishing a western lightning-war capability on the ground was in place and functioning. Armored divisions had swept the continent. Mechanized infantry had kept up with the armor and had taken over when terrain and heavy resistance negated the mobility factor. Strategic bombing and close support by tactical air completed the picture visualized by Chaffee and his fellow architects.

The deterrent to aggression in the shape of the atomic bomb was also in existence, its viability resting on American monopoly. Unhappily, it proved a factor of transitory effect, lasting only until rapid Soviet advances in the nuclear field and skill in the art of nuclear blackmail destroyed its value. Developments in small-yield "tactical" nuclear weapons, and in translating mobility from ground to air lay some years in the future.

Circumstances wherein the western world would allow itself to become embroiled in wars of attrition, fought at the end of a tenuous logistical lifeline and against an Asiatic potential of many millions of men, would have seemed incredible to blitzkrieg architects and practitioners alike.

The personalities who highlighted lightning-war actions during World War II were every bit as colorful and professionally brilliant as their counterparts of old, including the great Napoleon and the homespun Forrest. To them fell the task of putting the concepts of the "architects" into practical use. In many respects they were like spirited horses, held in check by masters not always worthy of the title, through the device of withholding political or logistical support. One may speculate on the results that might have been had they been allowed full and free rein.

Their traits of character, their methods of operating and their campaigns, furnish excellent guidelines for the development of a future national blitz in profusion! Rommel, Patton and Harmon have been chosen to illustrate the early implementation of modern lightning war. The vignette on Rommel is followed by an illustrative example from the 1940 Russian campaign of Hasso von Manteuffel, emphasizing the advantages of "command forward"; that relating to General Patton is accompanied by a story of a wholly different character, showing how command state of mind led to the German "blitz that failed" in the Ardennes. The description of General Harmon leads to a short exposition of Allied command errors and faulty communications that might have led to the success of the German blitz had it not been for the moral courage and strong leadership of Harmon and his associates.

Field Marshal Erwin Rommel is probably the most famous single exponent of modern mobile warfare, due principally to the fact that the North African campaign of 1941–43 was peculiarly his own. There, Rommel was essentially the supreme commander not only because he tended to ignore his nominal superiors, the Italians, but because he was given a great degree of independence, in marked contrast to the limited freedom of action extended by Hitler to the commanders on the Continent. Elsewhere the Fuehrer got into minute details of planning and execution, never hesitating to overturn decisions or prescribe exact courses of actions for his professionals.

There is more research material available on Rommel than on almost any other commander of similar prestige and responsibility. The subject of many studies and books and the author of others, his character and methods are set forth in a wealth of detail. Where questions might have arisen, it proved possible to interview Generals Alfred Gause, Hans Speidel, Siegfried Westphal, and F. W. von Mellenthin, all former staff officers of the Desert Fox and therefore intimates.

Rommel was probably more revered by his adversaries than by many of his compatriots. British commanders in Egypt found it necessary to issue official orders to troops to shun the prevalent idea that Rommel was the wizard mentioned in the then popular song from the motion picture "Wizard of Oz." Among Germans of the *Afrika Korps,* legends grew on the apparently charmed life of Rommel, either in the midst of hostile fire, or in the sometimes unaccountable cessation of fire when Rommel would appear in the battle areas.

In the German Army of today one finds conflicting views of the Desert Fox. In spite of the miraculous exploits of the *Afrika Korps,* there are many who remember him as a grandstander and a publicity hound, a man who wanted glory that he refused to share with his peers. He is known as an early admirer of Hitler, remaining close to the Fuehrer during the Polish campaign; he thus established himself politically and was given a command of a panzer division for the invasion of France in 1940. This political and personal association is also regarded as responsible for the freedom of action accorded him in North Africa.

True or not, these opinions are not shared by the younger officers of today's *Bundeswehr;* to them Rommel is still a hero. Certainly, there is no more tragic figure in military history. And, whatever his early ties with Hitler, his involvement in the 1944 assassination plot, culminating in his own suicide or murder, should absolve him from culpability for Nazi politics.

After talking to former staff officers of the *Afrika Korps* and *Panzergruppe Afrika,* it is inescapable that Rommel was a trial to his staff. Even more than Forrest, he overdid the practice of being far to the front for protracted periods, getting out of touch with the command post, and trusting to the experience of professionals like Gause and Westphal to take action in his absence.

He was once located after an absence of more than three days at an artillery position, absorbed in the mechanism of a gun. Field Marshal Albert Kesselring, air commander in North Africa, on another occasion arrived at Rommel's headquarters for a conference only to find him missing.

"Gause, this cannot be tolerated," fumed Kesselring to the Chief of Staff. "Rommel cannot spend his time in the front line like a division or a corps commander. He has larger duties and must always be reachable. Make sure of this!"

But Gause knew that front-line action was the secret of Rommel's genius. "He cannot be restrained," he replied to Kesselring, "he drives off and the radio trucks cannot keep up. We try to reach him at different command posts, though usually it is too late. Yet, here in Africa, Herr Field Marshal, everything must be decided at the front."

In contrast, however, General Hans Speidel, Rommel's Chief of Staff on the Western Front in 1944, and who later became head of NATO Ground Forces, Central Europe, experienced no difficulty; he first informed Rommel that he could not function unless kept informed of decisions and orders arising from visits outside headquarters. He also cited Rommel's reputation for keeping his own counsel. But, according to Speidel, Rommel at once recognized the validity of Speidel's statements and thereafter conformed to the requirements of the staff.

Rommel listened to his staff and respected its advice. However, most of his decision-making resulted from his own ideas. According to his staff, his was an aloof, stubborn personality. He held his Italian allies in the greatest contempt, and on the rare occasions when Italian (Allied) Headquarters issued orders, Rommel ignored them when they deviated in any way from his personal view.

In general, the staff described him as hard, uncompromising, and impersonal in dealing with matters of discipline or incompetence. In the latter case, the offender was immediately relieved of command, though General Westphal says that, where any doubt existed, a three-week trial period was unobtrusively resorted to.

The Field Marshal apparently resented any implication that he was a tactical gambler or given to rashness on the battlefield. The phenomenal success of his troops against sometimes heavily superior forces often gave rise to criticisms of overboldness. Rommel insisted that his was definitely a calculated risk and that he never moved without carefully weighing the probabilities. This belies the charge that he lacked thorough attention to detail, such as Napoleon exhibited, though that charge was frequently made.

Rommel's views as expressed in the *Rommel Papers* provide considerable insight into his character and his professional background. He was a thorough student of tactics and military history and published a number of works resulting from analyses of infantry action in the First World War.

He felt that tactical victory usually goes to the commander who immediately lays down a heavy curtain of fire, an action that rests squarely on a superb control system. He was a firm believer in independent thinking and certainly lived this belief in his campaigns; he emphasized the value of having a flexible mind, able to react instantly to unexpected situations. In this respect he regarded the commander as the prime mover in every battle to the degree that the troops must feel his presence. By implication, he insisted that the leader must sense the location of, and be present at, the critical point (*schwerpunkt*) at the critical time. His ability to put this into practice was the mark of his genius.

Rommel, like all famous lightning-war commanders, continually complained that there was never enough time, a standard lament that seemingly contradicts the oft-voiced "gripe" of the common soldier that combat consists of a series of hurry-up-and-wait movements. Under the great leaders, this type of grumbling was practically unknown. Every moment was precious and filled with some form of action.

Intense concern for supply and maintenance matters in the *Afrika Korps* was of course forced on Rommel by the difficulties of getting material across the Mediterranean in the face of Allied naval and air superiority. He felt strongly that an interest in logistics was an essential characteristic of any able commander. This gave rise to his aphorism that "success in mobile war depends upon equipment losses while success in static war depends on personnel losses." His experiences with Kesselring and the British, and the steady diminution of his air support gave rise to his firm belief that tactical air forces must be subject to direct control of the ground commander.

Rommel often talked to combat units, exhorting them to greater efforts; but, like most of the "masters," his inspirational appeal rested almost entirely on his professional capabilities and not on his personality. Similarly, his "color" was the result of his command habits and his unbelievable successes rather than any particular customs of dress and deportment.

His moral courage was exhibited constantly during the many months that the *Afrika Korps* was literally living by Rommel's wits. His every decision became a risk; any slip in the ensuing action might have meant defeat by a greatly superior enemy. He was thus led to undertake all sorts of deceptive measures, from the creation of dust clouds to simulate moving columns to the design of traps baited to lure enemy tanks into prepared antitank positions.

In spite of the criticism based on his tendency to get out of touch with his staff and headquarters, the Field Marshal in reality devoted extraordinary attention to his communications organization. In his visits to advance elements, Rommel was accompanied by a retinue of radio trucks that tried to keep in contact with all essential elements of the command. In contrast to the American system, his interest did not extend to the point where he handled his own microphone or telephone receiver. This was probably due to the greater distances at which control was exercised in the desert, generally putting the operator beyond effective voice radio distances and requiring radio telegraph service as the norm. While he saw the need for careful communications organization, it appears that he was not personally communications-conscious; at least he could be easily diverted into other aspects of combat. Otherwise his staff in Africa could not have been so exasperated with him, nor could General Speidel have corrected the problem so easily.

Rommel's life in the field was the epitome of austerity. As General Gause said, "his methods pre-supposed a robust constitution, disdain for personal safety and an almost ascetic frugality." During operations Rommel slept only a few hours each day or night in the desert—no tent and no trailer. For lack of cooking utensils, there was only cold food, and he remained in his command car for meals.

Such is the picture of Erwin Rommel: tragic genius, controversial, beloved of his troops and vexatious to his staff, idol of Liddell Hart and master of mobile war.

Others besides Rommel had figuratively sat at the feet of the great Guderian, and among these was General of Panzer-troops

Hasso von Manteuffel, a leader who was to serve brilliantly in Russia, North Africa, and Europe and who was to become the "24th Soldier of the Wehrmacht." Two examples, taken from later phases of the German race to Moscow, bring out the vital importance of force and judgment, based on command experience, on occasions when staff advice may prove fallacious.

In July of 1941 von Manteuffel's 7th Panzer Division was operating as part of Tank Group 3, under Colonel-General Hermann Hoth. The Group had broken through the "Stalin Line," only to face trouble in the heat of the Russian midsummer. The 7th Panzer found itself in a narrow pass between two lakes, on ground that had been strongly fortified and covered by the fires of heavy artillery and dug-in tanks. Attempts by other troops to storm the pass had failed.

From the viewpoint of the senior commanders, it was clearly an occasion for massing all the resources of the Field Army. Accordingly, a combined attack of tanks, infantry, and engineers, with massive artillery support, was set for July 10 at 0530 hours.

Von Manteuffel moved impatiently into position with a rifle regiment of the 7th Panzer on July 7. The heat of the day persisted and nights were now very short. Probes had been sent into the Red lines while waiting for the attack of the 10th. These had brought in a few prisoners, whose morale appeared to be excellent. Otherwise very little had been accomplished, as is usual when small patrols attempt to undertake large tasks.

There was still doubt whether the Reds would decide to make a stand in the advantageous terrain that they occupied.

Von Manteuffel's concern increased. In the darkness, and in the hope of minimizing possible future casualties through personal knowledge of conditions just prior to jump-off, he moved to the very front elements. There an interview was held with a company commander to gain any information that might be helpful.

"Well, sir," said the captain, "an enemy artillery battery located in that direction has not fired since midafternoon. It does seem queer, since before that time they fired steadily."

It was queer, the General agreed. "We must get the facts at once. I'll have a strong probing force move against that supposed position and ask its commander to report the moment they strike resistance. It is essential that we know whether the battery has moved or withdrawn."

The well-oiled machinery of the regiment began to move. The reconnaissance in force got under way. Another battalion of the regiment was alerted.

By 0300 hours, just as the northern midsummer sun was promising another hot and fair day, reports came back that the reconnaissance in force had met with no resistance. The enemy had left! And with that report, activity exploded. Von Manteuffel felt able to dispatch a full battalion in the wake of the reconnaissance elements, and when that battalion likewise hit thin air, another battalion was hurried in. By 0500 the entire regiment had reached the Witebsk highway, a line that had been the objective of the main attack scheduled for the day that was just dawning. And at any moment the German preparatory fires for that attack would get under way. The superb control system of the higher command cancelled those fires well before zero hour. At the same time the entire 7th Panzer Division mounted vehicles, with the infantry riding tanks, and swept far beyond the initial objectives, reaching the city of Witebsk before nightfall.

One might say that the 7th Panzer had had a lucky break. But a moment's reflection shows that it was a senior commander's presence at a critical point at the right time, his ability to sense the opportunity, and his responsive control system that allowed him to exploit the opportunity. It was in no sense a lucky break.

The Volga-Moscow Canal runs through a wooded area that in places presents very heavy going. It was here that the 7th Panzer met with what promised to be a sorry situation, as the short days of the coming winter ran out the month of November 1941.

Advance units, skillfully using the cover of the thick woods, had reached a point about two miles short of the Canal. Von Manteuffel had followed custom and had located his command car with the leading elements. Sensing a need for personal assessment of conditions, he stopped the column before it reached open ground leading to what was hoped to be a bridge over the Canal.

Assisted by the staff, he carefully scrutinized the terrain with field glasses and saw to his relief that the bridge was not only present but in good condition. It was heavily guarded, and whether it was also heavily mined remained to be seen. At this point the staff urgently recommended an attack without delay, before darkness made it impracticable.

But the commander reflected that vehicles were low on fuel. Troops were tired. He could see on the far side of the Canal a high hill to which troops could be rushed from Moscow to defend the bridge. And the Division advance units would have to capture the hill in order to provide protection for the crossing of the rest of the Division. For this, full gas tanks and rested troops were essential. So he elected to make a careful personal reconnaisance, holding troops under cover of the heavy woods. Protected routes of approach were discovered and appropriate tank-infantry teams assigned to them. By 0200 hours in the morning all was in order and a violent surprise attack was launched. The bridge was taken before it could be destroyed, while the Panzers moved on to the key hill and secured it before noon.

Within a matter of hours the 7th Panzer Division was well across the Volga-Moscow Canal.

This episode brings out the difference between audacity and rashness. It would have been patently rash to launch the attack the previous evening under adverse conditions, especially as the presence of the 7th Panzer appeared to be unknown to the Reds. The point is that the commander, by being on the spot, was able to make the decision based on factors he could see. Ponderous tactics, waiting in the rear for reports, might have resulted in a precipitate and costly attack that would have prevented any surprise and probably would have caused the blowing up of the bridge and a heavy fight for the key terrain.

General George S. Patton, who earned the sobriquet of "Old Blood and Guts" from his vivid descriptions of what should be done to the "goddam Krauts," is probably established in American opinion as the prime exponent of mobile war.

As in the case of Rommel, Patton enjoyed a greater reputation in the eyes of the enemy than in those of many of his countrymen.

Without exception German generals Westphal, Speidel, von Manteuffel, and others speak of Patton as the greatest of U.S. generals and even the greatest serving any Allied command.

A product of the American Cavalry, Patton inherited its doctrines and its methods and held to them with fierce devotion. Physically he was most suited to his role, for his prowess as an athlete was demonstrated forcibly in the 1912 Olympic Games, where he won fourth place among the military athletes of the world, competing in the grueling Pentathlon.

He served through the peace years in the cavalry, enjoying polo, horse shows, and hunts, which his personal wealth permitted him to do. Then, in the Tank Corps in World War I he established the basis for the real career that awaited him twenty-five years later. This service was not without setbacks. As Chief of Staff and a junior commander of the Tank Corps, Patton's impetuousness led to severe criticism and the threat of relief from duty. He responded with one of his many, many humble promises to do better.

In the period between the wars, one commander rated Patton as "invaluable in time of war, but a disturbing element in time of peace." Patton took this as a compliment, though it was not so intended. His efforts to promote modern tank concepts in company with Dwight D. Eisenhower have been mentioned, but at the time he was not in a position to do more than talk. As a result, his influence on the development of American armor never reached the level achieved by Chaffee, Van Voorhis, Scott, and Palmer. Fortunately for all, and for America in particular, it fell to Patton to put into battle practice the tenets advanced by these good friends whom he respected and admired.

He took over the command of the 2nd Armored Division from Major General C. L. Scott and with it created a furor in the several giant maneuvers that took place in 1941. This service was followed by his formation and command of the Desert Training Center in California, where Patton's flair for lightning-war tactics was imparted to the many leaders who succeeded to high rank in Europe in 1944–45.

But the most significant era of his life began with his nomination to head the expedition to North Africa, dubbed Operation

TORCH, that involved some 34,000 personnel and included his old 2nd Armored Division. Though surrounded by the doubts and fears of senior headquarters and politicians, it was largely his determination and daring that led TORCH to outstanding success and hastened the fall of Erwin Rommel.

Frederick Ayer in *Before the Colors Fade* relates a story of this time that illustrates the extremes of disposition of this mercurial character. Patton told his intimates of his belief that he was destined to lead a great army to smash the Germans and that God would not permit him to be killed until this had been accomplished; in contrast, and before TORCH, he spoke of a dream in which he saw himself going ashore in water filled with dead and dying soldiers who reproached him for their deaths. "You did this to me," they said. Patton exclaimed, "By God! I won't go!"

In March 1943 Patton was named to command the II U.S. Corps which had taken a mauling at Kasserine Pass. He rejuvenated the command amidst anguished howls from subordinates who felt the lash, but entered into the first of many periods of bickering with British commanders over objectives and methods. At this time Omar Bradley was assigned as a deputy to Patton, significant because of the later reversal of their positions and because their relations were always cordial.

Mid-1943 was a critical period for Patton. He was assigned to command the Seventh Army for Operation HUSKY, the invasion of Sicily, in cooperation with Montgomery's British Eighth Army, the whole under British General Alexander. It was Patton's firepower and mobility versus Montgomery's cautious "set pieces." Patton openly criticized Eisenhower for "selling out" to the British and was bitter against Montgomery. He refused to entertain any idea that the American system was not the best, being first and last a top-notch American fighting man.

But his talents could not be ignored when crises threatened. Operation OVERLORD, the great cross-Channel invasion of 1944, featured him in the planning stage in January of that year. There he at once spotted the planning flaws incident to OVERLORD's lack of provision for break-out and exploitation.

This work was interrupted by his assignment to the VI Corps when the Corps got into trouble at the Anzio beachhead. Patton

cheerfully accepted and implied demotion; he would do anything
to get into the fight. But the order was countermanded, fortunately, for Patton turned at once to organize and lead the Third
Army as it threw its weight into the Normandy invasion. On the
eve of commitment he briefed his staff to preach "L'audace,
toujours l'audace!" as the Third Army watchword, one that was
scrupously observed. In Normandy it was not long before his
VII, XII, XV, and XX Corps were attacking in four directions
simultaneously, a slashing bold action presaging the great pursuit
that ended only between Linz and Vienna.

With his accession to command of the Third Army, his scope
of command, or, span of control, exceeded that of most other
mobile commanders on the list of "masters." A force the size of the
Third Army, with several corps and often a dozen or so divisions,
cannot be given the personal direction associated with a single
leader. But he had experienced the whole spectrum of battle command. In Africa his forces were approximately the size of Rommel's whereas in Europe they were greater than La Grande
Armée, in effect, since the densely packed troops of the latter presented a lesser control problem.

Patton impressed his personality upon all ranks of the Third
Army in an unmistakable manner, once he had assumed command.
His was a dominating personality and one never had to ask,
"Who's in charge here?" at any gathering at which he was not
well outranked. Yet he was basically well disciplined, and more
or less cheerfully went along with the decisions of his superiors
where his own point of view was not accepted. In private he often
fumed, especially as his strained relations with Montgomery persisted. In the several instances where bad public relations followed
some action of his, quick apologies and promises to reform were
the rule.

Still, the press's injustice must have rankled. Once, when asked
jokingly why he was wearing his pearl-handled pistols, Patton
replied, "There was a rumor this morning that Drew Pearson
was coming up to the front, and I thought maybe I'd get a shot
at the son of a bitch!"

When the Bulge action was at its nadir, in the pre-Christmas
week of 1944, a meeting of senior commanders was held at Verdun

to discuss the grave developments. A pronounced defensive attitude pervaded the gathering until Patton arrived; there was
discussion of making a stand at the Meuse. But Patton, striding
in with his huge stars flashing from his helmet roared, "Well,
we've got the sons of bitches where we want them at last!" His
positive and forceful mien changed the entire atmosphere. Third
Army staff was even then anticipating a thrust against the south
shoulder of the Bulge salient; orders only awaited the green light.
With these orders implemented, and with General "Lightning
Joe" Collins' tactful evasion of Montgomery's roll-with-the-punch
ideas on the north, the fate of the German Ardennes adventure
was sealed.

Patton, like Forrest, insisted on a high standard, to include
neatness and cleanliness of men and machines. The portrayal of
the tramp-like figures of Willie and Joe by cartoonist Bill Mauldin
to typify the American combat soldier especially irked Patton and
there were few if any Willies and Joes in the Third Army.

At the same time Patton was more tolerant than most commanders with subordinates who did not meet his standards. Sometimes posts in other areas of service were unobtrusively found;
in at least one case, where a general had displayed a reasonable
degree of humility, he was not only retained in his job but was
promoted after a short period and then served with distinction.
But in any case, if relief was in order, and much as he disliked
having to do it, he almost always performed the distasteful task
in person, at least as far as general officers were concerned. He
would first go to great lengths to try to obtain a better performance, threatening, exhorting, cussing-out and sometimes pleading
over the phone. But if results were not forthcoming and his patience finally wore thin, he would take off with an aide and hurry
to get it over with.

On one occasion, late at night, he journeyed to the command
post of an unfortunate commander. Stumbling around in the
blackout, trying to locate his quarry, he stepped on a recumbent
form which promptly came awake, exclaiming, "Why the hell
don't you look where you're going! Can't you see I'm trying to
sleep?"

"By God," cried Georgie, "you're the only son of a bitch around here who does know what he's trying to do!" Patton was not attempting to be funny, but simply stating what he believed to be a fact.

A trait of major importance was his ability to judge the limits of endurance of units and commanders. Many commanders reported major gains on the battlefield with pride only to hear Patton's high-pitched bark over the telephone, "What the hell is holding you back?"

One general, who had made a splendid sweep to the Rhine River, was so flushed with success that he made an immediate report by telephone to Patton to say that he had "reached the bank of the Rhine." He was crestfallen when Patton sharply queried, "Which bank?"

In professional background he was probably no more competent than many other American leaders who had come up through practical experience in the Philippines, on the Mexican Border in 1916–17 or in France in 1917–18, augmented by schooling at the peerless American professional colleges. But he had color and flamboyance to spare and thus stood out among more quiet personalities. His colorful appearance, dressed to the nines and festooned with stars and pistols, was unquestionably studied for the effect it had on troops and journalists. He cultivated profanity and his many talks to exhort troops were laced with it. Unfortunately, the stratagem was not wholly successful, since many men, if not most, were repelled by it.

His views on training and combat reflect an ability to analyze and adapt doctrine and principles to modern usage. He said that "in war nothing is impossible if you use audacity in handling the American soldier." He had little use for anyone who took counsel of his fears rather than adopting a positive and aggressive attitude.

Of immediate interest in this day of attempting to control battles from the Pentagon is his concept of span of control. He felt that a commander should exercise command only one echelon down and know the dispositions of units two echelons down. No more. Thus a corps commander should command a division and know the location of the brigades; where this commander attempted to influence the actions of battalions, Patton believed the influence to be wholly disruptive. With this philosophy, he visited front-line units to include division and smaller commands, but, while monitoring each successive situation, never intruded on the command prerogatives of the local commander, nor tarried long in one place.

Of leadership, he said, "You can't push a piece of spaghetti!"— to exert command and control, a leader had to be at the front where his presence would pull the command along. He felt that command presence was to inspire, advise or determine requirements for additional resources, but never to *interfere*. Of a front line commander who was criticized for using too much artillery ammunition in the Bulge action, Patton said, "Let the son of a bitch alone, he's doing all right."

He took a dim view of commanders who lost freedom of movement through unnecessary exposure or became personally involved in actions which resulted in loss of contact with their own and higher headquarters. He said that such commanders were almost as useless as the ones who spent all their time back at their main command posts. He once said, "Be sure your stars are uncovered when you are going forward. Cover them on the way back."

Patton followed the pattern of his famous predecessors in the matter of austere living. His two truck-trailers, used as sleeping and office quarters, were elaborate when compared to Rommel's command car, but then Patton was not in direct tactical command. He expected his staff to work around the clock during periods of stress but wisely decreed that at other times overworked staff personnel would operate in shifts and take all possible rest.

His techniques of command were based more on the influence he exerted on people before rather than during the battle. He realized that at his level of command the only real way he could influence the outcome was by wise and appropriate distribution of resources. He sought therefore to get his philosophy of tactics and leadership across to commanders and troops prior to "H-hour." The dramatic exposition of his ideas and expectations to an entire division assembled for the occasion was something that no one present ever forgot, even later on the field of combat. The ranks knew what was demanded of them and how it was to be done. Few commanders have exercised such influence.

His almost daily visits to commanders of advance units gave him direct knowledge of the progress of the action at what he considered the key point. Though the size of the command precluded personal views of battlefields, he combined his local coverage with information passed immediately over a specially-organized radio net encompassing other divisions, corps and separate reconnaissance units.

As an example, the arrival of the leading battalion of Third Army at the so-called National Redoubt in Bavaria, the final objective of May 6, 1945, was acknowledged by Patton himself over the network within five minutes.

In the division, blitz techniques of German and American mobile elements followed the same pattern from 1939 through the end of World War II. The commander stationed himself well forward, accompanied by a small group of staff personnel, usually including artillery and air representatives; in Patton's Third Army, General "Opie" Weyland's XIX Tactical Air forces were on immediate call, while self-propelled artillery moved with the forward elements. The tactics of leading integrated groups of tanks, motorized infantry, and engineers contemplated automatic deployments from march column, with artillery, or air, or both, able to provide support within two to five minutes of the deployment. Command ability to integrate a massive blow eliminated the need for old-fashioned preparatory fires or strikes; the support was timed in seconds. As a result, the violence typical of a blitz attack was always on call as soon as enemy contact was made.

One of the most challenging requirements of the German pursuit into Poland and Russia, and that of American armored division pursuits into Germany was the need for frequent displacement of mobile artillery battalions, so that heavy weapons fire, either alone or in conjunction with tac-air, would always be within range of the advance battalion. On narrow roads, sometimes presenting a two-way traffic problem, it might be necessary to leapfrog artillery battalions, "side-lining" other advance units so that as soon as the artillery unit neared the point of extreme range to the pursued enemy, it could race forward to the head of the column, bypass the halted segments, and go into firing position just off the road. This use of artillery, paralleling Forrest's tactics at Brice's Crossroads, was a significant departure from textbook concepts of the day, which envisioned firing from one position for a day or more.

The mobile divisions also had attached artillery, usually doubling the normal allotment of each. In some cases, ten or more battalions of artillery, plus tactical air, might be applied in a single strike against a given point, a blow naturally requiring the commander personally to take an interest in the fire mission.

The wholesale use of artillery in this manner presaged the day of nuclear weapons, when a single rocket or gun battery will have the destructive force of ten or more battalions of 1945; for nuclear strikes having both military and political import, it seems certain that the Patton technique would involve command interest in the strike, and its follow-up maneuver, at corps and army level as well as at division.

It is interesting to speculate what might have been the course of World War II had Patton's influence been completely subordinated to the more cautious policies of some senior commanders. Slowdowns might have attended both TORCH and HUSKY. As the European campaign developed he had on more than one occasion to pound away at higher command tendencies to take a defensive attitude. Here delays could well have allowed the German introduction of highly sophisticated weapons then in the programming stages and at least permitted Hitler to bargain for terms.

Patton's influence on subordinates in peacetime and in North Africa was an important factor. Some of these commanders had had inadequate training and as a result were mentally inflexible. But those who survived went on to earn enviable reputations and in one way or another bore the Patton stamp.

# 8 The Blitz Failure in the Ardennes

The definition of blitzkrieg as a "state of mind" takes on real significance when one analyzes the strange Hitlerian gamble that became known as the Battle of the Bulge. The historical examples that have been offered portrayed lightning war as successfully waged by more or less inspired generals. It is only fitting to examine a situation in which all the qualities associated with decisive mobile war were present save one; and where irresolution at the divisional level proved disastrous.

There is no better example of the imponderables faced by leaders in fluid combat. Practically all the possible imponderables were present; weather bitter enough to freeze the soul, real fog compounding the fog of war, terrain rated as unsuitable for mobile combat, and kaleidoscopic shifts in the tactical environment to the point where friend was indistinguishable from foe.

Although correctly termed a gamble, the German Ardennes adventure was by no means an irresponsible and foolhardy leap in the dark. Desperate it may have been, for the Reich was under unbearable pressure in a British-American and Russian vise.

But rich rewards beckoned on the Western horizon—rewards in the shape of the tremendous booty to be had for the taking in the vast American supply depots spotted in the Belgian heartland, literally manna to the supply-starved German war machine. Then there was time, an ephemeral prize, to be sure, but one not to be dismissed lightly. For, by stripping the Belgian depots, the war in the West must come to an ignominious halt. Not only could the

98

German main effort be diverted to the Russian front, but there were strange new weapons being promised by German scientists. Jet aircraft were already in production in underground factories, capable of outflying Allied bombers and tactical planes. Rockets, mammoth in comparison to any then operational, were raining on Britain, and the secret of the atom might soon be unlocked. Time was indeed crucial.

These considerations were weighed against the known American dispositions and beliefs. The rough, canyon-crossed eastern region of Belgium known as the Eifel had become a rest area for American divisions badly shot up in the heavy fighting elsewhere. These were widely scattered and thinly distributed. Beyond the Eifel lay reasonably open terrain leading straight to Liege and Antwerp, the British-American logistical jugular. It was known that the suitability of this ground for mechanized action was not appreciated by Allied Intelligence, though earlier French views, as well as those of Liddell Hart, had held that it was indeed suitable.

The green light was given at high-level conferences held by Hitler with *Oberkommando Wehrmacht* (OKW) at Ziegenberg in early December. Orders for the secret concentration of all available armor and mechanized troops were skillfully carried out, and, though reports of the build-up were sent to Allied Supreme Headquarters by Colonel Oscar Koch (Patton's Intelligence Chief) and others, they were fated to be treated as rumors.

All was not well on the German side, however. The OKW meetings were shot through with private misgivings on the part of generals over the feasibility of the entire scheme. As late as December 2, General Hasso von Manteuffel, named to command the Fifth Panzer Army in the early meetings, asked and was allowed to see Hitler to make what the military euphemistically call constructive suggestions.

Even though General Alfred Jodl had declared the set plans to be irrevocable, von Manteuffel succeeded in persuading an irascible Hitler to make certain amendments, not an easy task after the abortive attempt on the Fuehrer's life in July 1944. Still, few of the commanders were optimistic. The Hitler reputation for omniscient intuitiveness had long since worn to the nub. Cer-

tainly no one would have forecast the tactical miscalculations to
be made by commanders supposedly steeped in the blitz concepts
of Guderian.

In spite of all the qualms that may have filtered through the
middle echelons of command, the operation was destined to penetrate American lines to a depth of some sixty-five miles, to smash
several American divisions and to come breathtakingly close to
achieving the full realization of the German hopes of overrunning
American storage depots.

The German storm broke on December 16, 1944, with mobile
divisions hurtling out of the Eifel area. The spearhead was pointed
at the battle-weary and green American divisions that had been
spread so thin along the road between Spa and Bastogne.

Long-range weather predictions for bitter cold and low over-
cast, with light snow on the ground, proved correct. The great
Allied preponderance of strength in the air was essentially nullified. However, the intense European cold, biting through the
stoutest garments, is a two-edged sword; it can dull the senses so
that the soldier cares little about life and death. For the general
it can sap the spirit that is necessary to sustain a drive.

The time-tested precepts of Guderian, a massing at a weak
point and punching with overwhelming power, were at first faith-
fully carried out by troops long schooled in the blitz environment
of Poland and France. The premise was the same—strike hard, bypass resistance, and sweep on to nullify enemy control centers
before reserves could be brought into play.

The flood brushed before it shattered elements of American
units and panicky individuals, streaming west on roads converging
at Bastogne on the southern flank of the drive. On the afternoon
of the 18th, leading elements, full of confidence and in good order,
reached a general north and south line about seven miles east of
Bastogne.

There was an immediate American reaction to the German
thrust although an evaluation of its impact was not at once available.

Colonel (later Brigadier General) William L. Roberts, commanding a task force (CCB) of the U.S. 10th Armored Division,

as one of the most conveniently situated elements for blocking German progress, was ordered to march posthaste for Bastogne. His was a pitifully small command. But Roberts was a professional of some thirty years' service and his calm but forceful presence was to prove a notable factor in the days that followed. He was able to deploy hurriedly three small combat teams of tanks and infantry to the north and east of Bastogne to reinforce them lightly with stragglers.

Bastogne was apparently cited by the American High Command more or less haphazardly as a rallying point. Because of its radiating road net in a country where vehicles took a chance elsewhere, it was truly, for friend and foe alike, a natural key to the situation. In the German view, to quote General von Lüttwitz of the XLVII Corps, "Bastogne must be taken; otherwise it will remain an abscess on our lines of communication. We must close it out and march on!"

While the handful of troops under Roberts were deploying late on December 18, other emergency American movements were taking place. The 7th Armored Division was rushed to the north flank where an epic stand at St. Vith was to occur, together with the 82nd Airborne; on the south the 101st Airborne Division moved piecemeal to Bastogne, first by truck and later by gliders. Divisions in the First, Third and Ninth Armies were alerted for movement that closed out the salient weeks later. First on the scene, however, and at the critical time, were Roberts and his team leaders, Lieutenant Colonels Henry T. Cherry and James O'Hara, and Major William R. Desobry, later to be augmented by the initial arrivals from the 101st Airborne, elements of the 501st Parachute Infantry under Lieutenant Colonel (now Lieutenant General) Julian Ewell.

These were the principal American figures who were to throw off the German timing to a critical degree and to find some important German leaders wanting at the very moment when skill and determination were most needed.

Major General Fritz H. Bayerlein was a stockily built man whose command of the *Panzerlehr* Division (tank training) was based apparently on his aggressive attitude in speech, an attitude not borne out by subsequent aggressive action. He was not-so-secretly scornful of his superior, Lieutenant General Heinrich von Lüttwitz, though von Lüttwitz had distinguished himself as commander of the 2nd Panzer in Russia, and was known as a leader especially devoted to his men. His opinion was shared to some extent by Major General Heinz Kokott, who led the 26th *Volksgrenadier* Division. All these leaders had been carefully briefed on the general concept that panzer divisions would bypass points of defense in order to cut deeply into rear areas and disrupt the control facilities of the enemy; meanwhile, slower moving units would clear out the pockets of resistance. Yet, Lieutenant General von Lüttwitz continued to emphasize the necessity of reducing Bastogne as a vital control center, before the Americans could bring up reinforcements.

From the December 16 jump-off matters had gone well. In spite of the marrow-freezing cold and the snowy roads and fields, the timetable was being complied with; this called for Bastogne to fall to German control not later than the 19th.

When the breakthrough was made, the *Panzerlehr* Division was following the lead divisions but soon was passed through Kokott's *Volksgrenadier* to take the lead. It was confidently expected that *Panzerlehr* could maintain momentum and take Bastogne itself, but in any event the 26th *Volksgrenadier* would if necessary strike the town from the north and east while *Panzerlehr* attacked from the east and south. Additionally, the 2nd Panzer Division (von Lauchert) was speeding on a parallel route, some three miles to the north.

At Longvilly village, as darkness fell on the 18th, Team Cherry of Colonel Roberts' forces, consisting of a badly depleted battalion of tanks, infantry, and engineers, was reinforcing a road block that had been established by some remnants of the U.S. 9th Armored Division. This unit had been parcelled out among infantry elements in the original defense line. Cherry's troops passed through Mageret (some three miles west of Longvilly) where a very poor road joins the Longvilly-Mageret-Neffe-Bastogne route from the southeast, a road that was to have an important effect in the next few hours.

Roberts had succeeded in snaring some 200 of the dazed strag-

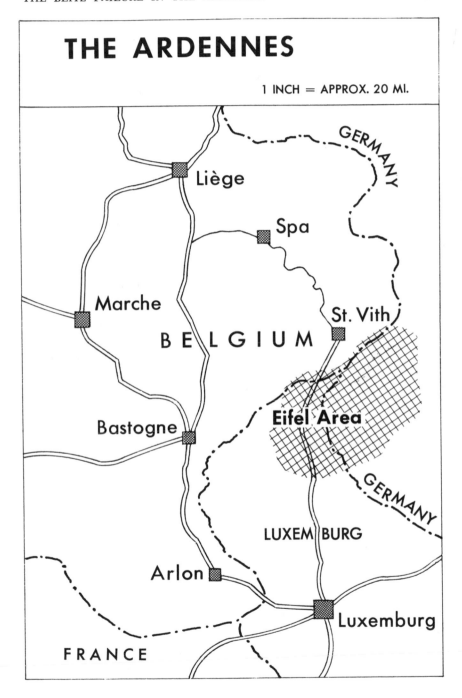

# THE ARDENNES

1 INCH = APPROX. 20 MI.

glers fleeing westward and after urging them into trucks sent them forward to Team Cherry. But all save about forty fled into the darkness upon arrival. The vehicles of the 9th Armored then pulled out leaving Cherry alone. Roads and villages were choked with stalled and abandoned motors, making travel more difficult both on and off the roads.

Amid this confusion, Cherry's command set up in a chateau west of Neffe, just over a mile from Mageret and four miles west of Longvilly, using a tank or two and a few infantry to protect the headquarters. Cherry, at about 2300 hours, having had no word of enemy contact, went to Roberts' command post in Bastogne to report in person as to his dispositions. Returning over the littered roads to Neffe, he learned that German forces had arrived at Mageret along the road described above, thus cutting his command post off from the Longvilly road block. Since it was apparent that Longvilly could not now be held, Cherry ordered a rear guard to hold on at Longvilly and cover the withdrawal of the main body of the team to Neffe. No one knew that the main column of the 2nd Panzer Division had turned northwest at the road fork just east of Longvilly. Hence the small holding detachment would not be seriously engaged for some time to come.

By this critical midnight of December 18–19, Colonel Ewell's regiment of the 101st Airborne had closed in an assembly area at Bastogne. All information on the true situation was confusing. The best Ewell could do was to lead out immediately with his battalions abreast, the first directed toward Longvilly via Neffe. It was Ewell's understanding that Longvilly was surrounded; the second Battalion advanced on the north on a wide front over the snow-covered ground, with the third paralleling on the south flank. The basic idea was simple—advance to meet the enemy and stop him. In effect, Ewell's forces were advancing to the attack.

Earlier in the evening of the 18th, Major General Bayerlein had halted about one and one-half miles south of Longvilly, seeking the best route into Bastogne. He was weary of coping with snow and mud, to say nothing of darkness. His original route had turned out to be a very bad road. He had been informed that conditions would improve if he went northwest to Mageret and then straight to Bastogne. He was wrong, for conditions worsened. True, he was with his lead elements, full of high hopes and keen ambitions to have the honor of taking Bastogne. But in a matter of hours his mental condition was to undergo complete inversion and his actions to become inexplicable.

His motorized advance elements closed on the Longvilly-Mageret-Neffe-Bastogne road at the Mageret junction shortly after midnight and it was this force that cut Colonel Cherry off at Neffe, while Cherry's rear guard still held on at Longvilly, and while his main force struggled over and around the choked roads in an effort to withdraw.

However, Bayerlein had a fateful conversation with a Belgian civilian at Mageret. This worthy glibly assured him that soon after dark an American force of fifty tanks under a "general" had passed through going east. He probably referred to the detachment sent by Cherry to Longvilly. Whether a deliberate lie or an honest mistake, the report shook Bayerlein. Moreover, road conditions, churned up by Americans going in both directions, continued to be abominable.

By now, Bayerlein was becoming extremely perturbed. Possibly the cold on top of fatigue was taking its toll. Or it may have been the mysterious events in the murk of this early winter predawn. American armor, probably Team Cherry's detachment trying to withdraw from Longvilly, and the remains of the 9th Armored road block, had been heard milling around in the foggy darkness to the east and north. But no German dared fire for fear of hitting Germans. Was this ghostly force moving to strike the rear of Bayerlein's division?

To add chaos to confusion, the German force in Mageret was considered by the Americans to be only a wandering patrol instead of the main strength of Bayerlein's division turning northwest into a supposedly better road. Cherry's team had been expecting a direct thrust straight down the road from Longvilly; instead the 2nd Panzer, apparently headed for this route, had turned northwest, putting out only weak flank protection.

Then, at 0400 hours German troops in Mageret began to draw fire from the north, compelling retaliatory fire for the better part of an hour. At this juncture General Bayerlein started his tanks

towards Neffe, again drawing fire from the north, in all probability from the 9th Armored Division tanks wandering to the
rear. Bayerlein's lead tank struck a mine and blew up, necessitat-
ing a mine-clearing operation. But, since no fire had been received from Cherry's command post area, the Germans assumed
that Neffe was not occupied.

Therefore, German infantry moved towards Cherry's chateau,
but without tanks, since it had become clear that any movement
off the road might mire the vehicles. It was this maneuver that
captured Neffe for Bayerlein. Yet, on reaching Neffe at 0700 on
the 19th, the day set for the capture of Bastogne, the column
halted for the better part of a highly critical hour, while Bayerlein occupied a command post in the Neffe railway station, a most
primitive establishment. It was critical because by 0700 Colonel
Ewell's battalions were just leaving Bastogne; in fact, the column
headed for Neffe was delayed some time by taking the wrong road.
Yet the hour's inexplicable wait had not been questioned by
Bayerlein, and in consequence his chances to hit Bastogne before
Ewell's movement got under way went glimmering.

As the timing went, the German forces had advanced no more
than 200 yards before coming under fire from Ewell's men. Another German halt then ensued, infantry pinned down and tanks
immobilized. Within the hour American artillery came into
action, killing or wounding some eighty Germans with concentrations that, in view of weather conditions, were most unlikely to
be the result of observed fire. And as luck would have it, Bayerlein
mistook the sound of the light airborne artillery pieces for tank
cannon. Instead of urging on the effort, Bayerlein retired to his
command post in the railway station, believing that he was opposed by armor in strength.

Another three hours went by. Fire was coming from his left,
probably now from Cherry's pitifully small force in the chateau.
Ewell's men threatened from mist-shrouded positions. At noon,
now convinced he was being pressed from all sides, Bayerlein
went back to Mageret. But here again was trouble. A road block
he had established against the fancied threat of American armor
(as reported by the Belgian) appeared to be under attack. Ludi-
crously enough, the "attack" amounted only to sporadic firing

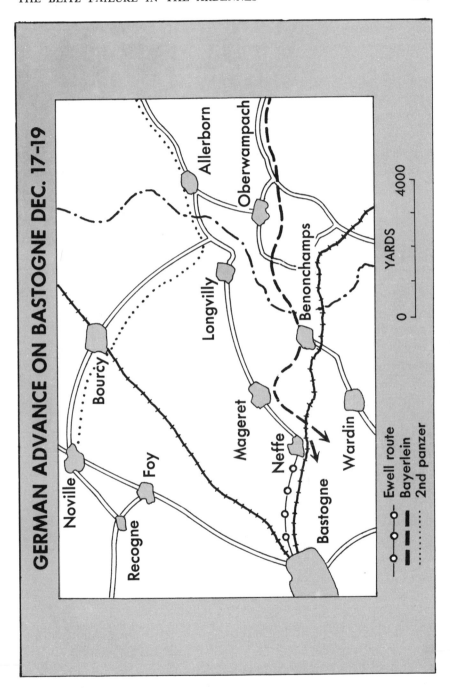

GERMAN ADVANCE ON BASTOGNE DEC. 17-19

Allerborn
Oberwampach
Benonchamps
Longvilly
Bourcy
Mageret
Neffe
Wardin
Bastogne
Foy
Noville
Recogne

YARDS

0          4000

Ewell route
Bayerlein
2nd panzer

from the elements of Team Cherry, trying to get back into Bastogne from Longvilly through the maze of mired and abandoned vehicles. Heavy fire could be heard from the northeast; more fire was heard from the south. Here Team O'Hara was engaging any and all comers between Ewell's southern battalion and a reconnaissance unit of Bayerlein's division, which had been charged with protection of the flank.

The general now no longer thought of pushing on to Bastogne with advance elements. He was imagining infantry battalions closing in on his front and flanks augmented by random tank fires aimed from behind snowy hills. Plainly, the capture of Bastogne would require a major effort by his entire division. He then called upon the division to assemble near the hamlet of Benonchamps, about a mile to the southeast of Mageret, a formidable and time-consuming task considering the road and weather conditions.

A similar development was taking place in front of the 2nd Panzer Division after its turn to the northwest from Longvilly towards Noville. Here Colonel Roberts' Team Desobry, with some fifteen tanks, had established a position near midnight and, since the defense had been based on after-dark reconnaissance, dawn showed the choice to be less than ideal. Small outposts had been set up to the north, east, and south. These were struck by the lead tanks of the 2nd Panzer at about 0530 on the 19th. A weird battle in the fog ensued. Before daylight Desobry had been reinforced by a platoon of tank destroyers from the 609th Battalion. The fog lifted momentarily to show Desobry practically the entire Panzer Division deployed over the hills and fields; but his men fought with renewed vigor through the morning. The lift in fog had shown Desobry, however, that the ground was even more unfavorable for defense than had been estimated in the dark. He therefore considered withdrawing, but the move had been foreseen by the indefatigable Roberts, whose decision was to stay.

By now the succeeding elements of the 101st Airborne had followed close on the heels of Ewell's regiment into Bastogne. A battalion was immediately dispatched to Noville, and these troops, reinforcing Desobry, aided in the conduct of a true epic of American arms. Instead of a withdrawal, a counterattack was organized to seize more favorable ground. In forty-eight hours of fighting the conglomerate group at Noville had accounted for at least twenty to thirty tanks and an estimated half regiment of the 2nd Panzer Division. Its own determination was measured by the loss of thirteen officers, including the commander, and 199 men out of the battalion of the 506th Parachute Infantry, plus eleven of Desobry's fifteen tanks. Most of all, the stand convinced the commander of the 2nd Panzer that Bastogne could be taken only by a coordinated effort of the entire XLVII Corps.

Desobry himself was wounded and was taken prisoner in the action.

The conviction of Colonel von Lauchert concerning the commitment of the entire Corps to the Bastogne attack was relayed to von Lüttwitz, the Corps commander, who was already discouraged by reports from Bayerlein's *Panzerlehr* Division. Yet von Lüttwitz continued to have confidence that Bayerlein could take Bastogne while the Corps concentrated on maneuvers to bypass the town and continue the plunge to the Meuse.

On the 20th, Bayerlein attempted to force another route by moving to the south. Here his forces were again repulsed by the combined efforts of Team O'Hara and Ewell's southern battalion. He was by this time in the mood to break out of a trap which in fact existed only in his imagination. His worries turned to the reduction of the road block at Longvilly. This concern resulted only in the pointing of the elements of three divisions against the road block, whose personnel had by now escaped.

To Bayerlein's fears, and those of the commander of the 2nd Panzer, were added reports of punishment inflicted on the 26th *Volksgrenadier* Division, operating in the interval between 2nd Panzer and *Panzerlehr*. These reports finally induced the Corps commander to plan a coordinated attack against Bastogne, coupled with an attempt to bypass it with other elements; however, all the plans proved to be a matter of too little too late.

Some of the probes were successful, notably to the south, but the success was not appreciated. Bastogne was bypassed, to be sure, on both the north and the south. The commander of the Fifth Panzer Army, General von Manteuffel, whose lightning-war

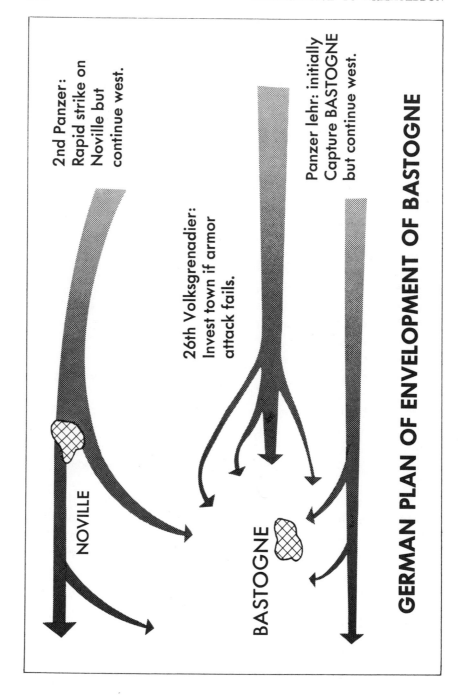

2nd Panzer: Rapid strike on Noville but continue west.

26th Volksgrenadier: Invest town if armor attack fails.

Panzer lehr: initially Capture BASTOGNE but continue west.

NOVILLE

BASTOGNE

**GERMAN PLAN OF ENVELOPMENT OF BASTOGNE**

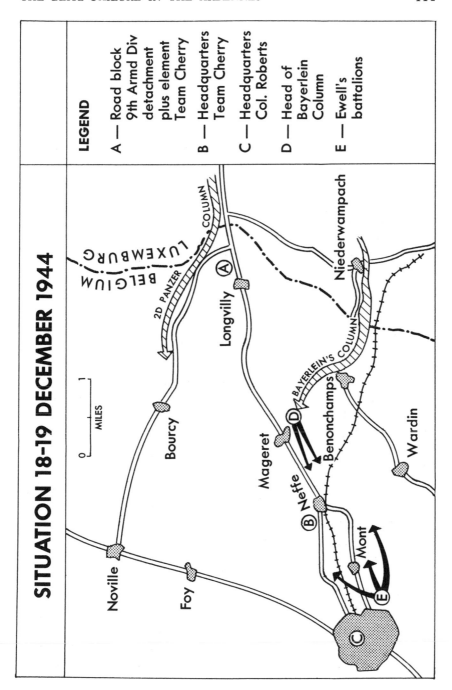

SITUATION 18-19 DECEMBER 1944

LEGEND

A — Road block 9th Armd Div detachment plus element Team Cherry

B — Headquarters Team Cherry

C — Headquarters Col. Roberts

D — Head of Bayerlein Column

E — Ewell's battalions

"state of mind" was unimpaired, himself rode with leading elements around the south flank about four miles west of the town without meeting anything more than small arms fire. (All clear for *Panzerlehr*). But the advance of Corps to its objective was certainly half-hearted and the American defense was undeniably stout.

All this time, up to December 21, Bastogne was by any measurement lightly defended. From the number of German dead who fell at its outposts there can be no criticism of the zeal and bravery of the small units under Bayerlein, or in the 26th *Volksgrenadier* Division or the 2nd Panzer. Without doubt, at the very moment the advance reached Neffe, Major General Bayerlein could have strongly reinforced an infantry dismounted attack in daylight hours straight into Bastogne, with the fog as an ally and not an enemy. American officers estimated that even as late as the 21st such an attack could have succeeded before American forces arrived in sufficient strength. Similarly, concerted action against Noville would have secured that strategic position. In most instances forces of a few tanks and 100–200 infantry held up the advance of a full division.

The defense forced the diversion of strong German units to assist in the reduction of the town, forces that had been earmarked for strikes far to the west at the Meuse River. But it was all too late. By glider, tank, and truck the Bastogne "garrison" was swelled even though it was by now completely surrounded. Then on the 23d the skies cleared and air support was forthcoming. Finally, on the 26th Lieutenant Colonel Creighton W. Abrams, heading a column of the Fourth Armored Division, broke through south of the town and opened up an avenue of supply and further reinforcement. (Abrams rose to become Supreme Commander in Vietnam.)

Causes of the "state of mind" that stalled the action are many: weather, cold, fog, and snowy and churned-up roads among them.

Von Manteuffel says, "The shortage of experienced officers, noncommissioned officers and soldiers due to the preceding five years of war showed its effect. Experienced personnel would have been able to effect close coordination of all weapons, which is a prerequisite of success and includes the timely dismounting of infantry to attack in close cooperation with tanks." This is the penalty of embarking on wars of attrition.

There is also conjecture as to the effect on the command of the pessimism that marked the final conferences with Hitler that took place at Ziegenberg on December 11–12. Senior leaders must have been affected, their confidence perhaps shaken at the outset. Yet failure came at the very time when the operation seemed to be going strong.

Bayerlein and the other division commanders were apparently "de-energized" at about the same time. Steeped in the Guderian tradition of dive bombers and close coordination of weapons and units, they were simply unable to function in an environment where this was not possible. They were at a loss for readily available alternatives. Bayerlein's movement to the rear at the very moment the spearhead should have been strengthened with men and firepower is only one of many instances when the consequences of ignoring timing were not appreciated. But others blundered, too. One may ask where the Corps commander, von Lüttwitz, was when he should have been keeping a tight rein on developments. His dilemma probably was one of inability to be in two sore spots at the same time, with either choice a bad one.

Note: The account of the Ardennes battle is derived from S. L. A. Marshall's *Bastogne, The First Eight Days* (Infantry Journal Press, 1946) and from personal experiences and contacts of the authors. General Marshall wrote from interviews with principal participants soon after the battle. General von Manteuffel rates Marshall's report completely accurate in describing the German point of view.

It is perhaps not too coincidental that the great epic of the Ardennes found the two American modern masters, Patton and Ernest Nason Harmon, concerned with the beginning and the end of the American counterpunch. When the German tide began to swell, and when little less than consternation reigned in the senior American headquarters, it was Patton who threw his divisions, and almost as important, his personality into the breach.

As the tide flowed onward the situation at the German spear-head became more and more touch and go. At one time leading troops were halted a matter of some hundreds of yards from a major gasoline depot. Had this been captured it might well have proved decisive.

But Ernest Nason Harmon's initiative and drive caused the end of the German gamble. General Harmon may well be taken as a model of the many able American commanders of mobile divisions; none was more picturesque or better exemplified the title of master of lightning war.

When he assumed command of the 2nd Armored (Hell on Wheels) Division, just before the invasion of North Africa, he told his officers, "I hear you think you are a pretty damned good outfit. Now the first thing I am going to do is to find out how good *I* think you are, which is what counts with me."

This came as quite a shock to an organization that had just finished a highly successful maneuver. It had run rings around its opponents; maneuver directors had found it necessary to handicap the division in various ways in order to keep the maneuver going for the allotted time and to keep it within set terrain boundaries. In addition, the previous division commander, prior to moving on to a higher command, had received from the President of the United States a letter praising the division and its accomplishments. Harmon's comment on this should be carved in granite. "What the hell does he know about it?" he asked.

Harmon found that he did indeed have a fine division, but his bluntness, his untiring energy, and his professional competence in terms of fundamentals were just what was needed at the time. It was not long before he was known to every man in the organization. His graphic language and his willingness to give a hearty slap on the back to anyone worthy of praise became legendary.

Second Lieutenant Harmon, as a member of the 2nd United States Cavalry in World War I, was no doubt one of the last horse soldiers to lead a mounted charge in combat. This unusual experience was the result of associating with some unusual horses and meeting an unusual officer in the Argonne.

The cavalrymen had been provided with French horses that

were by no means inspiring. Without them fields would not be plowed and tumbrils would not roll in Paris. Still, what passed for a cavalry platoon was formed and it was this motley array that Harmon led to the area of an American division engaged in the Argonne fight. Its chief of staff was a cavalry enthusiast who would one day be known as "Mr. Cavalry." To him, Harmon's platoon represented the exact answer to the problem posed by a German machine gun unit that had been holding up the entire infantry attack; it was Hawkins who had warned both the German and French cavalry schools in 1912–13 that charges by massed horseflesh were doomed.

But Harmon's charge was a deployed charge. The gross and ungainly nags thundered over the rough ground of the Argonne, surprising German gunners who did not have time to get their machine guns into action. The day was won handsomely and without casualties, while an entire infantry division was enabled to get moving again. Courage and dash had paid off, as usual.

This event undoubtedly did much to instill in Harmon the lifelong audacity, the desire to close with the enemy, and the unwillingness to give up the initiative that characterized his career in Armor.

Twenty-six years later he had come through a series of brilliant operations in North Africa and Europe, taking over commands where others had failed. Now in the Ardennes, even as a bewildered General Bayerlein was vainly attacking Bastogne, he led his division over 100 miles of sleet-covered roads only to be placed in temporary reserve at the very tip of the Bulge salient. He immediately began importuning his superiors to allow him to attack the German 2nd Panzer Division, which had bypassed Bastogne after its mauling by Colonel Roberts' Task Force Desobry. He was subsequently to have a large share in ending Hitler's dream of a new blitz.

Harmon was not a colorful leader in the sense of deportment and flamboyance, but he was highly individualistic. Known by sight by every man in the division, his hoarse, rasping speech earned him the title of "Old Gravel Voice." He would borrow a cigarette from a soldier and talk with him on any given subject, yet none ever became familiar with him. He was always "up front where the action is" but he let his commanders run their part of the battle. Ordinarily he used these visits to discuss with these subordinates what sort of additional resources he might make available to them.

Harmon's greatest appeal as a leader was probably his down-to-earth manner, his lack of pretense and the impression he gave in word and action of being intensely human. He was liked, respected, and obeyed without question. He had the attribute common to the masters of being able to get the most out of his staff and his subordinate commanders. He knew the ones who had to be urged with a well-placed if symbolic kick, as well as the ones who would go all out just from appeals to "help the old man with this damned battle."

He completely dominated his staff. He used them, but they worked out only the details. Plans and concepts were his, as well as the supervision of the planned action. An excellent logistician, he nevertheless never allowed logistic worries to bog down the operation. He expected his special staff to keep the fuel and ammunition on hand, and his maintenance organizations to keep the equipment going. Without interfering with them, he knew what they were doing.

Harmon's career did not end with his retirement, for his varied talents then found expression in his appointment to the presidency of Norwich University.

General Harmon's impatience to launch an attack on the 2nd Panzer Division when he, like General Forrest, knew full well that the assumption of the offensive is often the best defense, is understandable. The circumstances that held him in check are not so understandable. They do, however, add to the reasons why lightning-war battles are infrequent in history.

It is easy to criticize by hindsight. As a rule, the military critic rarely knows the conditions faced by the object of his criticism. He may judge a commander rash when in truth he acted only after carefully analyzing all available factors. Or he may fault a senior commander who is the sole recipient of information dictating caution when subordinates are eager to exploit what they believe to be a golden opportunity for decisive victory.

Be that as it may, Napoleon, who was by far the most experienced of commanders in every grade, emphasized that he never presumed to give detailed orders when he himself was not in a physical position to know the facts.

It is especially important to recall that Napoleon, if he did not have the facts, turned heaven and earth to get them. Between the Emperor and Berthier, the information needed for the decision-making was nearly always at hand. In the case of the British-American high command in December of 1944, evidence of real effort is lacking and the subject becomes fair critical game.

The failure to recognize that Harmon knew what he was talking about was countered only by Harmon's eagerness to close with the enemy and by the moral courage of General J. Lawton "Lightning Joe" Collins, commanding the U.S. VII Corps. General Collins took it upon himself to parry directives that might have kept Harmon on the defensive with consequent loss of the opportunity to smash the German thrust to the Meuse.

The episode provides insight into the workings of high-level staffs, when there is lack of confidence in the ability of the command structure to transmit critical information in a timely manner.

When German attacks had finally bypassed Bastogne and St. Vith and had rolled on westward, General Bernard Montgomery was hurriedly placed in overall command of troops on the north of the Bulge salient, to include the American First Army. The situation was fluid in the extreme. By December 24, 1944, the break in the sector of the U.S. VII Corps was about sixty miles deep and forty-five miles wide. Some German tank units were reported within four miles of the Meuse River. The entire flank of the First Army was endangered to the point where the Army Commander, General Courtney H. Hodges, shifted the weight of Collins' VII Corps from the left to the right flank.

The concept was one of keeping the VII Corps disengaged as far as possible in the hope of making an ultimate counterattack. But the German steamroller was going too fast. Two of Collins' divisions were heavily engaged. And while Harmon's 2nd Armored was being held in reserve, it had been tacitly understood that the division was not to be employed without First Army approval.

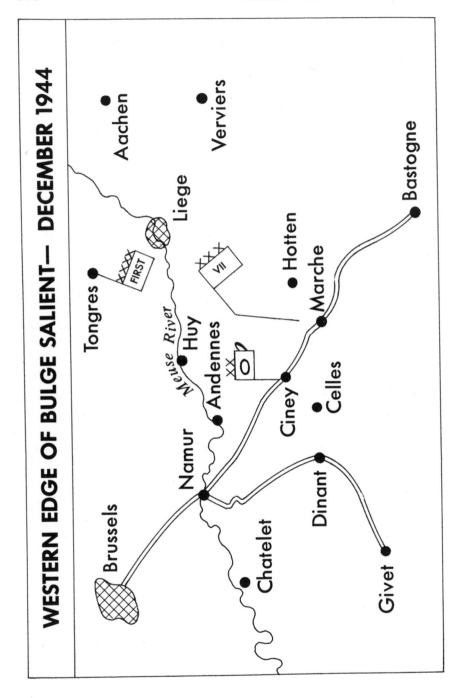

WESTERN EDGE OF BULGE SALIENT— DECEMBER 1944

Montgomery had visited Hodges and had directed that the right flank be "refused," or drawn back to the Andenne-Hotten line and that the line be held at all costs. He also gave the cryptic directive to "roll with the punch." It was then First Army opinion that Montgomery had anticipated a German breakthrough towards Liege and therefore wanted to shorten the front, but in any event, on December 23, Hodges considered the situation so critical as to require Collins' complete control over Harmon's division.

Collins left his command post at Marche at noon on the 23d to make a round of visits to his division commanders. On leaving, he empowered his Chief of Staff to take any action, in his absence, that was required. Apparently there was either little confidence in keeping radio contact with Collins while he was on the road, or disinclination to air sensitive instructions that could be subject to German intercept.

Harmon now began to phone VII Corps to obtain authority to strike the German 2nd Panzer Division, stating that some of its elements were known to be immobilized by fuel shortages.

The Corps Chief of Staff was torn between a desire to give Harmon a green light, and his understanding that Army was "keeping strings" on Harmon's division. He therefore sidestepped any decision by informing Harmon that Collins was en route to 2nd Armored Headquarters. This attitude persisted after a second call from Harmon pointed up the latter's frustration and impatience.

Some twenty minutes after Harmon's second call, the First Army Chief of Staff telephoned VII Corps to transmit several important items. It appeared that a colonel-courier, a member of the First Army staff, was then traveling to VII Corps with the list of decisions made at a conference between Montgomery and Hodges; VII Corps was not only authorized to use the Second Armored as it saw fit, but to alter the Corps defensive line as required. Most important, however, was the directive to refuse the right flank, drawing back to the Andenne-Hotten line, important because of the time-consuming misunderstanding of geographical identification.

The First Army, in an effort to minimize intercept effects attempted a spur-of-the-moment code, referring to Andenne and Hotten as "A and H" on the map.

But the Corps Chief of Staff interpreted A and H to mean Andenne and Huy, and was so appalled at the implications of such a marked withdrawal that he radioed to General Collins, recommending that he return to headquarters at once.

Collins meanwhile had conferred with Harmon and both had agreed on plans for a 2nd Armored Division counterattack. He arrived at his own headquarters some time before the First Army courier and went over the conflicting impressions of what senior headquarters really desired.

When the courier arrived, "H" was identified as Hotten and not Huy. Yet the entire attitude of defensive lines and rolling with the punch remained. Collins must have recalled the disastrous results of the visit of another courier in 1914, one Lieutenant Colonel Hentsch of von Moltke's staff, when an unauthorized retirement of the whole German First Army had taken place as a result. Collins then asked for and received a written memorandum from the courier to the effect that the VII Corps was released from all offensive missions (?) and was to fall back, as necessary, on the Andenne-Hotten line.

Collins was made of sterner stuff. He considered the eleven battalions of his own artillery located east of Marche, the immediate readiness of Harmon's division and the report that the Germans were short of fuel. His Corps had been bearing the brunt of the German attack in good shape. A withdrawal might well open up the entire top of the Bulge salient to the Meuse; Namur and Antwerp, the richest of rich logistical prizes, could fall. Finally, the 2nd Armored was to be used at his discretion.

The decision was to attack at once, employing both White's and Collier's combat commands of the 2nd Armored. As a hedge in case matters did not develop as hoped for, orders and map overlays were prepared for the defensive operation. These, however, were not issued to troops.

The courier returned to First Army with the outline of the proposed action. Later, General Hodges telephoned and reiterated that Collins was free to employ Harmon's division in any manner he thought advisable.

The counterattack destroyed the 2nd Panzer, and, with it the German hopes. The enemy withdrawal began at once and was reasonably successful, since American forces in the Bastogne and St. Vith areas failed to close out the base of the salient before the bulk of German forces had been extricated through the canyons of the Eifel.

The episode is as important for what it does not say as for what it says. One may infer a lack of communication between British and American headquarters that never resolved the real objectives, or analyzed the feasibility of the counteroffensive. General Hodges may have paid lip service to Montgomery's roll with the punch advice and secretly have hoped that Collins would assume the initiative. But more factual is the awkward communications break between Army and corps, and corps and division.

All mobile American tactical units of the day used simple voice radio codes, following Patton's principle that anything can be said by wire or radio as long as the enemy does not have time to react. Both General von Manteuffel and General Speidel have said of this eventful period that German interception and translation of Allied electrical messages was common but that the use of even simple codes destroyed the chance of timely response.

While Harmon danced in impatience, there were two high level staffs floundering over the letters A and H and calling upon a courier to transmit orders that not only were not clear but which ran counter to the professional opinions of experienced commanders who were on the spot. Few military analysts at this late date have appreciated how near the Hitler gamble came to paying off; without the force, decisiveness, and moral courage of Harmon and Collins, World War II in the West might have been prolonged to the point where new weapons might have guaranteed a German victory or at least established a basis for a negotiated peace on other than unconditional terms.

These episodes of the closing months of World War II offer an interesting comparison of command state of mind in opposing forces, as influenced by environment.

The German troubles before Bastogne have been linked to a negative state of mind on the part of Bayerlein and his fellow division commanders; cold, bad roads, combat weariness, and lack of faith in the mission were cited as contributing causes.

But Harmon had gone through many months of almost continuous combat, starting with an adverse situation in North Africa, and now being part of a force under heavy attack. Bad weather and terrain and lack of air support were common to both sides at the time. The difference in state of mind lay simply in Harmon's refusal, not to admit possible defeat, but to think that a counterattack could be anything but successful.

There will be many times when blitz action forms an important part of a defensive effort. Defense may even turn out to be the normal initial attitude of forces of the West. But it is plain that if a blitz-type army is to be a real deterrent to aggression, potential enemies must implicitly believe that western leaders are uniformly offense-minded, regardless of the tactical situation in which they may find themselves.

# 9  The Sinai Campaigns

The State of Israel came into being officially in May 1948 through a United Nations resolution of November 29, 1947, ending the British mandate over Palestine and dividing the country into Jewish and Arab portions, with Jerusalem declared an independent area under U.N. administration. Later the city was divided between Israel and Jordan.

It was a solution that solved nothing. The years during and immediately following World War II, and even going back to 1921, had been marked by political bickering and armed forays by Israeli and Arab groups, manifesting the deep hatred between the peoples.

Israeli had fought in considerable numbers on the Allied side during the war. A militia existed, termed Haganah, which was but one of several paramilitary or guerrilla groups that enjoyed official recognition. But because of such cadres, Israel was able to greet its independent status with a small, highly disciplined army of brilliant and experienced young leaders.

Forces of the Arab States of Egypt, Iraq, Jordan, Lebanon, Syria, and Saudi Arabia, however, vastly outnumbered the new army and were far better equipped. As to air power, the 1948 Israeli air force consisted of about forty pilots, with no fighter aircraft, as compared to the forty-six fighters of the enemy; fighter-bombers showed a thirty–three and transports a thirty–two disparity. The Israeli aircraft were mainly converted commercial types.

The Arabs attacked promptly on the birth date of Israel, May 14, 1948. At that moment few if any qualified analysts considered that an effective defense could be presented. Nevertheless a stub-

123

born resistance developed which held Jerusalem in the face of a three-pronged invasion. Then, after a four-week truce arranged by U.N. officials, the Arabs struck again. But now the fledgling army had found itself and, after only ten days of combat, defeated the Arab forces. Israel's President Chaim Weizmann explained that, in contrast to his countrymen, Arab soldiers were too lean and their officers too fat. This was a condition that was to persist for many years to come.

A third round ensued in mid-October, when the Arabs tried again, this time with Israel gaining control over a large part of the Negev. A fourth Arab effort was made in December only to have their despised foes capture the rest of the Negev down to the Red Sea, encroach on Egyptian territory, and threaten Jordan.

Ralph Bunche of the U.N. Palestine Commission finally arranged an armistice in February 1949 under U.N. supervision.

Other developments were afoot. When the last American tanks had rolled over the German *Autobahnen* after the close of hostilities in 1945 en route to storage depots, surplus war materials were acquired for Israel by the American-sponsored Joint Distribution Committee. This was a well-financed agency empowered to purchase enormous stores which were then moved into Israel even as the 1948 battles faded again into the status of raids.

The Soviets, too, were busy. By this time the U.S.S.R. had turned from its initial policy of urging the creation of the State of Israel. Now, because of British and American reluctance to offend the Arab world through the seeming espousal of the Zionist cause, capital could be made through a shift of support. Arabs began to bear Russian arms.

Curiously, the Israeli hint that blitzkrieg might be still alive appeared lost on U.S. decision-makers, who committed themselves to the first of the "no-win" wars of the fifties and sixties. In Korea, as the 1950s advanced, the experienced, mobile-minded field commanders who remained from World War II found themselves hamstrung by sets of artificial rules imposed by Washington politicians; these appeared to hope that by stabilizing the fighting front, some sort of settlement might be wrung from the hard-nosed North Korean negotiators at Panmunjon.

In spite of the brilliance of MacArthur's Inchon landing, a blitz

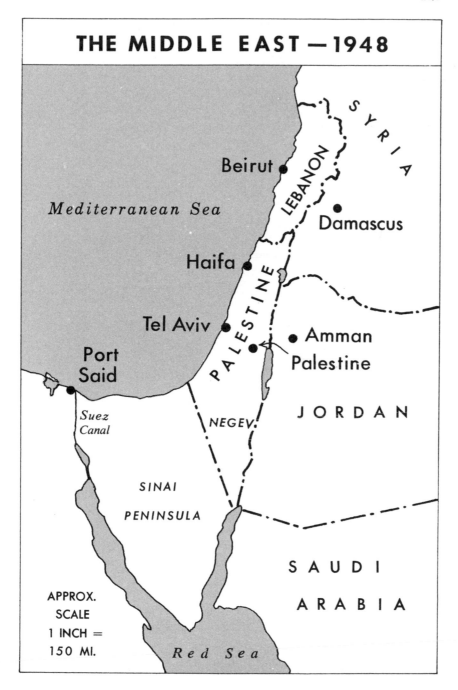

# THE MIDDLE EAST — 1948

*Mediterranean Sea*

Beirut ●

SYRIA

LEBANON

Damascus ●

Haifa ●

PALESTINE

Tel Aviv ●

Amman ●
Palestine

Port
Said

● 

*Suez
Canal*

*NEGEV.*

JORDAN

*SINAI*

*PENINSULA*

SAUDI

ARABIA

APPROX.
SCALE
1 INCH =
150 MI.

*Red Sea*

in itself, and the stunning Communist defeat which followed the 1953 North Korean–Chinese offensive and which brought the enemy into the open, the American field commanders were forbidden the orthodox counter-attacks, pursuit, and interdiction of logistical support bases that could have forced a decision, and perhaps discouraged the probes into Southeast Asia that immediately intensified.

For the West, or at least the United States, it seemed a long way back to the lightning wars of 1939–1945. The art of blitzkrieg appeared rejected, if not forgotten as an instrument of national policy.

The Israeli could not have failed to draw conclusions regarding the value of stablization or "de-escalation" while attempting to conduct meaningful negotiations. For their part, they carefully cultivated the blitz capability that had had its seed in Haganah. The result was not couched in those terms but the objective had all the right characteristics.

Israeli statesmen showed themselves to be hardheaded realists. There was none of the peculiar reasoning adopted by Neville Chamberlain in the pre-Munich days, of which Leonard Mosley wrote in *On Borrowed Time:*

He believed in low taxes and a balanced budget, and the idea that money should be frittered away on guns and planes instead of on peaceful purposes irked him. He did not think that rearmament was necessary; he believed that peace was attainable by reasonable discussion rather than through military strength. . . . "Eden became increasingly concerned about our slow rearmament," wrote Churchill. "On the 11th of November 1937 he had an interview with the Prime Minister and tried to convey his misgivings. Mr. Neville Chamberlain after a while refused to listen. He advised him to go home and take an aspirin."

Dr. Robin Higham, noted historian and editor of *Military Affairs,* takes a more sympathetic view of Chamberlain in *Armed Forces in Peacetime,* citing him as having worked assiduously for rearmament, after having cut military expenditures to the bone only to realize belatedly that the hour was indeed late. Chamberlain was unquestionably faced with reluctant colleagues and public apathy in 1935 and, as a businessman, probably never realized the enormous deficiencies. Dr. Higham points out that funds are never wasted which provide a deterrent whereby merchants can conduct their affairs in freedom; in contrast, it is war that is wasteful, war that can happen in any era when leaders and voters become apathetic about defense. But this was a lesson lost on Chamberlain.

The lesson was far from lost in Israel; there could be no public apathy in the face of constant Arab threats. Armament proceeded apace. In forming the army, inductees were not considered qualified for military service without thirty months of practical training. Battle practice was more emphasized than parade-ground work. Leadership development under highly competent commanders and instructors was exhaustive, with encouragement given to the acceptance of risk in battlefield maneuver. Israeli officers were sent to schools in England and France, but in view of what followed they could have gone to teach rather than to learn. A truly top-flight fighting machine resulted.

Threats, real and implied, and political pressures against Israel continued. By 1956 Egypt had received indirectly from the U.S.S.R. munitions totalling some 230 tanks, 200 armored personnel carriers, 100 self-propelled guns, 500 artillery pieces, 200 fighter aircraft and some naval vessels, bringing the armor and aircraft ratio about four to one against the Israeli—all in modern equipment. These developments forced Israeli planners to consider the risk of what might be a preemptive war.

As matters developed, the risk was immeasurably lessened by the Egyptian seizure of Suez Canal properties, closing the Canal to traffic. Britain and France then served an ultimatum on Egypt calling for all forces to be pulled back ten miles from the waterway, Israeli as well as Egyptian. At this time, however, while tentative Israeli deployments were being made, no forces were inside this limit.

Egypt ignored the ultimatum. French and British air and airborne troops then bombed and invaded the critical areas on October 31, 1956.

The air attacks served to permit initially cautious implementation of Israeli contingency plans for a blitz with only moderate fear of Arab air action. For propaganda purposes, a case might be made against either side for being the aggressor. But in what was known as the "100 Hour War," the Israeli thrust a multicolumned whirlwind into the Negev and Sinai, decisively smashing all opposition. Just a week after the firing of the first shot on October 29–30, 1956, nine brigades of crack Israeli blitz-trained troops stood unchallenged over all of the Sinai Peninsula, every enemy position having been overwhelmed.

The deterrent, resting almost solely on a corps of brilliant tactical leaders, had proved its soundness. In spite of sporadic raids and threats to shipping, the State of Israel had known a peace, though perhaps a troubled peace, for eight years; the threat, when it came, had been disposed of in hours.

United Nations intervention terminated all action in the Middle East and Israeli units returned to their borders. If this intervention was aimed at gaining Arab sympathy, it proved fruitless, for Egypt turned more and more to the Soviet, continued to control the Canal and to build up conditions that in another eleven years called for a repetition of the 1956 conflict.

In 1967 Israeli Intelligence forecast another Arab effort to conquer its territory; further, Egypt closed the Straits of Tiran to Israeli shipping. But although the situation closely resembled that which preceded the 1956 blitz, the Arabs had now been supplied with additional aircraft, tanks, transport, and weapons of late design. The odds, if anything, were worse against Israel than in 1956. And there was no possibility of taking advantage of outside intervention, as in the case of the 1956 British-French air action, to deploy ground forces with adequate air cover.

So it was necessary to risk the launching of Egyptian air against the armored columns, and it was unthinkable that Israeli territory should become the scene of battle. Therefore it became essential once again, to move to defeat the enemy in his own territory.

A four-stage strategic plan was laid out: (1) destroy the enemy air forces, (2) break through the strong Egyptian defenses in the Sinai (some having been bolstered over a period of many years), (3) make a deep armored thrust to the mountains just east of Suez to cut off Egyptian escape and, (4) destroy the scattered Egyptian Army.

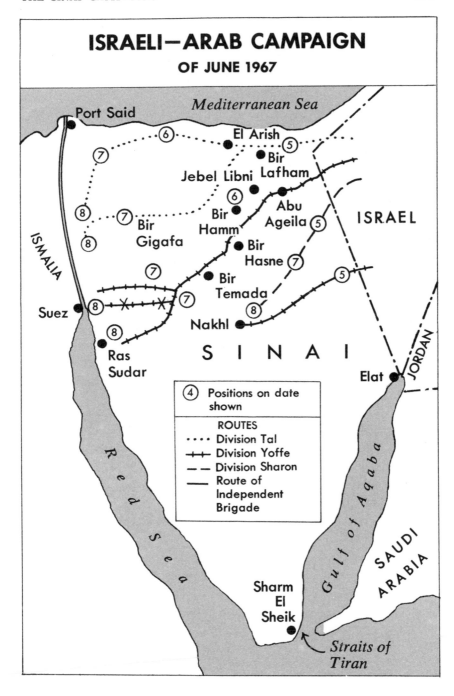

# ISRAELI–ARAB CAMPAIGN
## OF JUNE 1967

*Mediterranean Sea*

Port Said

⑥        El Arish ⑤

⑦        ● Bir
         Lafham
Jebel Libni
⑥  ●
         Abu
Bir      Ageila ⑤        ISRAEL
Hamm

⑧   ⑦ ● Bir
Bir          ● Bir
Gigafa       Hasne ⑦

⑧                     ⑤

⑦   ● Bir
    Temada
           ⑧
Suez ⑧ ╳━━╳ ⑦

⑧      Nakhl ●

Ras          S  I  N  A  I
Sudar                          Elat ●   JORDAN

┌─────────────────────────────┐
│ ④  Positions on date         │
│     shown                    │
│    ROUTES                    │
│ ···· Division Tal            │
│ ╂╂╂ Division Yoffe           │
│ ── Division Sharon           │
│ ── Route of                  │
│     Independent              │
│     Brigade                  │
└─────────────────────────────┘

*Red Sea*

*Gulf of Aqaba*

SAUDI
ARABIA

Sharm
El
Sheik ●

*Straits of
Tiran*

ISMALIA

All this was accomplished even more brilliantly than in 1956. A war on three fronts was won really in hours, though writers commonly call the campaign the "Six Day War." Between 0745 and 1035 hours on June 5 the Egyptian Air Force was destroyed, losses totalling some 500 aircraft, mostly hit on the ground. General Yoffe's "deep thrust" column was at Suez sixty hours after leaving Israeli territory and thousands upon thousands of tons of new Russian equipment were strewn over the wastes of the Sinai in one of history's greatest routs.

There is little doubt that increasing stores of Arab munitions and increasing belligerency, added to the conclusions of an excellent Israeli Intelligence system, justified drastic action whether it might be termed preemptive warfare or not. There was a critical threat; retaliation was swift and sure. The deterrent effect had provided another decade or more of peace, rather than igniting a general conflict of superpowers.

There were the usual attempts to call the blitz a "new kind of warfare" as Randolph Churchill intimated when he said that the strength of the Israeli lay in "flexibility and the use of tactics not found in military books."

In truth it was not tactics but techniques—Austerlitz and Cannae all over again. The tactics and strategy matter little. The important point is the careful establishment of the blitz capability and of having the commanders able to implement it.

The choice of one leader to typify Israeli leadership in the 1956 and 1967 wars is a task every bit as difficult as the choice of the other masters. Here were two miniature wars completed in days if not hours, and waged against an enemy who proved incredibly inept. Shall they be equated with the great campaigns of Napoleon or the near-cosmic efforts of World War II?

It is not necessary to equate the campaigns. Without any Arab forces being present at all, the swift deployment of the Israeli Brigades and Divisions over the forbidding terrain of the Sinai was a performance worthy of the best blitz commanders of other times. Possibly the Israeli had excellent Intelligence coverage of the Arab forces and, in the strategic sense, knew their weaknesses. Yet the troops could not make any such assumptions locally. The audacity and the firm control exhibited were in any case of the highest order.

General Yigael Yadon, Chief of Staff for Military Operations in 1948, and head of the entire effort in 1949–51 promulgated the doctrine that later bore so much fruit. Moshe Dayan was Chief of Staff during the 1956 war and General Itzhak Rabin assumed that post when Dayan became Minister of Defense just before the 1967 campaign.

Then there were Generals Mier Amit, Yeshuyahu Gavish, Israel Tal, and Haim Barlev, the last named considered the ablest of armored commanders by his associates. Colonels Aaron Doron, Ariel Sharon, Uri Ben Ari, Salmon and Avraham Yoffe were outstanding in 1956, most of them moving to higher rank and responsibilities in 1967.

General S. L. A. Marshall, former Chief Historian of the U.S. Army in Europe is the author of innumerable books on battle techniques in all theaters of war and is an expert's expert. Of Dayan he says in "Armor East of Suez" which appeared in the November–December 1967 issue of *Armor* Magazine:

The 1956 campaign was Dayan's masterpiece. Providing the best measure of his genius as a soldier, it still says too little directly about his command personality, which, by its radiance, energized a fighting system.

He speaks as well of Dayan's sparkling wit reinforcing an occasional biting criticism, a natural man, down-to-earth, forthright in speech and personal manner. Dayan's grasp of small unit tactics and broad strategy, his ability to estimate the enemy and his disdain for a staff officer "not dedicated to the front line soldier" are Israeli bywords. It is therefore tempting to select Dayan as a master. Although he did almost continually fly over the far-flung columns, visiting nearly all units in person, he was not in actual command.

Avraham Yoffe undoubtedly typifies the best of Israel's large corps of topflight commanders. His interest in command techniques especially commends him to any analysis of command and control. Further, Yoffe consented to a written interview with the authors of this book in which he subscribed completely to the principles and techniques that have been practiced by other famous leaders in the masters category.

So, at the risk of offending backers of other Israeli, Yoffe is presented as a most worthy exponent of blitzkrieg. Like Forrest, he has a commanding presence, being over six feet in height and weighing some 230 pounds, yet moving with complete grace, as might befit a heavyweight boxer. Of him General Marshall says:

No officer in Israel's Army knows more about the business of leading than this one; no other is more articulate or radiates greater good humor. Yoffe would probably wear well in any fighting unit on earth . . . he was nicknamed "Gideon" and the battalion that later formed the nucleus of the 9th Brigade was called "Gideon's Battalion," with the quotation "The Sword for God and Gideon" emblazoned on its emblem.

General Yoffe practiced the utmost in personal austerity while on campaign. In the 1967 war, for example, he ate only oranges and grapefruit, washed down with tea. Six oranges sufficed for the first three days.

He went into retirement for a second time after the close of hostilities to serve his government as the head of the Nature Reserves Authority in Tel Aviv.

The story of the flying Israeli columns in both the 1956 and 1967 wars is more an account of man's struggle against the elements than a tale of battles. The Negev is a forbidding land, generally a sandy, barren waste, with key points connected by caravan tracks that break down quickly after the passage of a few vehicles. The clinging sand is fully as effective as General Mud in bogging down motorized units.

The Egyptian Army had occupied the desert hamlets, apparently intending to back the forward outposts with strong reserves. These latter proved worse than useless. Either they never got into action at all or were surprised and overrun by Israeli aircraft or armored sweeps. In some cases the inflexibility of Egyptian planning was manifested by the abandonment of hundreds of vehicles on the pretext that the plans of the Egyptian commander had been "nullified."

There were exceptions. Many positions required mine-clearing operations. Others, such as the Mitla Pass area in 1956, were stubbornly defended; in this case a night attack against fortified caves proved essential to save elements of tank columns from the withering cross fire of antitank crews holed up on the cliffsides.

Usually the Forrest tactics of launching a smashing attack were employed, to some extent involving piecemeal action in cases where columns were strung out for miles over the desert trails. Each action called for choosing between risking disaster by a premature attack or losing momentum by delaying until stronger forces and adequate artillery had been assembled at the critical point. In two instances the rising and the setting sun served to blind defending Egyptians while Israeli tanks simply barrelled down the road to the gates of the fortified position.

The 1967 operation differed from the 1956 war in that a divisional organization was employed rather than that of the smaller and more austere Brigade, thus providing more staff assistance and better integration of forces.

For example, the task of Yoffe's Division in 1967 called for him to protect, initially, the left flank of Division Tal by clearing the way to Jebel Libni and Bir Hamm. Yoffe and Tal conferred briefly at Jebel Libni to coordinate their actions and to prevent the repetition of one or two cases in 1956 when one Israeli column had mistakenly fired on another. Following this momentary pause, and freed from intercolumn responsibility, Yoffe sped to Mitla Pass and Suez. Interestingly enough, even after the lessons of 1956, Yoffe's route was considered impassable by the Egyptians.

Yoffe was blessed with a highly competent Chief of Staff, Colonel Bren Adan, who had served as Commandant of the Israeli Armored School and who was an excellent foil for Yoffe's technical inexperience with armor. At the same time, Yoffe was presented with a problem similar to that recorded for the German General von Lüttwitz at Bastogne; one of his major commanders lacked the punch needed to keep up. It was not an unusual command problem in the complex history of the blitz. Yoffe readily solved it by changing commanders, a course that less positive leaders frequently fail to take. In any event when the erring brigade ran out of gas and lay dormant, the Egyptians failed to capitalize on their opportunity. The leading brigade proved adequate for the mission, urged on by Yoffe. The arrival at Suez, only sixty hours after crossing the border of Israel, proved more or less icing on the cake, since the mission of cutting off the escape of the Egyptian Army was wholly redundant; the Egyptian Army was already decimated.

In spite of the decision to commit air forces to counterair missions at the outset of operations, the Israeli flew 200 sorties in support of the ground action of Division Tal alone, on June 5, 1967. And artillery support was ever present. Self-propelled guns, in contrast to the towed cannon of 1956, kept well forward in the columns, so that on hostile contact they provided almost instant and direct support to tanks and infantry.

It was, to quote Dayan, the proper kind of war, fought in a suitable place with methods adapted to the enemy at hand.

The Israeli battle doctrine was summarized in Moshe Dayan's *Diary of the Sinai Campaign* to include the following:

Commanders went with the advance elements of their units.

Speed was the prime factor—Sinai had to be conquered in two weeks.

Plans were (and are) based on a huge measure of independence to field commanders.

Steam roller operations were planned, with planes followed immediately by assaulting tanks and personnel carriers. Positions were captured one after another.

Dayan contrasted the Egyptian command techniques with those of his own troops. He described the schematic nature of Arab practices with headquarters placed far in the rear. Changes in dispositions required many hours—time to think and to receive reports through many echelons of command, time to obtain a decision and to filter orders down again. The Israeli, however, acted with flexibility; commanders were on the spot; orders contemplated only the general mission, with actions and results left to local commanders.

Much of the doctrine profited from the experience of 1956.

Then it was realized that much remained to be done in war gaming and in large scale maneuvers. The need was filled. As a result, when 1967 arrived, all had been worked out. It was only necessary to apply lessons already learned.

If the Israeli won because of their battle techniques, it is another of the many cases when the defeated have appeared irresolute or inept when facing the bold and the skillful. It is thus reasonable to ask what might have happened had two skilled adversaries met. Suppose that both sides had been blitz-oriented. What is the antidote for the blitz? One may as well propound the hoary question of what happens when an irresistible force meets an immovable body. It is an argument that can go on forever.

But the mid-East situation poses a concrete case of what might develop should the Arab States produce tactical leaders of the caliber of the Israeli. Here one must add that leadership is not all there is to it. Leadership must be able to evoke an immediate and effective response from its air forces and its maneuver and fire-support ground elements. Response is a question of training; leader and led must play an integrated tune.

There is the added factor of luck. Which side gets the breaks on the imponderables—the weather, the rivers, the bogs and the accidents?

Napoleon confronted by Quatre Bras and Ligny may be recalled. He was, initially at least, personally active in keeping contact with Grouchy and Ney and his was a brilliant mind. Yet he got little response. Had his persuasive powers deserted him? Had they lost faith? Or was everyone simply too jaded to answer with intelligence and force? Perhaps Chaim Weizmann's observation applied: the men were too lean and the officers were too fat.

Training requires time and must rest on sound concepts. As this is written, war clouds in the Middle East have grown very dark indeed. But until Arab leadership and Arab training match the blitz doctrine of the Israeli, victory should prove illusory regardless of the sophisticated supplies and equipment that may wind up in Arab hands. It could take many years. For the moment, however, the blitz doctrine remains sound and the deterrent is working.

From the sketches of the masters, Napoleon through the Israeli generals, it is evident that their personal characteristics and their methods of command are set pretty much in the same mold. It is encouraging that most of them were not born geniuses, but rather acquired talents through study and field experience. What they have done, others can do.

If any one trait stands out above the others, it is their common and acquired attribute of "knowing their job." The knowledge is particularly applicable to their ability to mass and coordinate striking forces at what they correctly sensed to be the critical time and place.

The masters were all strong personalities, able to dominate battles. But because they were supremely professionally competent, they were able to do so in a quietly persuasive manner, neither becoming choleric nor martinets. Their temperaments were down to earth and included the realization that they must keep a sense of humor to save their wits amid the whirling problems of mobile battle.

Their feel for exquisite timing was enhanced by the habit of keeping up front where the action is, far enough forward to see battle developments at first hand, yet not so far forward as to risk being pinned down by enemy fire and thus being incapable of exercising normal control functions. In his *Diary,* Dayan says, "I like to be at the forward command post of a fighting unit. I do not know whether the commander enjoys having me at his elbow, but I prefer to follow the action (and if necessary intervene in its direction) while it is happening, rather than to read about it in dispatches. . . ."

Being in a forward position did not mean that they were out of touch with their own headquarters, except for the lapses noted in the case of Rommel. Horsed messengers had kept contact in pre-radio days, and the advent of the latter made any loss of contact inexcusable.

They cheerfully accepted responsibility for the frequent decisions made necessary by the many imponderables that always test the moral courage of a field commander. There was no passing of the buck. The great majority were highly creative in their thinking and used this trait to adjust matters so that the enemy was more often surprised than not; in the absence of orders, they assumed the responsibility and, in fact, preferred to operate on their own. They were invariably able to draw the line between audacity and rashness. While their collective motto may have been the one word "Risk!" all adhered to Rommel's habit of carefully considering alternatives before arriving at a decision.

All had a talent for sensing the limit of endurance of their troops and, when the need arose, of pushing them to that limit without compunction, thus usually avoiding an occasion of even greater stress at a later hour.

The close supervision of battle necessary to enhance the appreciation of timing and integrating the effort was expanded by the uniform use, in a tactful manner, of aides ("gallopers," or "cowboys," depending on the local terminology) to act as the eyes and ears of the commander at various critical points. They were all in direct communication with him and assisted the flow of critical information. Napoleon, to his grief, suffered a lapse of the practice at Waterloo, and modern times make the use of very senior officers on such duty impracticable. Nevertheless, it is an essential technique, with suitable adaptations, for past, present, and future lightning war.

Patton's Third Army, other World War II mobile divisions, and the Israeli appear to have been imbued with another of the manifestations of the spirit of constant drive. One of the marks of its lack is the halting of a march column without arousing the forceful pressure of every officer and noncom to find immediately the cause of delay and to press for correction. Vehicle drivers can fall asleep, make wrong turns or lose distance, as frequently happens, especially at night. Undoubtedly a circumstance of this kind was behind the delays in Yoffe's column in the 1967 Sinai campaign with the consequent relief of a commander.

Finally, it would be expected that anyone with the attributes of these brilliant leaders would be colorful. It is possible that many of them assiduously cultivated practices that made them especially subject to comment. Patton's violent language and his wearing of glittering stars some sizes larger than those of his contemporaries, to say nothing of pearl-handled pistols, offer one example. And Rommel's reputation for grandstanding was not entirely the result of jealousy on the part of his fellow commanders. Harmon had a comradely way with soldiers; Napoleon made a great show as he galloped around the battlefield in brilliant uniform; Forrest's penchant for personal combat earned him no end of publicity in the ranks; Yoffe personalized the "Sword for God and Gideon."

It is perhaps unjust to say that all this was deliberately contrived; probably it was natural. At the same time the methods of personalizing themselves gave great impetus to the morale of all ranks. Coupled with their known professional skills, appearances at the critical point would always give reassurance at the critical time. Deliberate or not, it was effective.

# 10 Functions of the Mobile Staff

With the end of the war in the Sinai, the analysis of the highlights of ancient and modern blitzkrieg and its leaders theoretically terminates—theoretically only because conflicts of similar type and environment in the immediate future cannot be ruled out.

Having extracted from the annals of mobile battles whatever lessons may be relevant to the age of the supertank, the helicopter, the giant air transport and the electronically equipped headquarters, it remains to determine whether this gadgetry will in fact enhance the command function or stultify it. The authors must now rely to a great extent on battle and research experience. But, since unsupported opinion is always risky, opinion will be based, wherever possible, on current war gaming. It is a good base. For example, the Naval War College used to plot a possible battle for Saipan and Tinian. When the actual battle occurred some years later, the gaming script proved surprisingly accurate. In general, gaming examines all contingencies.

Successful commanders operated in close conformity to the doctrine expressed for the Israeli in the previous chapter. Through all the years, the doctrine has been essentially unchanged in spite of striking improvement in matériel. It follows that the pattern should furnish valuable guidance in developing or perfecting a general national capability for applying lightning-war methods to the solution of future emergency geopolitical problems.

If a major power is to plan for such a capability within its armed forces, it must reach well beyond the Israeli basic principles. It must procure weapons systems suited to future combat environments and train even more rapidly a corps of leaders to conduct mobile operations.

The collapse of an enemy after less than six days (in some cases only hours) is a tribute to blitz methods. But the Sinai conflict did not test the national capability to reach trouble spots thousands of miles removed from the homeland, to sustain an effort requiring massive transport of re-supply items plus heavy outlays of mechanical and human maintenance facilities; nor did it call for the exercise of a general staff system capable of supervising global as well as local combat and administrative activities.

A major power with worldwide responsibilities adjudged to be in the national interest must visualize such expanded functions. It might be hoped, especially where a brushfire incident is concerned, that all would be over in hours. But with major confrontation, even where a blitz victory may be scored in an initial battle, the size of the confrontation would inevitably entail follow up by such actions as exploitation, wide encirclements, or rapid shifts of reserves, all adding up to a series of lightning-war engagements to reach a final decision.

A look into the crystal ball to determine the future of the blitz in the closing quarter of the twentieth century must therefore involve two general areas of concern: first, the impact of the new mobility as exemplified by more powerful vehicles and more versatile aircraft; second, and equally important, the type of staff support suitable for some future master in planning and controlling a stepped-up tempo of operations.

It will become evident that past blitz leadership methods are in fact being applied to a limited degree in the actual and conceptual operations of the airborne and airmobile commands that have come into being since the Korean conflict. At the same time, the complexity of mechanized war is such that these methods become more and more dependent on effective though unobtrusive staff effort.

Just about every organized human activity requires that a body of specialists assist the director of the activity by contributing knowledge of a particular area of interest, and generally by overseeing the conduct of business within that area save for the actual exercise of command.

Whole shelves of books and manuals are available to provide

technical instruction in military staff duties. The objective here is simply one of pointing out certain aspects of mobile command and staff work that either differ somewhat from more conventional or static types of combat or must be emphasized if the lightning quality of the blitz is to remain applicable.

The distinction between command and staff personnel can become especially marked in mobile warfare. Among combat troops a staff officer is sometimes viewed with contempt, sometimes with dislike, rarely with confidence and always with suspicion. It is a natural situation. The staff officer, in close contact with the commander, tends to identify with his chief and perhaps to assume an air of importance. He has, as a rule, personal interests to serve. A reputation for brilliance, for being always or usually right or for "protecting" his commander from unnecessary burdens earns him rewards in the form of coveted assignments or promotion. Responsibility can be shared with other staff officers. Blame can be shifted or absorbed. The stark mistakes or bad luck that sometimes beset a commander are easily avoided by a shrewd staff man. By dint of skillful political maneuvering he may carve out a complete career without ever risking his prestige on a decision that is his and his alone. Thus, from the viewpoint of the subordinate commander a staff officer often represents an interposition between him and his commander, through which his own point of view can be, and frequently is, distorted.

A story of the late Brigadier General Samuel D. Rockenbach is illustrative. He was a soldier of the Old Army and had served in many of the frontier Indian posts as a young man. During World War I he rose to head the embryo Tank Corps, justifying the star he now wore. Above all he was practical.

In the thirties he had led a brigade into maneuvers in the great Brasada of South Texas, where the mesquite grows tall and all plant life bears thorns as sharp as the good General's tongue.

It was the General's luck to be away from his command post when a husky young lieutenant wandered in leading an "enemy" patrol, thus capturing the entire brigade staff, a feat which was to engender some caustic comment at the final critique. To staff protests the umpire said, calmly, "You may not have been surprised, but you were certainly astonished."

Rockenbach was not the least flustered. Indeed, as he answered his critics from the platform it became plain that he was most unsympathetic with staff practices then being taught at the War Colleges. He was evidently under the impression that the lieutenant had done him a favor.

"As soon as I got rid of the goddam staff," the General explained with relish, "everything was simplified. I sat down with my aide, wrote out a few orders and finished the goddam war without any further trouble."

Much of this resentment can be ascribed to beliefs holding over from World War I when the static nature of operations permitted staff action to influence excessively, if not to override, commanders. Some of the resentment is the result of the importance very properly attached to high level staff instruction in special military schools, especially when that is followed by assignment to coveted posts.

It is certain that the command personalities of the so-called masters made for ideal relationships both within and outside of their own headquarters. They demanded a spirit of courtesy throughout. They supervised their staffs in a positive manner, acting of course through the Chief of Staff. They always provided a general directive that set up the plan of operations to be expanded in detail by the staff. They accepted the responsibility for whatever developed. They courted and listened to advice, but in no case were they creatures of their staffs.

The result always pointed to a real team effort. The commander was not figuratively kept in an ivory tower from which he emerged occasionally to sign a paper prepared by the staff; he participated instead in all actions except those involving obvious details or those not pertinent to decision making. No staff member was ever at a loss to know his commander's position on a given matter and the Chief of Staff was always kept informed, as Speidel finally persuaded Rommel that he should be.

Again, these conditions should prevail whether mobile war or a state of siege is in progress. In the static environment, lapses from such an ideal need not necessarily spell trouble; under blitz conditions they spell disaster.

A brief review of the Napoleonic staff system provides an excellent insight into appropriate practices, though it may seem strange that the methods of the Little Corporal are pertinent to problems of today or tomorrow.

Napoleon and his great Chief of Staff, Alexandre Berthier, established a lightning-war system of command and control at the dawn of the nineteenth century that would in many cases operate more speedily than electronically equipped commands of 1970. Certainly Moshe Dayan would testify that the Egyptian forces could not cope with its modernized version. The simplicity of the system serves to highlight the essential principles of staff work that must prevail for the mobility and control needed in tomorrow's blitzes.

Napoleon was careful in selecting officers to serve on the staffs of La Grande Armée. It will be recalled that General Girard, an otherwise highly qualified officer, was initially passed over until he had had more experience in command of troops. The same criterion was applied through all ranks. Staff personnel were drawn from officers of demonstrated command ability, bravery in combat, coolness of judgment, initiative, persistence, and physical stamina. Only these were considered fit for the mobile operations favored by Bonaparte.

The modern staff officer must have many more qualities than those specified by Napoleon. There is technical excellence to be considered, there is an overwhelming requirement that the staff officer get along well with others, and there is a pressing demand for men who understand the techniques of branches other than their own basic discipline. It is more and more difficult to pick and choose. Still, Napoleon's requirements for personnel appear to stand up currently as guidance for selection criteria.

Neither manuals nor studies were available to guide the ambitious officer seeking a coveted staff assignment at the end of the eighteenth century. Staff education came in the form of letters from senior experienced officers and from on-the-job training. This affords an interesting comparison with modern military education, where whole libraries and professional schools deal in staff instruction, while the command function is essentially left to practical field practice.

A prominent officer of the period, General Thiébault, realized the difficulties and published two volumes not long after the beginning of the Napoleonic era. These were titled *Manuel des Adjutants Généraux,* and *Manuel Général du Service des États-major Généraux et Divisionnaires dans les Armées.* These summarized and updated staff practices common a short time earlier under Ségur. They were said to reflect the thinking of the Emperor; in any event, they became standard reference works.

While the times were relatively simple, it would be a mistake to assume that bureaucracy was unknown in La Grande Armée. With the staffs of the artillery and engineers and general administration including health, finance, postal services, transport and printing, as well as the security forces, Napoleon's major headquarters employed some 400 officers, 5000 men and 500 horses.

The Napoleonic entourage may have been the first instance of the employment of what is now called a command van or trailer. The mobile headquarters was housed in a specially constructed wagon or coach, requiring eight horses to move it about at the speed he liked to travel. It appears to have been the last word in traveling comfort for the day; there were folding tables, a seat capable of being transformed into a bed for the Emperor, a place for Chief of Staff Berthier to doze en route, a map compartment, and a larder. The coach was escorted by relays of chasseurs and orderlies who formed a guard ring around it during halts when Napoleon and Berthier busied themselves on the ever-present situation maps.

In bivouac, two tents carried on a wagon were set up. One was used as a command tent; the second had bedding facilities. An aide slept in the second and a shift of one-half the orderlies remained in the first. A full battalion of the Imperial Guard was detailed as a security force.

Carried along were the meticulous records used by the Little Corporal to make his decisions; data on every unit and every major commander, including strengths, characteristics, sick lists, desertion rates, and battle records were available to reinforce the Emperor's great powers of recall when decisions were in the making.

Napoleon's personal staff consisted of three major generals and two brigadiers, used as equerries and secretaries on missions of great confidence. As battle aides, there were also three major generals and two brigadiers, each having his own orderlies and string of horses. In addition there were groups of orderlies and grooms for ordinary tasks. Particularly important, however, were the civilians to whom Napoleon dictated administrative and operations orders, Count P. A. Daru, the Intendant-General, and L. A. de Bourienne, the secretary. Baron L. A. Bacler d'Albe, as engineer-topographer, drew up and maintained maps, posting the situation map at convenient intervals.

Members of the personal staff were entrusted with delicate tasks concerned with the control of battle. These roles appear to be at once common and peculiar to blitz leaders. Napoleon, however, frequently employed junior officers on commissions of trust. An oft-chosen courier was de Castellane, then a simple lieutenant, who on a typical occasion was given the following order:

Castellane will proceed to Linz, where he will deliver the attached letter to the Duke of Danzig; he will then go to Bayreuth to take the letter to the Duke of Abrantes. At Bayreuth he will acquaint himself with the identity and dispositions of the troops making up the Corps of the Austrian General Kienmayer. He will report to me, similarly, the situation of the Duke of Abrantes with respect to Infantry, Cavalry and Artillery. During his return trip he will examine the fortifications at Passau and Linz and prepare to report their character. In passing he will take despatches to General Bourcier. [Napoleon at Schonbrunn, July 21, 1809]

Castellane's diary proved him to be one of the most caustic critics of the Emperor, doubtless tried beyond his patience on numerous occasions when he recorded rides of eighty miles or more at top speed, starting at any hour of the day or night. His experiences suggest that the Emperor had, in common with Forrest, Patton, Rommel, and the others, the ability to estimate the powers remaining in an apparently exhausted man or troop unit and he never hesitated to call on them.

As Chief of Staff, Berthier maintained a cabinet of a personal secretary, engineer officer, aides and two civilian commissioners of war. After the dispositions of La Grand Armée had become continent-wide he supervised a chief of troop movements, with six civilian assistants, plus a secret section of civilians with a quasi-intelligence role.

Berthier wrestled with and at least partially solved a vexing problem of modern times, the almost inexplicable disruptions of military organizations caused by levies of needed personnel to fill presumably greater needs elsewhere, or through the normal turn-over of personnel through rotation or by battle casualties. Berthier insisted on the use of civilians who were not subject to the same degree of turnover in staff positions where administration, includ-ing combat administration, was concerned. These handled the evolution of orders and the routine around headquarters which can often cause serious blunders if in the hands of green or untrained personnel.

Berthier was Chief of Staff until shortly before Waterloo. Bona-parte therefore had no need to exercise selection criteria for this important post. He did state that a Chief of Staff must be a man who (1) understood maps, (2) appreciated the value of reconnais-sance, (3) exercised care and *force* in the processing of orders and information, (4) was able to brief the commander in simple terms as to the dispositions and movements of forces and (5) who had a personality suited to the commander he served.

In the statement of requirements the word "force" is empha-sized, since Berthier's role was to see all, know all, and bring to the Emperor's immediate attention any information pertinent to current decisions. This most important function involves a com-munications problem by no means solved under conditions of modern electronics.

A suitable personality means of course an ability to work in harmony. But harmony in many cases may mean an alter ego of an entirely different character; in many cases a hard-boiled general will purposely select an affable and easygoing Chief. In mobile tactical commands, however, top flight generals are neither hard-boiled nor easygoing.

There were three "bureaux" in the staff itself:

1st Division. Charged with handling daily orders, letters, troop movements, situation reports, assignment of commanders, and general correspondence.

2d Division. The lodgment of the headquarters, police, subsistence, hospitals.

3d Division. Prisoners of war, military government, conscriptions, councils.

In addition, generals functioned as chiefs of cavalry and artillery and engineers, with supervisory roles over these branches.

Most of the functions charged to a modern staff are contained in the foregoing account. Napoleon was generally his own plans and operations officer, with the administrative elements of this function absorbed by Berthier's cabinet. The intelligence function at that time was severely restricted. Information came almost wholly from paid spies or local informers, sources that dried up in the later campaigns when the French Army became anathema to the people in occupied areas. Battle information was almost always obtained the hard way, from probing attacks or raids.

In battle all the excess impedimenta and personnel were left in the rear. Facilities to operate two command post sites were brought to the combat area. After the usual personnel reconnaissance by the Emperor or members of his staff, an advance command post was formed consisting ordinarily of Napoleon and two aides, two orderlies, the Chief of Staff and one of the general staff. The composition of this group varied according to the requirements of the moment.

Because of the limited range of the weapons of the day, it was possible to station another group only about 400 meters to the rear of the advance command post. This group split into two parts, one with aides and orderlies and another with Berthier's aides, staff bureau heads, and the chiefs of artillery, cavalry or engineers, according to the degree that each of the branches was in use. Another half mile to the rear were stationed their remaining staff members under the direction of a general officer.

Qualified staff officers were used throughout the field of action in roles that would be unthinkable in modern times. For example a staff officer always rode with the advance guard; other missions included supervision or monitorship over assembly or deployment of troops.

In general, the aides served as the Emperor's eyes and ears in spots that he could not conveniently reach himself. Their missions frequently called for the utmost in bravery, intelligence, and tact. Among these were: verification of the situation or condition of troops, leading columns on routes decided upon during the battle by Bonaparte, commanding task forces, reconnaissance to flanks, commanding massed artillery or cavalry.

The aides spoke in the name of the Emperor, justified somewhat by their advanced rank; they were invariably respected as having the confidence of Napoleon and the ability to relay his desires precisely. Napoleon's leadership was such as to permit that system to operate with, apparently, the complete support and even the cordial cooperation of the subordinate commanders. Aside from the battle roles, the aides often went on distant missions far more dangerous than Castellane's. During the Peninsular Campaign they had to traverse country infested with guerrillas and otherwise completely hostile, where capture meant death. They were young men in the thirty to thirty-five-year age bracket, sometimes younger, but necessarily old enough to have the judgment and experience the task demanded. There can be little doubt that Napoleon's use of aides was one of the major factors in the success of his command and control system.

In any summary of Napoleonic precepts as to the operation of a model headquarters, three principles would undoubtedly stand out. The first would be Berthier's adage that *speed is the most important consideration in general staff action.* This might shock professionals of the World War I and Montgomery schools of caution, but the shock might be eased by emphasizing that the reference is after all strictly to a tactical general staff and not to the planners of vast strategic ventures of the OVERLORD or TORCH variety. Inherent in this principle is a second—*that control of tactical operations must not be stultified by command preoccupation with administrative details.* Again inherent is a third, implying the essence of staff efficiency is the *immediate provision to the commander of all information that relates to a command decision.*

It is of course easy to cite principles of this kind and quite another matter to put them into practice. In the electronically equipped modern headquarters, the problems back of the three principles have not been solved. The reason is simply that the amount of information that had to be sifted by Berthier and his assistants to get to critical items is a far cry from the mountains of data that accrue in a complex modern world.

It is perhaps misleading to say that lightning-war staff practices vary from those associated with conventional or static war. They are, it is to be hoped, identical in careful attention to detail. The differences, where they occur, really lie in the amount of emphasis that time, that ever-present bugaboo of the mobile commander, allows for planning and execution.

While a series of volumes could well be devoted to the subject, special consideration in lightning war must be given to the intelligence, logistical, combat supervisory, and headquarters organizational functions.

The blitz intelligence problem centers on how much time a commander has available to seek information that will justify a course of action, usually offensive action.

At the divisional and corps echelons, that is, those most concerned with blitz tactics, the headquarters absorbs information from above and passes it down the chain of command. Conversely, subordinate units in contact with the enemy, friendly aircraft, and electronic devices pick up information which, when evaluated by experienced personnel, is defined as intelligence. Appropriate portions, usually most if not all of it, are transmitted up the chain of command. It is a vast network. Today modern computers of the highest speed and memory capacity are hard put to store and print out the availabe information.

Unfortunately, and particularly at the divisional level, the information from above is rarely specific enough to promote sound decision making for a divisional operation. And information from below is only infrequently general enough to meet the same requirement. This is especially true in fluid warfare.

As a result the blitz commander usually must go ahead with an operation without having the information he really needs. The battle examples in earlier chapters are replete with this sort of dilemma; risk immediate action into the unknown or wait for information that may never come, while in the meantime the opportunity is lost.

Once an attack is launched and has promise of success, valid information begins to pour in, to be passed on to senior headquarters. With a good control system, commanders respond quickly to indications for changes in plan. Bold action becomes at once a source of intelligence and a means of capitalizing on it; Nathan Forrest was an apostle of this creed.

While none of the urgent requirements for the development and transmission of intelligence are lessened in lightning war, it is axiomatic that the blitz leader must become reconciled to getting along with little or none until the action starts. The usual state of affairs is the basis of the Israeli slogan of "risk, risk, risk."

As a corollary, mobile troops must be trained in battle drills in which tactical moves are carried out with dash and violence on signal, much as an American football team operates. Although the drills are designed for small units of a battalion or reinforced company size, their use by elements in the lead of advancing columns are vital to the success of divisions; instant fire action coupled with maneuver will either overrun opposition or will generate immediate intelligence for use by the next senior commander.

Logistics problems are subject to similar considerations. That is, the commander must frequently risk action with less ammunition gasoline, or other necessary supplies than he would like to have or may actually need. To this end many commanders treat the Assistant Chief of Staff for Logistics (G-4) as a combat officer rather than an administrator. As such he is found at or near the operations command post of the unit during critical phases of the battle, where he is able to sense immediately and in person the needs of a rapidly changing tactical situation.

Recently the United States Army recognized the special logistical requirements of mobile war by forming Logistical Commands, which in essence permit the allotment of resources to a combat unit in proportion to the severity of its engagement. Under the old concept, for example, an armored division might be in reserve, together with a relatively idle complement of motor maintenance agencies. Though it now enjoys a degree of organic maintenance support, the typical combat unit will have minimum support when not committed and maximum support when fully committed.

The Napoleonic system of control through skilled aides has never been practiced as such by western nations, though Forrest came near to copying it. It will probably never be employed in detail in modern times, for the system depended upon the use of very senior general officers; the technical complexities of today make it unlikely that officers of similar rank could be spared for the duty.

Patton used a system of radio-equipped officers who accompanied major columns and reported their location at intervals directly to "Old Blood and Guts." Von Manteuffel employed officers he called "cowboys" who performed an eyes-and-ears role and who reported directly to him on battle conditions observed in areas von Manteuffel could not personally visit.

The present American organization of the combat division provides for a deputy (or assistant) commander, a general officer, who could carry out the "aide" mission, or perhaps supervise a group of aides without exciting the resentment and suspicion of subordinate commanders. The role of the aide can be made palatable by using him as a means of furnishing rapid additional support for the subordinate unit without going through command channels. The aide, in direct contact, can make recommendations to the senior commander immediately; the subordinate usually hesitates to call for help. Basically the system saves precious time in getting critical information to the commander.

Finally, the aide system of eyes and ears, when tactfully used, is a silent and effective means of encouraging factual reporting. Commanders often go overboard in either pessimistic or optimistic ways. An on-the-spot observer motivates them to second thoughts.

The aide system should not be confused with the common practice of sending liaison officers from a lower headquarters to a higher to bring back critical information to their own commander and thus short-circuit routine channels. The aide system works in the reverse direction; the aide in a sense represents the senior commander, whereas a liaison officer has no authority whatever. He is simply an especially qualified messenger.

Napoleon provided for the organization of La Grande Armée Headquarters to the end that administrative or routine information could be separated from that pertinent to decision-making.

There was always a main headquarters, an advance and a rear. The principal change in the last 160 years has been the inclusion of a Tactical Operations Center (TOC) within the command post as a wholly operations-intelligence agency concerned, as the name implies, with tactical operations. The change has been necessary because of the complexity of measures aimed at coordinating maneuver- and fire-missions in a nuclear age.

Generally the blitz commander establishes an advance command post near the site of the main effort of the command. In so doing, he has close and possibly personal contact with the principal subcommander of the moment, and coincidentally provides some headquarters security by reason of proximity to a combat unit.

The staff personnel manning an advance command post or a TOC are always minimal in number, being confined to those directly concerned with the operation. The artillery officer or his representative (directly connected by radio with the Fire Support Coordination Center (FSCC)), is always a member of the party. As required, the operations, intelligence, engineer and other specialists may be present, though if the TOC is in "advance," operations-intelligence personnel are mandatory. The end in view is that of minimizing the time of information exchange. Blitz practice would appear to dictate the location of the TOC in the advance command post.

The dependence of the blitz commander upon superior communications is self-evident. The only way of insuring that communications are indeed superior is for the commander to take a personal and technical interest in everything relating to information flow, from the organization and transport of the headquarters to the ability of communications personnel to speed up service. The commander should interest himself in the number and type of radio channels available, the composition of the various nets, the matter of priorities and the question of who is responsible for insuring immediate delivery of critical information.

It is well to admit that many persons, even military professionals, would regard risk-taking in the intelligence and logistics areas foolhardy in the extreme. The tendency of Montgomery of Alamein to wait until mountains of supplies and presumably accurate information had been built up comes to mind at once. A Patton might ask, of course, what might have happened had Rommel been able to take advantage of the time to receive more tanks, petrol, weapons, and personnel. But these examples bring out one fault in the history books—they relate to high level strategy, whereas blitz battles at the division level are most sensitive to the time element. Minutes, sometimes seconds, count.

Most blitz leaders have felt that by sacrificing a degree of intelligence or logistics support they gained a greater advantage in the areas of surprise or massing of effort at a critical point. No commander attacks unless he feels that he can win, though on occasion defeat locally may help to gain victory elsewhere. But the decision to attack means that the factors have all been weighed and that superiority lies in better morale, better control for the massing of effort or for quicker reaction, or better weapons. Control is often a more than adequate substitute for intelligence and speed a substitute for supply. There may be risk, but there is no rashness, where advantages outweigh disadvantages.

# 11 The Combat Environment: Fancy and Fact

A true picture of the problems of command at the divisional and corps levels suffers within military circles from the fact that few persons ever get to see it at first hand.

Definitive data on day-by-day command problems are lacking to an even greater degree than on the general subject of blitzkrieg itself. Today's military writers tend to deal with the adventures and the problems of soldiers at the levels of direct enemy contact, or they become preoccupied with the great strategic aspects of warfare and neglect the levels at which the real business of war is carried out.

Where history and research fail, it is necessary to invent it by describing fictionalized events occurring over approximately one day in the life of a typical division. Events are simply those that affect decision-making, bringing out more forcibly some of the principles that have been developed from battle and personality sketches. At the same time a depiction of typical combat environment will assist in reaching an understanding of how developments in the nuclear age make it all the more imperative that potential leaders be trained to cope with the increasing tempo of mobility and control.

The situation to be described is what might be termed quasi-mobile—selected so that more staff action can be highlighted than that normally associated with the conduct of rapidly moving combat. It depicts a river-crossing operation, one that will continue to plague ground commanders for all foreseeable decades.

154

The accounts are designed principally to portray two different command personalities faced with identical circumstances. One, like Napoleon's Marshal Berthier, is an estimable officer better adapted to staff duties than to dealing with problems of mobile command, the other an experienced combat leader. Both are decidedly dedicated human beings, doing a job for which they are qualified in varying degrees.

Major General Charley Dare, commanding the 68th Mechanized Division, was opposed by a highly sophisticated enemy. The 68th had an excellent reputation and General Dare, though charged with a tough river-crossing mission, felt that here was a golden opportunity to add luster to the brilliant record he had made during his years on staff duty in the Pentagon.

But at division headquarters there was some evidence of restlessness. "What have you heard from General Dare, Chief?" asked Lieutenant Colonel Al Sponson, the assistant chief of staff for operations. "He's been at Corps Headquarters over two hours!"

"His aide arrived and gave me a fragmentary order for the Corps river crossing," replied the Chief. "Let's get the staff together. The General is having lunch at Corps and wants us to have detailed plans ready for him when he returns."

Sponson gazed morosely into the distance. He had trouble adjusting to the present environment. General Dare was unpredictable. He alternated between moods in which the staff was expected to act without guidance to those in which Dare assumed control of everything. Sponson knew that the Chief of Staff had served in the Pentagon with Dare in Research and Development, where Dare was wont to take over part of a project and become immersed in it. And a nice guy, really. As for the Chief, he was easygoing and tolerant. Nothing bothered him.

General Ekko Foxx, the assistant division commander, excited Sponson's pity. Foxx simply sat around. It was half understood that Foxx might one day lead an emergency task force into action, but nothing had ever been done to arrange a staff for him or to discuss eventualities.

Two hours later the staff meeting was in full progress and Sponson took his turn in a series of briefings. It was an elaborate setup, a thing that Sponson was good at arranging, however much tongue-in-cheek. Beautifully drawn situation maps, in color and on sliding frames, were festooned with colored tapes and pins, all enhanced by lighting effects. Dare liked his command post to be impressive.

Lieutenant Colonel Joe Bogie led off with a long discussion about enemy capabilities. Sponson grew more morose; he didn't see what difference it would make to the division, considering the rapid changes in enemy dispositions that would be taking place before the river crossing began. But later his own tentative plans were accepted without comment, and talks by logistics and the special staffs droned on. Even the chaplain got into the act by suggesting precombat religious services. A general wrangle ensued after the briefings, and a staff consensus was finally reached. The General was called in, had matters explained to him, and approved the plans without so much as a question. He directed the Chief of Staff to draw up orders, mimeograph them, and send them out by liaison officers. Sponson's recommendation that air messenger service be used was turned down on the grounds that aircraft could not be spared. As finally decided, Task Force Lion (Colonel Texton) and Task Force Tiger (Colonel Rhoadus) would move to crossing sites, brushing back resistance, with TF Zebra in reserve.

General Dare retired for the night. At his regular 0600 briefing he was told that TF Lion had been delayed for more than two hours. It was explained that Texton had called in to ask for instructions and this had led to a search for a missing liaison officer. The unfortunate captain's vehicle had been wrecked, along with the radio, and the entire crew seriously hurt. The long suffering Sponson had therefore alerted both Texton and the Task Force and dispatched another copy of the order.

Then the Chief of Staff called another meeting. "Gentlemen," he said, "the Division Commander proposes to visit Task Forces Lion and Tiger in turn. He has directed that the staff study the situation and prepare alternate sets of plans for the succeeding phases of the operation after we have crossed the river. He is concerned at the possibility that distinguished visitors may arrive and wants to be advised at once so that his helicopter may bring him back here immediately.

"Some of you have asked about a forward command post. He does not think one suited to this river crossing. He wants written orders for every contingency and to that end we shall remain here at Main and work on our planning. The General will join us later and will receive reports of the action here from the big situation map."

Task Force Lion, after its two-hour delay, made up for lost time and, with the gods of war apparently trying to even matters, hit the river having met only token resistance. Assault boats were ready and, although sporadic machine-gun fire and a few mortar rounds made things uncomfortable, the leading company got to the far bank and opened a small bridgehead. When he saw how easily the crossing site was being secured, Colonel Texton began to bombard Lieutenant Colonel Sponson and the Chief of Staff for immediate provision of the bridge company under the supervision of the division engineer.

"The engineer is attending a conference at Corps Headquarters, Colonel Texton," replied Sponson. "I'm trying to reach General Dare, who is supposed to be with Rhoadus and Task Force Tiger, but he doesn't answer the radio."

Texton immediately sent a staff officer in a car to find General Dare. This courier reached TF Tiger's area to find a highly confused state of affairs. Troops were scattered over the area, sitting down from a column of three's formation, apparently awaiting orders. Near the grove of trees a small knot of officers was gathered and in their midst the division commander was giving orders in a loud tone of voice. Colonel Rhoadus, the Task Force commander, was standing idly by, his face a thundercloud.

"General, I have a message," began the courier, when the General cut him off. "Damn it, young man, don't interrupt. I'm giving orders here."

And so he was. The courier was of too tough a fiber to be abashed. It seemed evident, however, that General Dare had taken command of Tiger. Whether Rhoadus was relieved or not could not be determined at the moment. But the need for bridging equipment at Lion was too acute and the thick-skinned young officer returned to the attack. This time he was successful.

"Why didn't you say so?" roared General Dare. "How should I know what he needs? Nobody ever tells me anything. Now, listen, Rhoadus, I'm going to have to run over to Texton's people with this officer. Press on here and let me see some results."

"General, I think you should get a replacement for me," said Colonel Rhoadus. "You have countermanded most of my orders and I don't believe the Task Force can continue to have confidence in me."

"Nonsense, Rhoadus," snapped General Dare. "I've just been putting a few things right. You'll have no trouble now. Go ahead."

But if Colonel Rhoadus had misgivings he was not in the dilemma facing the Chief of Staff. The latter was being overloaded with requests for bridging equipment. He had called on the assistant division commander, Brigadier General Ekko Foxx, for a decision after nearly twenty minutes of trying to reach the division commander over the radio and by phone.

"I'm sorry, Chief," said Foxx heavily, "I'd tell you in a minute to go ahead, but in that instant General Dare would rescind the order and we'd be worse off than ever. You know he wanted that bridging equipment in support of TF Tiger. I'll not be the one to cross him. I'm really surprise he's not staying in the command post as usual."

By this time several new developments had taken place. First, Task Force Lion had come under heavy artillery fire, causing Colonel Texton to get on the radio personally to ask the division artillery officer for close support fires; the latter, as was the division custom under General Dare, was at his fire direction center. He was under the impression that General Dare had gone to Task Force Tiger, because Tiger was supposed to be the main effort. Texton's request was therefore cut to a battery concentration in anticipation of massing fires in support of Tiger.

But when the fire request was cut, with the explanation that General Dare was with TF Tiger and wanted the bulk of fire there, Texton exploded.

"That's ridiculous," he shot back. "My liaison officer is guiding

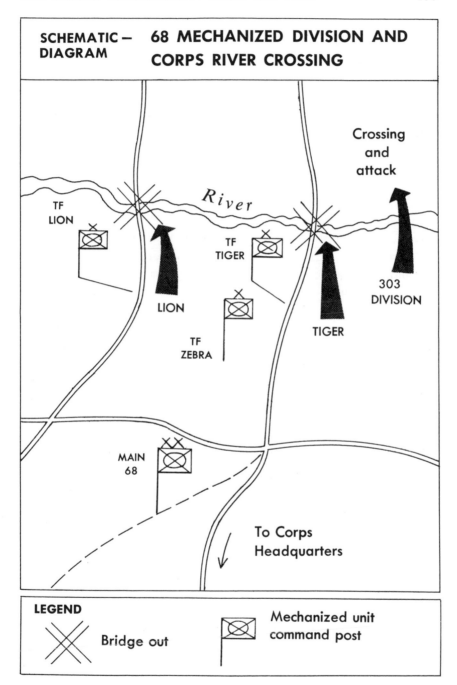

**SCHEMATIC — DIAGRAM**

**68 MECHANIZED DIVISION AND CORPS RIVER CROSSING**

Crossing and attack

TF LION

River

TF TIGER

303 DIVISION

LION

TF ZEBRA

TIGER

MAIN 68

To Corps Headquarters

**LEGEND**

Bridge out

Mechanized unit command post

General Dare here right now. I need the fire. Let's get going."

"The Chief has been unable to locate General Dare," said the artilleryman with a shrug that could almost be seen over the ether, "when we get organized I'll see what can be done."

Within a matter of moments General Dare arrived at Lion and immediately assumed command. He was incensed that the engineering equipment was not already at the Lion site and openly criticized the Chief of Staff, Lieutenant Colonel Sponson, and the engineer for not so arranging affairs. Troops were milling around the area, while sporadic artillery and mortar rounds burst at random in the woods and over the open spaces.

At this juncture the long-lost engineer officer arrived and was told to take charge of the effort to cross the river in assault boats. In spite of the confusion arising out of General Dare's assumption of command, somewhat more than a company of infantry made it across without suffering extensive casualties. But they were soon counterattacked and their situation became desperate. Their plight was brought home to the division command post and the artillery fire direction center; heavy artillery support and an air strike were thrown in to balance the scales.

Then enemy artillery fire, accurately placed in the river, destroyed most of the assault boats and such equipment as had been assembled. Bridging was now impossible.

General Dare, never one to shirk danger, crossed the river in an undamaged assault boat and joined the portion of TF Lion that was heavily engaged there. He was again without his radio but lost himself in his interested conduct of the local operation. Enemy probing was constant through the heavy brush that covered the river banks for nearly a half mile inland; artillery fire increased. After some twenty minutes General Dare was hit by a shell fragment and seriously wounded. Colonel Texton arranged to have him taken back across the river and decided that withdrawal at nightfall by the entire task force was essential to save it from annihilation. Texton was told by an orderly that the Chief of Staff was trying to reach him by radio, but Texton could not reach his command vehicle because of the heavy fire. He tried to pass the word to his driver to report developments to Division.

Meanwhile Task Force Tiger, reorganized after General Dare's departure, had reached the river, found a good crossing site and urgently requested bridging equipment from Division.

The Chief and General Foxx now shared a dilemma. It was the old half-witticism of "who's in charge here?" General Dare was not the type to have his orders superseded without losing his temper, but where was he?

The liaison officer sent by the Chief to the 303d Infantry Division on the right reported by radio that an excellent crossing site had been secured. The leading elements of the 303d were crossing.

"I suppose that Dare will be furious that we have been outdone by the 303d," said General Foxx, "but I can't see what can possibly be done here. I'm sure he'd rather implement Tiger's crossing, yet it seems simpler and less expensive to tie in with the 303d. Let's wait another fifteen minutes and . . ."

He was interrupted by a stir outside the command post and turned to find General Kirstone, the corps commander, and his small party.

"I changed into a command car I had waiting for me back about a mile," said Kirstone. "I didn't want to bring my chopper up here where there is so much shelling. But I could see from the air that things are not going well for you. Where is General Dare? And what's the trouble?"

"We're having some radio trouble," the Chief began nervously, his easygoing manner for once deserting him. However, Kirstone cut him off. "You people seem to be always having communications problems," he barked at the group. "We are wasting valuable time on stupid nonessentials. I sent word up here an hour ago that I was coming but it seems to be a surprise. Where's the message?"

As General Foxx attempted to explain a matter that was certainly not his immediate responsibility, Lieutenant Colonel Sponson appeared. In a voice that was transparently unconcerned he announced that General Dare had been wounded and evacuated. Meanwhile Texton was suffering from a lack of artillery support and his troops across the river were under heavy pressure. Sponson reported that Texton was planning to effect a withdrawal back across the river under cover of darkness.

General Kirstone's face was darkening rapidly. "How long have you been out of touch with General Dare?" he demanded.

"Nearly an hour," reported the Chief of Staff, "but . . ."

"No buts needed," cut in Kirstone. "Now, listen. Hereafter, should any question of command arise, the next senior will take command and until he is on the spot the Chief of Staff must take temporary responsibility. You are in command here. Foxx, I want to have the reserve, Task Force Zebra, move at once to the 303d Infantry for attachment to them. Regroup the 68th Division and be prepared to exploit the crossing of the 303d by nightfall. Try to expedite the withdrawal of TF Lion so it can catch up by the time Tiger starts across. Meanwhile displace and mass artillery so Lion's withdrawal can be supported. If possible try to shift fires to assist the Corps and the 303d Division Artillery for the support of the 303d . . ."

Kirstone continued in his incisive manner while his aide took notes for later transmittal to the Corps Chief of Staff.

But a look more morose than ever had settled on the face of Lieutenant Colonel Sponson. He was under no illusions about the failure of the 68th. The Chief and General Foxx hadn't come out of it too well either. He only hoped that he was far enough down the scale so that his own record would not be affected. He was by no means optimistic, reflecting that the old expression about the sins of the fathers all too frequently applied to generals.

Thus was the operational phase of a river crossing by a mechanized division brought to an unhappy conclusion. General Dare had by turns overdelegated responsibility in the planning phase of the battle, only to reverse himself in its conduct to the degree that he seriously infringed on the command prerogatives of experienced subordinates. Control was lost in the chain of command because those who might be expected to assume forceful charge in an emergency were reluctant to do so. It was a situation that probably would have produced excessive and needless casualties.

What might have happened if a different personality had been in General Dare's shoes? Here is an account of the way things might have broken for Major General Tex Goodspeed.

Major General Tex Goodspeed had an agile mind which permitted him to consider other problems even while assaying his options for his next move. How the country did fall into these wars where the other fellow had the initiative! A tough river crossing was the immediate prospect for his crack 68th Mechanized Division, with crossing sites well protected by enemy troops. How to dispose of them? The obvious ploy was to turn himself into an airmobile division but that seemed a problem for the scientists.

At the moment Tex was in his helicopter, en route to XXX Corps Headquarters to hear Lieutenant General Kirstone, the Corps commander, outline his plans for the operation. Before leaving the command post of the 68th, Tex had directed his chief of staff to alert all major units for the expected movement and to have their commanders prepare to meet him at division headquarters on his return. He checked into the division command net, as well as the special net linking the staff that he had set up, making sure that communications were functioning and using the simple voice code of the day. Tex was proud of his staff. He had trained them thoroughly as a team, relentlessly squelching the few evidences of bickering, or of friction between staff and the brigade commanders.

General Kirstone was brief as befitted an old pro. He invited comments when he had concluded. These were brief too; the engineer suggested that bridging elements should be moved farther forward in view of their expected use, into positions he himself had selected. This was approved. General Wedge, commanding the 303d Infantry Division requested the attachment of another artillery battalion from Corps to his division. Kirstone patiently gave reasons for denying this: he would place an entire group of artillery at Wedge's disposal for his attack, but would keep Corps strings on it. All routine. Kirstone had been at his positive and incisive best.

Tex Goodspeed and his aide had made notes and had marked their maps with the proposed phase lines and unit boundaries and with the numbered circles that indicated possible artillery and air strikes. It would be necessary, if the need arose, only to call for the proper number.

As his chopper left Corps headquarters, Tex radioed his chief of staff to assemble the major unit commanders, he mulled over

164          ALTERNATIVE TO ARMAGEDDON

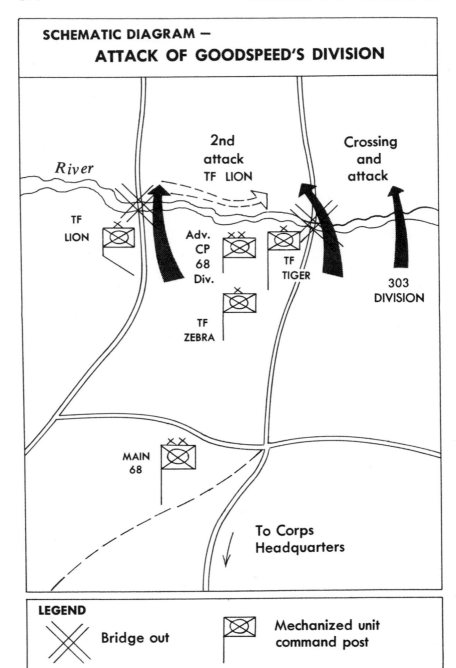

SCHEMATIC DIAGRAM —
**ATTACK OF GOODSPEED'S DIVISION**

*River*

2nd attack
TF LION

Crossing and attack

TF LION

Adv. CP 68 Div.

TF TIGER

303 DIVISION

TF ZEBRA

MAIN 68

To Corps Headquarters

LEGEND

Bridge out

Mechanized unit command post

several plans for the 68th Mechanized to seize a crossing site, bridge the river to allow passage of heavy equipment, and then exploit the advance on the far side. Meanwhile the chief and the staff had been busy considering details of all eventualities.

By the time of his arrival, commanders and staff were looking over the display map flashed on a screen, and Tex had come to his tentative decision. He first asked what changes, if any, had occurred, especially in enemy activity.

"Reports have been pretty meager, General, since we haven't been able to get sizable force across to get a significant contact," said Lieutenant Colonel Joe Bogie, the intelligence officer. "We have only the summaries from Corps and Army."

"Well," sighed Tex, "that seems normal enough, Joe, but I appreciate your difficulty. We'll punch hard tomorrow and you'll be able to tell Corps and Army all about it. Now, here's what I have in mind. . . ." He broke off and outlined his plan for the employment of three task forces, TF Lion, TF Tiger and TF Zebra.

Colonel Frank Texton said with some asperity that he needed more infantry for TF Lion. Texton was a burly, rough and ready veteran of the Pacific campaign and Korea. He was not too enthusiastic about mechanized warfare, though there was no doubt that he was a bold and adjustable leader. But Goodspeed demurred with the assurance that he would have the reserve commander right at hand in case immediate need for more infantry arrived. "And I want you gentlemen to get this," he added, rapping his knuckles on the table for emphasis. "I'm not going to reinforce trouble! Take your objectives with what you have and we'll exploit with reserves where the breakthrough occurs. You all know my principles on that!"

A not unnatural silence ensued, followed by Lieutenant Colonel Al Sponson, the division operations chief, briefing the group on the other ideas that had been evolved. This order of business was a peculiarity of General Goodspeed's, who believed that by allowing the staff to present suggestions and choices the major commanders might feel freer to comment; he sought general discussion as long as no radical departures from the point at issue occurred. Sponson talked, however, without much confidence, and drew the reply he seemed to expect. "No," said General Good-speed, "I thought of those too. But I appreciate your bringing them up, Al. You never know. Just the same, we'll go as I have outlined."

Rather unexpectedly TF Tiger requested a change in its route of approach. "I got a chance to look the ground over with a chopper," said Colonel George Rhoadus, a wiry and deceptively mild character. "What I suggest will make easier going after the rains."

Goodspeed gave his okay. Then simple map overlays were readied, showing the objectives, routes, and boundaries. The numbered Corps artillery and potential air strikes were brought down below division level. This again was standard procedure.

As the meeting broke up, Goodspeed called Colonel Texton and Brigadier General Ekko Foxx, the assistant division com-mander. "Texton," he said, "when action starts you will have General Foxx near you to observe the action of TF Lion. You know this system. But, I repeat, the relationship is between you and me. Foxx is there to help. If you feel that he is spying on you let me know, because he isn't. I am going to watch the action of TF Tiger. We both know that Foxx's presence will speed up getting what you may need!"

Texton grinned and said that he was really glad to have the help. As he left, the Chief of Staff came up to suggest the move-ment of the command post some two miles up the road and the setting up of the advance post, or Tactical Operations Center (TOC), with its intelligence and operations personnel near the crossing site of TF Tiger, the location of the main effort of the division. The Chief stressed that he was stationing Lieutenant Colonel Waggoner, the logistics (G-4) staff assistant with the ad-vance group in order that Waggoner could judge for himself when to move up additional gas, oil, and ammunition for the ex-ploitation.

"Okay," concurred Goodspeed, "and for this action I want the artillery officer, the air liaison and the engineer with me in the chopper as the commander's group. We'll locate up where we can see Tiger get started and keep in the area of the Tiger com-mand post. Foxx is going separately to Lion. Open the special staff net connecting the command post, the TOC, Sponson, Foxx, and myself. I may want Sponson to have a look at the crossing site of General Wedge's division."

"I think the artillery officer wants to stay in the fire direction center this time," said the Chief. "He wants close control over the battalions."

"Okay if he can send a good advisor with me," snapped Tex. "What the hell can he do in the FDC that he can't do with his radio from the command group? I need lots of fire for this one. We may just probably need ten or twelve battalions, in place of nuclear fires that are not practical for this crossing. And we'll also need tactical air to boot—in quantity. But he's running the artillery!"

There were no preliminary artillery fires aimed at the so-called softening of the enemy positions. Goodspeed would have been the last to employ of the World War I style of artillery support which really went out before that conflict had ended. He knew that this sort of pseudo-punishment rarely did anything short of swelling the profits of the ammunition manufacturers. He had trained his artillery to respond instantly to calls on or near numbered points on the maps already prepared.

The Goodspeed chopper and the specified staff took off in sunshine, welcome enough after the rains. The weather and the lush terrain below gave the General the opportunity to reflect on the stupidity of war, as most professionals from time to time do. Here he was, risking not only his own neck but those of 15,000 others. But he quickly shifted his mood. Firemen had to fight fires they didn't start; generals had to wage wars they had hoped to avoid.

In the meantime TF Lion had jumped off and was reported as making excellent progress. Goodspeed had this from General Foxx over the staff net in the voice code of the day. He did not feel that he had to bother Colonel Texton who had his hands full with combat duties. He was immediately concerned with TF Tiger which, as he could plainly see, was having trouble with the forces defending the bridge site, who were aided by most favorable terrain. Shelling was heavy and bursts were visible all around the seemingly confused array of troops and vehicles that always form a part of a combat situation.

So Goodspeed directed the engineer to have bridging equipment brought up on the axis of TF Lion, only to have the latter counsel a hedge. It seemed to him that the ground now held by enemy troops facing Tiger might offer a better opportunity for bridging.

Goodspeed, with the sagacity that came from dealing with several varieties of engineers, countered with the idea that the bridging equipment be brought to an area where trails leading to either site were available. When this suggestion was given engineer assent, Goodspeed sighed. He thought for the thousandth time of the futility of vast plans and orders. He was too old a hand not to know that changes are always demanded only minutes after the action has started.

He now directed that massed artillery fires be directed in support of TF Tiger. Support from a tac-air squadron was arranged for and in the fine weather all this was timed to the minute if not to the second. TF Tiger launched its attack and appeared to be knocking out all resistance ahead of the near bank of the river.

Goodspeed then called the Chief of Staff to tell him that the commander's group would now move to the zone of TF Lion. He had heard from General Foxx that some elements of TF Lion had already crossed the river but were sustaining heavy casualties from artillery fire and enemy tank action. The Chief verified the fact that he had monitored these transmissions and added that General Wedge's 303d Infantry Division had attacked on the right of the 86th Mechanized and had had relatively easy going; light elements were already across the river by ferry.

When the command chopper neared TF Lion's area, Goodspeed took over General Foxx's duties of observation and directed that Foxx return at once to the TOC. On the same radio the Chief of Staff was told to make a short visit to TF Tiger and check the situation, but first to alert for movement TF Zebra under the command of Colonel Frank Turett.

From the vantage point of the chopper, so far exceeding the observation capabilities of Napoleon's day, General Goodspeed could see the dirty splashes of artillery shells falling on both sides of the river, though he could hear little of the actual din of the battle in the crackle of static coming through the earphones of the chopper's radio. A few of the assault boats serving the initial attempt at crossing were moving in each direction with their limited cargo of men and small arms.

"What do you think, Mike?" he asked his artillery officer, who had thought better of staying in the fire direction center. "Had we better jump one or two medium battalions forward so as to reach farther into those enemy tank formations? Or maybe your artillery had better do that and also get ready for exploiting a breakthrough once we get over in strength; I can get some tac-air for the antitank role while the weather holds."

"I go along with displacing the two battalions," said the artilleryman. "There seems to be a lull of sorts. My staff has already selected tentative positions and I'll have them under way in a few minutes. I'll also ask Corps artillery for some added support. We don't want to forget Colonel Rhoadus and TF Tiger while this displacement is going on!"

"Just a minute, General Goodspeed," interrupted the engineer officer. "I've changed my mind. I'm glad that we have provided for slanting the bridge in either direction. This ground to the south looks as good for a crossing site as the one in front of TF Tiger. I'll get the move started right away, if it's all right with you."

Tex Goodspeed was more than glad that they had hedged on the possible use of the bridging equipment. But these engineers! Why couldn't they get a fixed opinion for once, why . . .

At this moment the Chief of Staff broke in excitedly on the special staff net. "General Kirstone is on his way up to our advance command post. He left his chopper back somewhere and is coming forward by car. The message got delayed somehow in message center. He may arrive at any moment."

"Damn it, Chief," swore Goodspeed, "that's the third time an important message has gone astray. Have Joe Bogie meet the Corps commander if you can't get there yourself. Tell him I'm pretty well tied up here but will come back at once if he wishes. I'm joining Texton at the Lion command post in a minute or two. And, get this, Chief, we're going to reorganize that message center right now. I want General Foxx to check into it personally. The signal officer must arrange to show General Foxx every single message that is not routine. And I mean every one. Foxx can train an officer to take over for him, but in the meantime he is to see to it that every critical message gets to me at once. Got it?"

The Chief was crestfallen and realized a basic error in his own procedural setup had come to light. "I'll get back to attend to the Corps commander right away," he said.

Goodspeed found Colonel Texton's command post adjacent to a tank battalion, useless until the bridging of the river was complete. Texton had already been across the river himself, making a personal reconnaissance. "I've got one company over," he said, "but they are hard pressed without heavy equipment. They are doing well to hold on. When can we start bridging?"

"We're going to try a site some 800 yards south of here right after dark," replied Goodspeed. "If we are able to get the tank battalion over, and you can put in your entire force, I can run TF Zebra through to exploit. We can see whether you should keep on or go into division reserve."

As they were discussing plans, two command cars drove up and General Kirstone, the Corps commander, dismounted. "Looks as though you've drawn the short stick, Tex," he said, with reasonable amiability. "Wedge and his 303d are having a comparatively easy time. What have you got in mind?"

Goodspeed took heart. Apparently the boss understod the situation and was not disposed to be overcritical. But, as Goodspeed outlined his plan for the employment of TF Zebra, Kirstone began to shake his head. "I'm sure you can do the job in time, Tex, but I feel it would be faster and less costly to cross Zebra over in the ferry now in use by Wedge's 303d. Here's how it stacks up," and he began to draw figures in the dirt with a stick.

"Here we have Lion, and just to the right is TF Tiger; then we go further to the crossing site of the 303d. If Zebra crosses at the site of the 303d it can move at once to a position. Do you think that Lion can hold its own here, even if it cannot advance?"

Goodspeed glanced toward Texton who nodded. "Yes sir," Texton replied, "we'll go ahead with bridging here in hopes of having a firm crossing by dawn. But we'll certainly need a tac-air strike about the time the crossing is ready."

"Okay, Tex, and I think we can also send up some more assault boats to speed it up. If they can't get here by dark I'll let you know. I'll be getting back now and perhaps I can borrow your chopper to get me back to Check Point 109; my own is meeting me there."

The fine weather held and General Goodspeed longed for some of the foul weather he had experienced in other times and in other places that had provided needed screening. There was smoke, but the wind was wrong. He impatiently awaited the return of his chopper and was airborne within seconds of its arrival.

The staff and the commander of TF Zebra were awaiting him. He brought them up to date and they, in turn, briefed him on the actions of other parts of the division as well as the success of the 303d Division on their right.

As soon as the air liaison got the daylight air strike request into the mill, General Goodspeed got in a few winks of sleep. Toward morning the G-3 duty officer woke him with the cheering news that all of Lion except the tank battalion and the personnel carriers were across the river. It was expected that the tank battalion could cross over shortly after daylight.

Goodspeed promptly moved his advance commander's group to the TF Tiger area. Lieutenant Colonel Sponson, the G-3 Operations staff chief, was directed to the Lion zone of action to take over the duties performed the previous day by General Foxx. TF Zebra began its move, traffic arrangements for the immediate use of the 303d Division crossing having been made by representatives of the corps and the division staffs. Lieutenant Colonel Bogie, the intelligence officer, accompanied Zebra and its commander, Colonel Frank Turett.

They profited from a break in the weather finally. A fine mist was falling and the ceiling had lowered to the point where ground movement was reasonably screened; at the same time, air operations and artillery observation were curtailed.

By 0900 hours the tank battalion of TF Lion had established itself on the far bank and was ready for maneuver. But the air strike had been called off and was sorely missed. Shortly Lieutenant Colonel Sponson got on the air on the special staff net using the daily voice code.

"General Goodspeed, things don't look too good at this moment," he said. "We have a good sized force across, but enemy air has been able to find the site even if our boys can't take off; also heavy artillery has registered. As a result more than half the bridging equipment has been destroyed and the rest is not adequate."

Goodspeed thought fast. "Get on the command net," he replied, "and listen to my instructions to Texton."

When Texton reported into the net Goodspeed gave code orders for TF Lion to work its way along the far bank to positions as close as possible across from TF Tiger. Meanwhile a major effort in support of Tiger would be made by TF Zebra and by artillery and air (if the weather cleared). The engineer units were directed to salvage as much bridging equipment as possible and to bring it to reinforce the Tiger crossing site. He asked for comments from Texton, who agreed that the move was feasible. Goodspeed's aide was given the task of informing the Chief of Staff of the new development.

Now there was little to do but wait for the new moves to get under way. Changes of this kind always gave Tex Goodspeed wry amusement. They took him back to the days of staff college when students would wrestle all day concocting a division field order in writing, under the supposition that it would solve everything. In the cold light of practical experience it was just the beginning.

Near the end of the day both Lion and Zebra reached positions opposite Tiger. General Goodspeed, with the artillery officer, took to the air in the helicopter to observe conditions on the far bank. The engineer had been left to coordinate the reassembly of the bridging material. The chopper was able to land at the command posts of both Lion and Zebra. Coordinated artillery fires were established; with the lifting of the weather, two strong air strikes were made against the crossing site and, timed to all this fire effect, bridging operations proceeded rapidly. Air cover to protect the site was provided and as the aircraft orbited overhead Goodspeed got on the air to order Tiger to be ready to move out; he then went back with the chopper to pick up Colonel Rhoadus, the Tiger commander.

As they gained altitude Goodspeed pointed out the terrain. "See that road, George?" he asked. "I want Tiger to barrel down it and exploit this bridgehead. Don't stop for anything. Turett will follow you with Zebra. Be ready to fan out when you hit opposition. Lion goes into reserve and I'll be on the road axis right behind you with the advance commander's group. We'll put the TOC just on this side of the river, bring up the Main and displace all artillery in echelon . . . but you can be sure of having the medium battalion in direct support of your advance."

These two accounts illustrate a typical sequence of events in a division battle day and night. The techniques applied by commanders of differing backgrounds are variable indeed. The story of General Goodspeed shows a commander making the best of a series of adverse developments that are unfortunately all too common. Procedures are equal to events if not ahead of them. The likeness to the operations of the famous leaders of history is evident.

General Dare's situation is admittedly overdrawn, though Dare is real enough if considered as a composite. His troubles were rooted in an inability to trust his staff or his immediate subordinates to carry out a mission in their own way. He not only allowed his staff to dictate the operation but also insisted on getting into the act. In so doing, he lost control over the team effort of his division. It might be protested that the communications failures in Dare's case were inserted here in order to make an unfavorable comparison with General Goodspeed. This is not necessarily so; preoccupation with specific events leads to the slighting of overall communication. There are many cases in recent history as well as in yesteryear where commanders have interfered with subordinates, trying to command their units for them. The invention of the helicopter, for example, helpful as it is, provides the General Dares with an aerial platform from which they can radio a stream of unsolicited advice to some hapless commander under heavy fire below. Such people have little appreciation of the real communications function. They usually fail to make a strong demand for the top speed necessary in all communications flow; if they are stubborn rather than strong, forceful characters, their staff associates are reluctant in the absence of the nominal leader to take the initiative and guide necessary action.

There are, of course, variations on General Dare. One of the most pernicious is the affable, charming personality with a flair for political infighting. His talents usually bring him choice staff assignments at high level. These in turn can lead to a mobile command for which experience has afforded him few qualifications. His competence in organizational management allows him to act confidently; that he acts too slowly is concealed by his plausibility and charm. Altogether an unsound selection for the conduct of a blitz.

Another and even more pernicious variation is the type so vividly portrayed by C. S. Forester in *The General*. Hitler was said to have been so fascinated by the principal character that he made the book required reading in the German Army of the late thirties. Forester recounted the swift rise, in early World War I, of a relatively undistinguished officer conspicuous for what seemed to be strength of character. He remained firm when others broke down, the very epitome of the British bulldog. His was a will to win. He was assiduous in training his men and in inspecting for high standards. He was brave, taking his risks with the best. All these virtues were unfortunately the reflection of a completely inflexible mind. Determination was in fact obstinacy. In common with the real life generals of the period he produced only the appalling casualty lists attending a war of attrition that the British high command was determined to wage at the very time it could least be afforded. The nation was allowed to run down the drain for lack of appreciation of maneuver, of timing, of the implications of new weapons, of innovations of tactics and of deception. In command of tactical divisions and corps these leaders are themselves worth many divisions—to the enemy.

The theoretical problems of Generals Dare and Goodspeed, whose persons and command facilities were either fairly or highly mobile, provide an opportunity for comparing attempts to control forces in a nuclear environment. The risk of being surprised by enemy use of mass destruction weapons is obviously unacceptable.

It was generally agreed by western authorities that the picture drawn by Comrade Prusanov is a reasonably accurate forecast of future war. Dynamism and violence, widely dispersed formations, and opportunities for striking sudden and decisive blows are to be expected. In other words, it is the same environment, as far as control operations is concerned, that has been associated with lightning-war battles of the past. And it is an environment for which an entire corps of mobile leaders must be prepared if a western deterrent is to be at all effective.

One extreme school of professionals has argued that because of the sensitiveness of the control function and the probability that all air and ground headquarters will become prime targets, command posts should be placed in elaborately prepared positions, dug deep into the ground and fortified with concrete and steel. Secure in these bastions, generals might direct combat operations by means of television circuits enabling them to view any part of the battlefield. The proponents of this concept hold that there is no alternative. Command posts may not live without massive fortifications. Whatever troop casualties might occur from tactical nuclear weapons, the loss of a headquarters would reduce surviving troops to a mindless animal.

Technically and practically the television-central idea has many flaws. It is technically suspect because of its dependence upon electronics in an environment that may well preclude all radio or wire transmission. The explosion of high yield bombs in the upper air could produce ionization and block all communication for many hours. Should this occur, any headquarters committed to a static position would be almost wholly out of action.

In the practical sense, the concept nullifies the control techniques made famous by the masters, even without the nuclear blackout. Troops would hardly be inspired by a leader walled up in a cellar. Not even a very large remote-controlled television network could provide the panoramic detail necessary for a firsthand assessment of battle development.

The same concept exists in modified form through peacetime attempts to automate the high level command process. Many headquarters above the tactical level have already planned or installed large-scale digital computer data-processing systems, placing a giant computer in a separate building in the headquarters area. These perform essential peacetime services but of course would be out of action at the outset of any conflict since they are not protected in any way. The transition from this kind of setup to a field posture is out of the question under current conditions.

Another modification of the hole-in-the-ground concept may be found in continued proposals to locate mobile command posts in public buildings with strings of telephone wire, much as was done in World War II when conditions were quite different. The idea was sound enough when enemy air was relatively powerless and long range rockets nonexistent. Today it is a simple matter to knock out installations of this kind with conventional weapons alone. It calls to mind the fact that the United States Army is essentially without experience in operating under conditions of enemy air superiority.

The most viable modern headquarters is therefore one which is completely mobile in vehicles and aircraft, which operates in several segments with one or more choices of action, and plans on displacing frequently to avoid the consequences of detection. This is simply another way of saying that future headquarters operations are going to be patterned exactly on the methods of the masters.

It is essentially the same system that is employed by the new airmobile units and for the Strike Command. A general tour of units in Europe will show that the Standing Operating Procedures of their headquarters also conform. The issue here is not entirely one of headquarters organization. Assuming that there will be segmentation and that dispersal and frequent displacement will be the rule, the question is one of determining what advantage can be taken of the latest improvements in electronics to fill the unprecedented demands on the control systems.

# 12 Automation of the Command Function via the Military-Industrial Complex

A discussion of technology, in the shape of automated command centers, marks a necessary milestone on the way to an analysis of the nuclear age. It also marks the uses of the so-called military-industrial complex in applying the principles used by the great leaders of the past for command and control. They are the same ones that guided Berthier in implementing mobile operations and can be summarized in one adage: *Maximize the speed of information flow and the amount of pertinent information available, while insuring the isolation and immediate delivery of items requiring command decisions.*

Inherent in the summarized principles are several questions that relate to the problem of automating the command process.

(1) What is a minimum standard of speed? (2) What is an adequate amount of information? (3) What is pertinent information? (4) What kind of information bears specifically on command decisions? (5) What sort of organization is best suited to processing information?

The answers are almost entirely a matter of military judgment. The answers do not solve the problem; they merely define it. For the rest, scientific technicians must determine speed capabilities and organizational effectiveness, while industry must produce the hardware.

The task falls to a small portion of what has recently become

known as the military-industrial complex. The term was coined
by President Eisenhower as he cautioned the Congress to beware
of it. He has since been quoted out of context, considerably dis-
torting his meaning. But he might well have warned that it is the
hidden scientist who puts the price tag on the engines of war. And
it is the price tag that furnishes ammunition for the critics of
programs that are vital to national defense.

The current relation between the military structure and its
scientific support leaves much to be desired. Unless a better understanding of the fundamentals of the command and control problem can be reached, the Rommels, Forrests, and Pattons of the
closing years of the twentieth century may be unable to cope
with the growing complexities of the day. The nature of the relationship, how it got that way, and how it can be improved are
therefore basic factors of an automation program.

The inflexibility of the military mind up to the advent of
World War II, and to some extent beyond, needs no elaboration.
The stories of the great analysts have borne eloquent testimony
to the power of uniformed mental immobility. But it was in that
era that science really began its major role in modernizing warfare as well as making it more lethal. Radio, nuclear energy, and
the transistor are but a few of the innovations that have contributed to greater operational speed; that they were not summarily rejected by General Staffs is a mark of progress.

Still, the scientific-military relationship has been one of saying,
"Here, we have produced this gadget. What do you propose to
do with it?" The process of analyzing conditions to determine
military requirements and then presenting the general specifications to science and industry was more or less neglected.

The influx of science into the United States Department of
Defense well antedated the Kennedy Administration, yet really
came into flower at that time. In many respects the association
has not been a happy one, perhaps because each profession is
marked by a certain arrogance, possibly inherent to the military
and possibly acquired by the scholar during the pursuit of his
Ph.D. The arrangement is in reality a marriage of convenience.

The bonds are no less binding because they are forged by billions in research funds.

One of the early ties was pointed up a generation ago by Army Project VISTA, a program that led scientific personalities to call attention to the lack of data on which to base the evaluation of new ideas on organization, equipment, and procedures. The flood of advanced theories and proposals made some form of evaluation essential, especially with regard to cost.

A Congressional group, the Haworth Committee, urged the creation of field laboratories in which new concepts could be quantitatively measured. Both these efforts displayed an uncanny appreciation of the weak points in the development programs of the services. They highlighted the undeniable fact that earlier wars had been entered into on the basis of ideas formulated about the previous conflict.

On such notes the trumpets sounded for the Ph.D.'s. Save the Army from itself! Get the Air Force and Navy on the beam! With the passage of time the climate became more and more congenial for the erudite. The millions that flowed from a complaisant Congress when the Secretary of Defense cracked the whip became the lifeblood of research foundations such as RAND (U.S. Air Force), Operations Research Office (Army), Institute for Defense Analyses (JCS level) and many independent contractors typified by Lockheed and Stanford Research Institute. Various headquarters and combat organizations were assigned the services of a "staff scientist."

Fortunately studies aimed at the development of hardware were generally rewarding. Unfortunately operations research, or the evaluation of such abstractions as the combat effectiveness of different troop units and variations of tactical methods, has never really proved effective in spite of continuous efforts over the years. And it is in operations research that objective evaluation of most of the requirements for the automation of mobile tactical headquarters must take place.

Tactically speaking, the primary cause of the discord in the military-scientific relationship is the frequent inability of the scientist to grasp the fundamentals of operational control of maneuvering troops, an inability too often shared by presumably informed professional military. The combat officer and even the staff specialist in the Pentagon tend to be awed by the scientist and his jargon and to be reluctant to display their own ignorance by questioning scientific proposals. This makes it difficult to define clear objectives for a given line of study. A few examples of scientific fuzziness in the tactical operations field will serve to illustrate the problem.

Professor A, an expert in computer applications, has designed a computer routine to evaluate several antitank weapons systems by means of a mathematical model of a phase of battle. He has calculated carefully the kill probabilities of each antitank gun and has lodged their grid-square map positions in computer memory. Positions for a number of attacking tanks are also entered, along with associated vulnerability factors that are at best highly speculative. The grid squares are identified in computer memory by factors assigned in accordance with the amount of cover available on that portion of the map. Other factors apply to tank attitude, mobile or immobile, and the game progresses in a series of moves.

The professor can vary the number and type of tanks and antitank guns in the systems and, by measuring the time required to kill off all the tanks, can determine the "best" antitank system. It would seem to be a sound analysis.

Unfortunately it has not been explained to Professor A that no tank commander in his right mind would attack without some kind of supporting fire from artillery, aircraft, or other tanks, which would have demoralizing effect on the antitank system. The professor would probably have no way of getting these abstract support factors into the computer even if he allowed for progressive maneuver decisions by the tank commander. So, not unnaturally, the lights in the computer have no more than blinked, when all tanks are killed and all antitank guns active.

His results might conceivably be taken seriously enough to call for a high-level change in tank-design policy or perhaps the termination of an entire tank-production program. Professor A's routine is actually valid only as a shooting gallery operation, possibly illustrating what can happen to a stupid tank commander. It is dangerously useless for evaluation in real life terms.

Doctor B, learning of Professor A's difficulties with the effects of support fire in suppressing enemy weapons, determines to do something about it. He conceives the idea that, since innumerable firing tests have provided data on the lethal power of various concentrations of artillery fire, these data can help to measure the degree to which a defender might be deterred from firing his weapon under various circumstances of morale. He reasons that out of a total of some 500 battle-experienced soldiers, he can individually interview a sufficient number of them to estimate the distance at which incoming shells would inhibit them from firing. A computer program would place groups of defenders under the same cover and attitude factors used in Professor A's model. The attacking tank commander would then call for support fires against Point X, the suspected location of the defending unit. The computer would then, in milliseconds, calculate the aiming and other probable errors, apply the kill probability and distance factors obtained from the interviews, and come up with a realistic evaluation of the systems. The game could be played hundreds of times to level off the probability factors.

An excellent concept and a great improvement on Professor A's game. But it now develops that Doctor B decided to make what he considered an improvement; he interviewed only very experienced battle veterans, men who had earned the DSC or the Silver Star. No one told him that these men are uncommon in a normal battle and that they would not be subject to fear to the degree experienced by the average G.I. His study is therefore of little account.

Mr. C is a brilliant industrialist with top-level decision-making responsibilities in the Department of Defense. He inspects an Army unit in the field, becoming interested in a weapon capable of delivering a small-yield nuclear shell. His questions show that he is under the impression that this small but powerful weapon is programed in the manner of an intercontinental ballistic missile fired by the Strategic Air Command (SAC). Explanations from the commander that the weapon is not fired until a suitable target appears during combat do not alter the feeling of bystanders that this eminent industrialist has little or no idea of the basic functions of a most important ground weapons system.

Examples of this kind, based on factual cases, must not be taken as an indictment of the scientific community. Where was the professional military opinion when each concept was evolved? Why did the scientists concerned work in isolation? Where did the industrialist get his ideas?

There is already a high and rapidly increasing percentage of Ph.D.'s among officers of the several services. While most are in the specialist fields, there is no reason why an officer or soldier versed in combat operations cannot earn an advanced degree in areas which include operations research, mathematical statistics, behavioral sciences, computer technology and, most important, military history.

That kind of soldier-scientist is badly needed to bridge the gap between the scientist who is trying to absorb the military art and the soldier who considers that science has no battlefield application.

With this state of affairs prevailing, it would be the height of folly to attempt to automate a combat headquarters without very close cooperation between the professional military (who must define the requirements), the scientists (who must determine the applicability of existing tools and methods, or design those not yet evolved) and industry (charged with creating the tools).

The need for practical military advice from senior leaders with exhaustive experience at the division echelon in mobile combat would appear to be obvious. One must not only outline the requirements, but also be ready to curb the scientist who may otherwise create a complex and expensive electronic system where only a man waving a flag is required. This suggests that it is not so much a question of failure of the military to communicate with science as it is one of not communicating at the proper levels in detail. This can be expensive.

General W. C. Westmoreland addressing the Association of the U.S. Army in October, 1969, said: "Hundreds of years were required to achieve the mobility of the armored division. A little over two decades later we had the airmobile division. With cooperative effort, no more than ten years should separate us from the automated battlefield."

Even if close cooperation is assured, the task of automating a headquarters remains formidable. There is a question of whether there are business-oriented devices on the market that can meet requirements at acceptable costs or whether new objects must be designed. The question involves research that may or may not be competitive in a high-cost field where industry tends to push its own products. The technical aspects are usually beyond the ken of military men normally charged with monitoring the studies.

Among the devices or machinery or potential use to field headquarters are:

The digital computer or automatic data processing device
Electronic display devices
Television
Aerial command posts, electronically equipped
Facsimile communications
Satellite communications on superhigh frequencies

In the description of General Goodspeed's day of combat there were typical opportunities for using some or all of these control tools. General Goodspeed and his Corps Commander used helicopters as flying command posts. The control equipment within such aircraft will become more sophisticated as well as more compact as time goes on and will unquestionably include all the other tools listed. In either ground or aerial headquarters, for example, in place of the numerous and space-consuming maps, a push on a button might have flashed the appropriate map section on the screen for simultaneous viewing by all the staff. Display panels in fighter aircraft could flash target data to the pilot, eliminating the foldout charts that once smothered the cockpit of an aircraft supporting a field army. Boundary lines and other attack data could have been transmitted by television display concurrently to several units with appropriate remarks by General Goodspeed, in keeping with the Patton dictum that transmission in the clear is permissible as long as the enemy does not have time to react. Facsimile telegraph could also transmit tabular data and sketches for a permanent record. Use of a satellite would have resulted in improved broadcast signal quality, even with a heavy volume of traffic and nuclear high altitude burst ionization.

The digital computer could make the most significant contribution provided that its capabilities and limitations were recognized and that it met design specifications for the needs of a mobile tactical headquarters. Since it can be linked with other devices, it has broad applications.

In business life many companies buy computers because it is the thing to do and not because there is any real need for the service. Is this true in any lightning-war headquarters? Or are there echelons where it may be valuable or desirable and others where it is useless or even an impediment to the rapid exchange of information?

The several battle accounts of blitzkrieg history have shown that life in a mobile headquarters revolves around a series of decisions, punctuated by planning for the next phase of the operation. As in the Napoleonic era, a tactical staff divides up the planning chores, advises the commander and other staff sections, draws up implementing orders, prepares voluminous reports to higher headquarters, and assists in supervising the action once it is under way. Altogether a tedious and time-consuming list of duties in which the weight of administrative requirements, especially information-gathering, often threatens the correct and timely execution of the planned action.

The volume of work can be astronomical. Not long ago, Headquarters European Command was hard put to it to take the field for maneuvers and still render daily and other periodic reports demanded by Washington and NATO. One might well speculate on what real war could bring—perhaps a division of loyalty between reporting and the prosecution of the conflict.

With an amused yearning for a way out of the modern maze, the late Major General Max Johnson, then commanding the Army War College, once told a scientific gathering at the University of Michigan that he aspired to have his portrait hung in Cullum Hall, at West Point, where the likenesses of many distinguished graduates are displayed. He both hoped and feared, said General Johnson, that his own portrait might show him with his hand on a large IBM computer, with the caption, "Johnson and Staff, after losing the battle of the Polar Ice Cap."

Since the duties of a human staff boil down to the process of gathering, storing, retrieving, and disseminating information, it is in this area that a digital computer promises the greatest rewards.

There is no mention here of the word "compute." In fact, there is little of a computing nature involved in a tactical headquarters in the sense that artillery computers are used in the fire support coordination centers. The specific nomenclature is therefore Automatic Data Processing Service (ADPS), a phrase that is quite familiar in business and industry. This is best illustrated by a very general description of what has been and is being done, on a gradual scale, to automate the headquarters of the Seventh U.S. Army in Europe.

The following extracts from official, unclassified publications will indicate the planning trends. This does not mean that the extracts represent either wholly attainable, or even wholly desirable goals. They do, however, outline the objectives and provide a general idea of system organization for preliminary field tests in the U.S. Seventh Army in Europe and for service-wide uses in the mid-70s time period.

In early 1964 the Seventh Army, with monitoring from the Chief of Communications-Electronics, U.S. Army, convened a study group of specialists to begin developing realistic, cost-conscious answers to the automation problem in terms of hardware. The group was supported at one time by eighty or more scientists.

The group defined the effort as being "based on the increased demands and concepts of modern war, [since] as projected, manual methods cannot handle the great volume of data produced by improved collection and reporting means in widely dispersed and fast-moving situations of conventional or nuclear battlefields of the future."

Dubbed the Tactical Operations System (TOS), the system development is explained in an undated publication issued by the U.S. Army Automatic Data Field Systems Command, Fort Belvoir, Virginia, which exercises supervision.

In concept, TOS is a *secure,* automated information system designed to assist commanders and staffs in the conduct of tactical operations. It provides (1) a central information repository available to all users of the system; (2) updating of the data in the data base as required, and (3) processing of data. Thus, up-to-date dynamic information is available to commanders.

To provide the information services required by military users it was necesary to determine and identify those classes of information comprising the heaviest manual work loads in current Tactical Operations Center activities. . . . Some eighteen separate functional areas were analyzed and incorporated into initial TOS requirements, to include:

Friendly unit information        Enemy Situation
Nuclear Fire Support             Enemy Order of Battle
Effects of Enemy Nuclear Strikes

Within the system there are three basic types of data processing equipment:

(1) User Input/Output Devices (UIODs). These have keyboards and page-printing capabilities similar to a teletypewriter, and a cathode ray tube type screen upon which are displayed formats that are called up at will by the operator.

(2) Remote Station Data Terminals. These are intermediate message processor-transmitters located between the UIODs and a central computing facility. The RSDT, which includes a computer, computer peripheral equipment and secure communication equipment is contained in shelters mounted on two 2½-ton trucks.

(3) The Central Computing Center (CCC) stores the TOS data base, processes all messages transmitted by RSTDs, performs TOS computations and transmits output messages to the RSTDs. The equipment is carried in one forty-foot van and two thirty-five-foot vans, two with expandable sides. The computer equipment is mounted on floating floors to ease the shock of travel.

The TOS has the following capabilities:

High speed switching of tactical messages
Rapid storage and retrieval of tactical information
Automatic routing of tactical messages
High speed computation facility
Automatic report generation.

The proposed system for general use throughout the Army is described in the TOS Technical Bulletin (undated and unclassified) titled "Tactical Operations System—1975, (TOS-75)" and issued by the same agency as the Seventh Army publication referred to above, The U.S. Army Automatic Data Field Systems Command at Fort Belvoir, Virginia.

The scope of TOS-75 involves the application of automatic data processing to selected functions in intelligence, operations and fire support coordination to improve command combat effectiveness. It is to be an on-line, near real time system.

Objectives are similar to those of the Seventh Army system:

(1) Improve the reception, processing, summarizing, disseminating, displaying, storing, and retrieval of selected information needed for decision-making,

(2) Provide computational capability to reduce reaction time,

(3) Improve means of dissemination of operations-intelligence information,

(4) Free personnel from routine functions to improve the estimating and evaluation process,

(5) Provide a mix of display and query devices to permit more rapid grasp of the situation by command and staff.

User access to the system within the division is accomplished through remote input/output devices located at the appropriate elements at each echelon.

Functional areas are necessarily beyond those contemplated for experimentation within the Seventh Army.

| | |
|---|---|
| Enemy Situation | Biological Contamination |
| Friendly Unit Situation | Airfield Location and Status |
| Nuclear Strike Effects | Air Defense Information |
| Reconnaissance and Surveillance | Barrier-Denial Operations |
| | Tactical Bridging Status |
| Enemy Order of Battle | Intelligence Collection |
| Tactical Air Support | Intelligence Analysis |
| Army Air Operations | Strategic Intelligence |
| Air Space Coordination | Chemical Contamination |
| Hostile Air Defense | Electronic Warfare |
| Terrain Intelligence | Internal Defense Matters |
| Weather Data | Psychological Warfare |
| Tactical Troop Movement | Unconventional Warfare |
| Communications Planning | Engineer Construction |
| Target Intelligence | Status |
| Counterintelligence | |

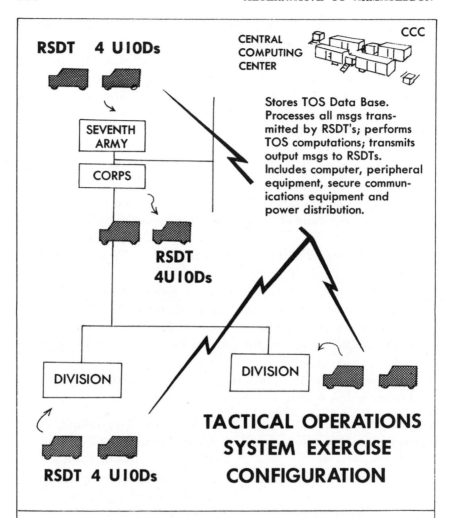

**RSDT   4 UIODs**

CENTRAL
COMPUTING
CENTER                                                    CCC

Stores TOS Data Base.
Processes all msgs trans-
mitted by RSDT's; performs
TOS computations; transmits
output msgs to RSDTs.
Includes computer, peripheral
equipment, secure commun-
ications equipment and
power distribution.

SEVENTH
ARMY

CORPS

**RSDT
4UIODs**

DIVISION

DIVISION

**TACTICAL OPERATIONS
SYSTEM EXERCISE
CONFIGURATION**

**RSDT  4 UIODs**

**UIOD....**  User Input/output Device

**RSDT....**  Remote Station Data Terminal;
intermediate msg processor-transmitter
between UIODs and central computer.
Includes a computer, peripheral
equipment and secure communications
equipment.

Programs of the selected functions will receive inputs from and provide output to more than 30 transmission and receiving remote stations within the division (including battalion level).

The TOS Bulletin cites a typical query to the system:

Division G-2 desires a summary of all reports of enemy tank locations within a 25 kilometer radius of the division objective since 0800 hours. He specifies enemy tanks, a geographic location, the radius of 25 kilometers and the time period. The computer answers the query by giving a summary of every reporting of tanks in that area for the period.

The computer is programed to route new information to users who have requested such information on a continuing and automatic basis. As information enters the system, the computer will update its own files and also provide a graphic display.

TOS-75 interfaces with the Tactical Fire Direction System (TAC-FIRE) and the Combat Service Support system (CS). Interface with other systems is in the planning stage.

Information in one divisional sector, when entered into the system, immediately becomes available to all system users. However (and this is important), indiscriminate access to the data is controlled on the basis of established clearances *and the prerogatives of the various commanders.*

Complete automation of tactical headquarters must come gradually and with suitable experimentation as in the case of the Seventh Army prototype system. ADPS has many advantages but there are elements connected with its organization and employment that can enhance its promise as a major boon to a commander and staff or, on the other hand, place men in bondage to a machine. This situation has frequently arisen in the past in communications planning for mobile operations—the inexperienced commander may allow his own, possibly sounder, system of operations to become dependent upon a communications doctrine more appropriate to static warfare, rather than insist that he be served through suitable adaptations.

There will be a great advantage when commanders and staffs are relatively free from onerous reporting and when a com-

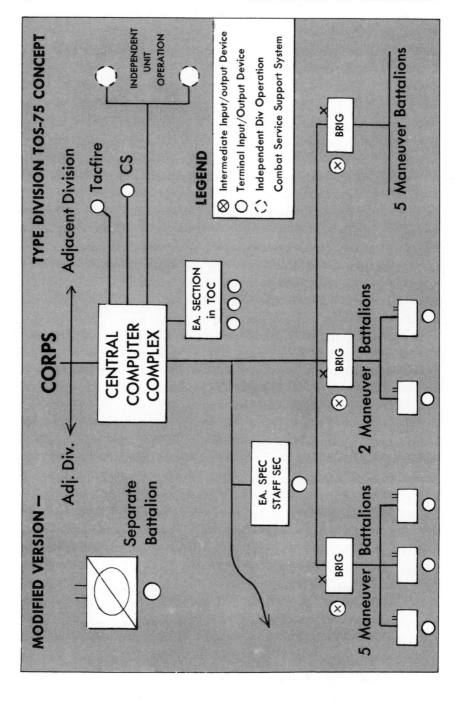

mander can avoid being snatched away from critical operational duties by a senior who wants a question answered, perhaps a routine question.

When the purpose of the system is misunderstood and its organization is unsuited to mobile warfare, it will harm the very thing it is designed to serve. The complexity of the listed functional areas appears to be at odds with the blitz characteristic of simplicity. It is difficult to imagine a Rommel or a Patton moving around a battle area with the weight of all this information burdening his mind. It might be supposed that a Patton would either sweep the system away with a burst of profanity or would pay lip service to the system while directing operations without it. If the system, however, is visualized as a tactical tool in support of command, it would be incredible that any of the masters could fail to emphasize its advantages and minimize or eliminate its dangers.

Visualization as a tactical tool can be thought of as the collective brains of all command and staff personnel in the units served. If all this brain power is housed in one place at headquarters and each brain continues to amass and reject information, any decision-maker can query the "brain room" and get a quick reply. Human minds would assess the relevance of information to a given question. They would not answer queries concerning engineering with a medical dissertation. The danger with the computer is in assuming that it has the brain capacity (memory) of the human mind and can be relied upon to discriminate as to what information it accepts, rejects, or transmits. There is a tendency to regard computer-released information as accurate and timely; it may well be neither.

How long will it be before the computers, sensitive memory mechanisms, can be constructed ruggedly enough to withstand frequent displacements of division headquarters over secondary roads, trails, or rough terrain? Can they continue to operate while in motion and, if not, how long after reaching a new location can they be made operative?

Most of the masters might have held that decision-making at the division level in combat is so simple that a computer facility (other than UIODs) would prove more of a liability than an asset. Their minds would have been concentrated on essentials and the ever-present time problem. They would not have allowed the availability of mountains of information to inhibit the mobility and violence of their attacks.

A typical problem of speed and accuracy can be illustrated by a possible report, from a ground unit in the vicinity, of an enemy tank battalion located at Point X. If this item enters the data bank, what of a report concerning the same enemy unit made by a reconnaissance aircraft, citing a company instead of a battalion and a location at Y, near but not at X? Can the computer resolve this difference mechanically?

Timeliness is affected by the number of echelons making input.

A data bank at Division Main, for example, would be subject to input from the battalion and perhaps as far down as the company, where a punch-card system might one day originate; data would in theory progress instantaneously up the chain of command through the intermediate links. These links could not be bypassed, for no intermediate commander would permit direct reporting by machine any more than he would let a captain make an individual report to the division commander. This is sound, inasmuch as a company that had been badly shot up might render a gloomy report although the parent battalion was on the whole successful. The system must allow for intermediate command consideration and that means delay. People and not electronics, which may be capable of millisecond delivery, are the real cause of delay in passing along information.

Tactical data input to an ADPS bank at the end of a chain of command must be considered as running well behind the actual situation at critical points. Before ADPS, the sluggish flow of information was the reason why mobile commanders organized advance command posts and took positions of direct observation, ground or aerial. Evidently the systems of the masters will apply even more forcibly with ADPS since it is essential that these people pass input directly to the data bank so that critical command-oriented data in the memory bank will be updated promptly.

Who will determine what information goes into the system and what should be rejected? The trivialities that now pass through tactical headquarters without ADPS should warn those who know that computer memories have limitations. When critical information is involved the input operator must be highly knowledgeable. He may perhaps be a private first class; at other times perhaps he *must* be a brigadier general.

According to the best current information, there is no sure way that an ADPS system can be programmed to separate essential decision-making information from routine information. Some counterpart of Berthier's entourage must determine what is essential and how its further transmission can be expedited. Exercises in large headquarters overseas have brought out glaring errors in message handling where hundreds of transmissions, all labeled FLASH (or topmost priority) have been stacked up for hours awaiting delivery. This situation cannot be tolerated anywhere, especially in tactical commands, or another case of Napoleon before Quatre Bras can be expected.

An interesting sidelight to message priority is the development in recent years of Pentagon involvement in minor tactical matters thousands of miles away. During the Korean War, a senior commander was called to the telephone by the Pentagon to explain why he had relieved a squad of infantry from an outpost position. Naturally the call had highest priority. But it is doubtful that it would ever occur to a master to account for a squad movement to a computer. Even more unlikely would be a query from, say, the Joint Chiefs of Staff, to a field army computer with the expectation of getting an answer to a problem of a squad of perhaps eight to twelve men. But geopolitical factors in modern times make for sensitive feelings in national capitals; Napoleon's principle that he never interfered when not in a position to see things for himself appears to be a matter of ancient history.

Because ADPS devices can play chess, many suppose that they might be programed to provide a tactical commander with a ready-made, printed-out decision when queried. Many war games have been contrived for the purpose. But playing a war game in a computer, even one of company size, involves so many parameters on the actual battlefield, increasing in almost geometrical progression as the action develops, that the largest computer cannot handle them. A commander, even the most timorous, would court disaster by entrusting his decisions to a machine when hundreds of units are affected by his decision.

Any data-processing device operates only on the data entered into it. Garbage in—garbage out (GIGO) is the now hackneyed phrase. It would be unwise to rely on a machine when its data might or might not be comprehensive or when some elements should have more weight than others.

To go back to the analogy of having all the brains of command and staff personnel centered in one room and subject to questioning, what is the likelihood that any one commander or staff officer could come up with factual answers? Yet these are the very people who are expected to make inputs to the TOS system.

Finally comes the question of operating under potentially nuclear conditions. The enemy use of high yield-high altitude bursts would probably provide enough electromagnetic pulse (EMP) effect to knock out and even fuse many radio and wire circuits and equipment. Risking the data base and reporting system against this possibility, without a human back-up system, would be unthinkable.

To satisfy all these requirements, the computers and associated devices must obviously be small, compact, portably rugged, able to operate immediately after displacement, if not operable while displacing, and at the same time have a large memory capacity. In plain language, for the moment "there ain't no such animal." The commercial market has yet to meet criteria of this kind, at least wholly. Yet cost considerations may in the end dictate the use of the least objectionable commercial designs rather than the development of a special-purpose device that would be used only in limited quantities.

In the meantime it is necesary to experiment. These caveats which have been raised are by no means insoluble problems. Aircraft pilots once were highly skeptical of the reliability of the dials on the instrument panel and now cannot operate without them. What is important here is that the solution of the automated command and control problem be based, at least initially, on the same command system whose principles have proved immutable through the ages.

This exposition of the general characteristics of the coming tactical operations systems (automated) has had for its purpose the nature of the additional demands to be made on tomorrow's commanders and the obvious need for practical field experience in handling the system.

The relation between the scientist and the military must be more clearly defined. The scientist must serve as a staff member of the military team; he recommends but does not lead, nor does he dictate courses of action until requirements have been clearly delineated. Conversely, more scientifically oriented personnel must appear in the ranks of the combat units. It is one thing to have command and control facilities available and quite another to find commanders able to employ them skillfully.

Professionals of the Air Force and Navy (except Marines) sometimes have difficulty in appreciating the complexity of ground-battle control problems. Accustomed to the entity of a crew-served aircraft or ship, with extraordinary communications facilities, they fail to understand how dozens of factors not present on the sea or in the air can cause chaotic conditions. If a ship or aircraft could conceivably break into hundreds of pieces while in motion, and could conceivably be reassembled by an able commander, a reasonable parallel could be drawn.

# 13 The Air Age:
## The Airborne Concept

"When sea power finally gives place to air power in transport and war, we shall have seen one of the greatest basic revolutions in History."
—Will and Ariel Durant, *Lessons of History*

The threat to the free world by Sino-Russian pressure has been discussed in general terms, but it is well to review the implications of the geopolitical trouble spots.

Provocations have far outnumbered the occasions on which an effective response has taken place. Within fifteen years Cuba has been established as a Russian base. The war in Vietnam was protracted on the somewhat naive assumption that negotiations could be successfully concluded without a military victory—in spite of the fact that Korean War negotiations of sorts are still going on. Lebanon and Central Africa have seen landings by American forces. Various incidents have been contrived to test western will without causing a positive public reaction in the United States.

Two philosophies have evolved from these commitments and incidents. On the one hand, the State Department has occasionally shown itself disposed to intervene arbitrarily, though with executive approval, in different global areas. On the other hand, the undeniable overcommitment of United States resources in both Asia and Europe, as well as in sensitive spots elsewhere, has political figures and most thoughtful Americans questioning the ability of the United States to police the globe either practically or emotionally.

Between these views comes the philosophy expressed in this book. No positive intervention is warranted unless a so-called

196

trouble spot can definitely be shown to compromise interests in a manner explainable to the Congress and the people; possible risk of nuclear war must sometimes be accepted.

It is conceivable that the expanding efforts of the Communist bloc will sooner or later bring about a major confrontation that will have to constitute an acceptable risk. Whether the acceptability of the risk is defined under past or future criteria, the means to meet the challenge must be available in the form of a viable deterrent.

In global areas amenable to U.S. influence, American strategic concepts have organized deterrent forces within defined areas of responsibility and have assigned a "Unified Command" to each. Hence, the Pacific Command (PACOM) with Army, Navy, and Air Force elements unified under the Commander-in-Chief, Pacific Forces (CINCPAC) conducts operations in the Pacific and Asia. Similarly, there is EUCOM and CINCEUR for Europe, CINCLANT for the Atlantic area and CINCSOUTH for the Latin American territory. Of course no infringement of national sovereignties is contemplated in the normal course of events. But the great distances separating the Unified Commands and the fact that many areas of the globe are not either under western influence or, as yet, that of totalitarian powers, requires a troop organization that can respond quickly in a reinforcing role to disturbances in one of the Unified Commands or can move into the unassigned areas to operate on its own. The requirement has been met by the development of the United States Strike Command.

The characteristics of the required force are those of high mobility, ready deployment, versatility, adequate air and sea lift, and, in addition, sufficient flexibility to permit landing in an objective area and tying in with the global communications networks under U.S. control, by a force tailored to meet the particular military problem presented. Recognizing these needs, Secretary of Defense McNamara on September 19, 1961, issued a directive to organize a command which "could contribute to our ability to deal effectively and swiftly with any limited war in a manner and on a scale best calculated to bring it to a conclusion, while minimizing the risks of hostilities broadening into general war."

Implementation of the directive created the Strike Command, or STRICOM, and charged it initially with the emergency mobilization and deployment of forces destined for the support of, and under the command of, one of the Unified Commanders. Later a new command responsibility was created because of the realization that there were certain areas assigned to CINCLANT that were inappropriate for the Navy. In consequence CINCMEAFSA came into being, denoting the Middle East, Southern Asia, and all of Africa south of the Sahara. Since these areas could be reached quickly only by STRICOM, and were those in which emergencies of the Lebanon type were most likely to occur, CINCSTRIKE and CINCMEAFSA were merged into one.

The concept was truly breathtaking, encompassing over half the world and entailing staggering logistical problems as well as those of communications, notwithstanding the existence of the Defense Communications Agency and its worldwide system.

Considering the nature of the problem, it was only natural that STRIKE should be organized as a joint command. The Army furnished elements that would enter ground combat at the objective; the Air Force provided the transport aircraft for the airlift, and fighters for the air-ground support of the Army in battle and for the protection of the airlift during the deployment and subsequent action. The Air Force would also require a substantial contribution of logistics and administrative support personnel and equipment for its own effort. Finally, there would be many occasions when a significant part of the transport and supply problem would devolve upon the Navy. Or, conceivably, a naval amphibious operation might for geographical considerations have to be combined with an airborne action.

For the mobilization and training of troops CINCSTRIKE was given two major deputies: a) CINCARSTRIKE, the Army component commander, whose normal job was that of commanding the Continental Army (Training) Command, and, b) CINCAFSTRIKE, the Air Force component commander, normally head of the Tactical Air Command. The Navy was given no specific role other than the contribution of a large number of personnel, serving at STRIKE Headquarters at MacDill Air Force Base in Florida and providing planning assistance for contingencies that concern the Navy.

The principal ready force of STRIKE is made up of the XVIII Airborne Corps with its two included airborne divisions and support troops. But the III Army Corps with two armored divisions and four other infantry divisions is also subject to employment by CINCSTRIKE.

Air Force elements comprise the 9th, 12th, and 19th Air Forces, the last-named being a planning element, all totaling eleven tactical fighter wings, four assault airlift wings and air reconnaissance and Special Warfare units. Standing back of this force are the immense resources of the Military Airlift Command (MAC), the Air National Guard and the Civil Reserve Air Fleet.

STRICOM operations emphasize employment of the "Joint Task Force" or JTF.

STRIKE has the capability of forming JTFs of Army and Air Force elements in various strengths and proportions. For example, a small JTF might consist of an airborne infantry battalion, with a proportion of supporting artillery and other Army units, and a Composite Air Striking Force (CASF) consisting of a squadron or two of fighter aircraft with its own support in the form of reconnaissance, maintenance and control facilities. At the other extreme, the JTF might run to an army corps of two divisions with great fleets of airlift and several CASFs, plus the appropriate logistical support agencies.

In tailoring the JTFs to meet specific situations, a package system is used, where a unit of designated size and composition forms a package. Several packages make up a medium or large JTF, with each calling for a package type Headquarters for the JTF.

COMJTF, COMARFOR and COMAFFOR are acronyms denoting the overall JTF commander and the heads of the Army and Air Force contingents, respectively.

STRICOM efficiency is measured in great part by the current and projected capabilities of the transport and fighter aircraft necessary to carry and protect troops en route to and at the objective, and by the sophisticated control devices for directing the task forces at all stages of the operation.

Within a span of five years airlift potential has increased astoundingly. The C-135 (Boeing 707 of the airlines), which itself dwarfed the propeller-driven craft of the preceding decade has been in turn dwarfed by the C-141 and the projected C-5As.

The C-141 will accommodate about 154 passengers, or some thirty-two tons of cargo at 425 knots. The C-5A (Lockheed) is to have a rated speed of about 440 knots (maximum 470) and a war-time load of 132 tons. It is programmed to carry fifty-five tons for 5500 miles non-stop or 110 tons for 2700 miles. More than 500 personnel can be carried, troop loaded. These figures far over-shadow the data associated with the familiar Boeing 707, which has a load limit of only nineteen tons, though much larger aircraft are entering commercial service.

Unfortunately, a plane loaded with 500 personnel, or with 50–100 tons of supplies, means a lot of eggs in one basket in a combat zone. Risking this load in a highly speculative air assault is obviously a matter for serious consideration.

It is also obvious that giant aircraft require landing runways that are lengthy and that can support the weights of a long suc-cession of massive landings. Design characteristics of the new aircraft will, however, permit landings in areas well below the standards set for commercial planes.

Every tool of war has limitations as well as powers. In spite of these drawbacks, it is evident that the transport aircraft is an ideal vehicle as far as modern strategic mobility is concerned. The entire strategic concept of the United States may be radically al-tered by it. Forces stationed in Europe, for example, could be withdrawn to continental America with great savings in overseas expenditures; in emergencies troops could be flown to points where heavy equipment, such as tanks and carriers, is stored and could deploy at once. The concept has already been the subject of experimental airlifts.

A vast strategic airborne operation makes unprecedented de-mands upon the command and control function both in the air and on the ground. The Strike Command has accordingly con-ducted studies to determine the requirements for the highly com-plicated electronic gear that must go into a new transport to make it suitable for command post use. The size of the aircraft of course permits a great expansion of the facilities that were described in the previous chapter.

In addition to aircraft, a major JTF resource is the communications networks of the Defense Communications Agency. The DCA was formed by amalgamating existing and far-flung networks of the Army, Navy, and Air Force. The system permits rapid contact with the Pentagon and the White House from various global key points. A JTF operating in the MEAFSA area has several possible DCA relay stations to work with; considering the great importance of its mission in terms of world politics, there will inevitably be a high volume of critical traffic between its headquarters and Washington.

While STRIKE as an entity is important as an international fire brigade, and is trained along fire brigade lines, there is only one aspect of its operations, air asault, that is of interest in lightning war. STRIKE is ideally deployed to a distant objective which features landing sites controlled by friendly agencies. Troops are deplaned and proceed overland to the combat area where the conflict may be either mobile or static. This kind of operation does not differ in any way from a movement by train or truck, except for the fact that STRIKE deployments are initially strategic, though they are followed by combat of a tactical nature.

On occasion deployment must be made to an area where hostile forces control the landing sites. Here an air drop of parachutists must ordinarily be made to secure an "airhead" for the subsequent landing of follow-up troops and supplies. The entire operation, from the approach to the objective through the establishment of the landing site, calls for the most skillful blitz leadership on the part of the Army and Air Force elements involved.

STRICOM has engaged in countless exercises to acquire and maintain a fire-brigade ability to respond instantly to emergency measures where minutes may count, even though a flight of several thousand miles may take place before troops are actually committed. Planning is meticulous. Airborne or other divisions may be trucked to rendezvous air fields, or transport planes may deploy to home stations of the divisions, such as Fort Bragg or Fort Campbell. Each troop contingent is assigned to a numbered aircraft according to its capacity and is loaded rapidly. The deployment is then made, with one aircraft following in trace of another, to planned staging areas overseas. Composite Air Strike Forces may have to cover the air movement as well as the air assault at the objective. Communications and navigational teams will usually precede, so that beacons and relays can be emplaced as needed. Air Warning and Control aircraft (AWAC), equipped with highly sophisticated radar and other electronic gear will assist in locating intruding aircraft for the CASF fighters protecting the vulnerable airborne formations. It is a complex array of combat strength, finely tuned to the smooth execution of awesome missions through sound planning and frequent practice.

Typical among many STRIKE domestic and overseas exercises were DELAWAR (to Iran) and DEEP FURROW (to Greece and Turkey).

DELAWAR, held in April 1964, demonstrated the ability of the United States to come quickly to the aid of a country which is a party to a mutual security treaty. It aimed at obtaining experience in bilateral (Iran and U.S.) operations and at perfecting operational procedures.

The U.S. and Iranian forces involved were of approximately equal size. Iran deployed an infantry brigade plus an airborne company, supported by two fighter squadrons of F-86 aircraft. U.S. forces, emplaning at stations in continental U.S., and staging at Incirlik Air Force Base in Turkey, consisted of a two-battalion brigade of the 101st Airborne Division, and two tactical fighter squadrons (36 F-100 aircraft) of the 832d Air Division. Certain American and Iranian naval units were also included. Logistical and personnel support were provided by various headquarters of the European Command. Aerial tanker refueling services were furnished for the fighters.

Twenty-three Military Airlift Command (then Military Air Transport Service) C-135 sorties carried the bulk of the 2346 Army personnel. Forty-eight MAC aircraft lifted 560 tons of heavy equipment. Some of the risks of actual combat were raised by severe turbulence in refueling areas and by blowing desert dust at air drop sites. However, 1000 sorties over oceans and mountains were carried out without accident; out of 1800 paratroopers dropped, only nine minor injuries were sustained. No serious illnesses occurred among the 6800 participants. A major event was the air assault involving 1500 men in thirty-seven carrier air-craft, supported by fifteen fighters, made at Vahdati Air Force Base in Iran.

To General Paul Adams, CINCSTRIKE, the most valuable lesson emerging from DELAWAR was the demonstrated effectiveness of the Joint Task Force Headquarters in controlling the elements of all services, an observation of special interest to students of lightning war.

The command and control of an aerial Joint Task Force calls for all the skills exhibited by the great blitz masters, and, in an air assault, poses timing problems that would provide a severe test for the best.

STRICOM Headquarters Standing Operating Procedure calls for the fielding of both an Advance (ADVON) and a MAIN segment of JTF Headquarters, capable of functioning either in the air or on the ground. Headquarters aircraft have been the subject of ex-haustive study and feature the latest in electronic gadgetry. COMAFFOR is also assigned a command aircraft from which he must control the initial deployment, the staging, and the trans-port aspects of the assault. The Army Commander (COMARFOR) rides in a regular transport but can communicate while airborne with his subordinate commanders in the event tactical changes are necessary before the assault takes place.

There are certain risks and pressures which inevitably must be faced by the lightning-war commander, and these are worth enumerating when an air-age deterrent is under consideration.

To reach distant world trouble spots, such as the mid-East, there must be a well-organized staging area capable of furnishing items of resupply, maintenance, and other services. The maintenance of good will with countries like Greece and Turkey is of great im-portance. Without this friendly support, operations in the mid-East would be all but impossible at any time and certainly im-possible in an emergency.

A deployment from Incirlik, Turkey, to Teheran typifies risks elsewhere in the world where a confrontation with a major power is possible. In an exercise like DELAWAR, or under potential war conditions, American command authority in Washington presumably would have concluded that such a confrontation would not occur, or else a small and aerially vulnerable JTF would not have been committed. The JTF commander cannot depend upon any such assumptions and conclusions; en route he must constantly weigh alternatives in case a massive enemy fighter attack is launched against the transports, resulting in serious losses.

Weather becomes a crucial factor. Blowing dust forced the cancellation of an air drop during DELAWAR. This could be fatal to an actual combat mission. Improved forecasts and weather readouts from satellites will be demanded. A weather section is already integral to STRICOM and JTF headquarters.

Fighters do not have the range of transports and may require refueling during some of the most delicate periods of deployment and combat. Refueling may not be ideally conducted at the altitudes and locations suitable for transports. These are all decision-making factors, perhaps spur-of-the-moment decisions.

The air assault is a touchy operation. If an airhead is defended by antiaircraft guns or missiles, many strikes by supporting fighters must precede the air drop and landing. If the timing of troop arrival is upset, there will have to be immediate decisions and orders to re-route or orbit aircraft.

The air drop and subsequent combat must receive careful command attention and observation to determine when and where air landing operations can take place. The sequence of landing must have been carefully planned, but may be based on erroneous assumptions. Should antiaircraft units be unloaded and set up first? Or should engineer troops begin work on damaged runways in order to get the transports down at all? If assumptions are wrong, plans must be changed at the last minute and implementing orders received in a timely manner when seconds count.

What effect will the loss of one or more transports have on the operation, especially if they carry 500 soldiers?

These are just a few of the questions that impose unprecedented responsibilities and finely timed control on COMJTF and COMARFFOR. Their jobs are not for vacillating and slow thinkers.

It is plain that events develop in an air assault even more rapidly than in the highly mobile ground battle, the tempo of which frequently overtaxes the ablest commanders. It is equally certain that personal observation by COMJTF, by COMAFFOR, and by key command and staff personnel is an absolute must. At critical times ADPS is no substitute.

Command requirements are fully recognized by STRICOM Headquarters Standing Operating Procedure. This document, though undoubtedly created independently, fully reflects the control patterns established by Napoleon, Rommel, Patton and the other masters.

STRICOM and its tailored Joint Task Forces unquestionably provide an effective deterrent to foreign aggression of the brush-fire type. STRIKE may indeed form an ideal nucleus for the great overall deterrent of complete fighting force, imbued with lightning-war precepts and able to prevent or to win a major confrontation.

# 14 The Air Age: The Airmobile Concept

The airborne strategic joint task force in the aerial assault to capture an airhead is a special form of lightning war and a special application of a national deterrent to brush-fire aggression in distant areas. In contrast, the airmobile force is simply a helicopter-borne cavalry with the usual historic roles of cavalry and armor such as reconnaissance, security, wide envelopments, delaying action, and pursuit in support of less mobile troops. Armor, with its tanks and heavy carriers, is capable of physical assault in combat vehicles—airmobile forces are not.

The advent of the helicopter, or chopper, adds a new dimension to the combat team. Seemingly a cranky and delicate vehicle, it has proved in the crucible of combat that it can operate and—under conditions such as those in Vietnam operate more effectively—than other kinds of transport. To students of the blitz it has clearly demonstrated two things: its freedom from terrain restrictions suggests that the airmobile concept will be a potent factor in making a national deterrent viable, especially as helicopter-borne units are themselves capable of participating in STRICOM joint task force operations when transported either in giant C-5A's or on naval carriers; it forces a tempo of operations demanding the training of great numbers of General Eisenhower's "special type of leader."

The helicopter functions of lifting troops, supplies, equipment, and wounded are familiar to all readers of the news. Tactically, however, the rotary-wing aircraft is used habitually in ways little

appreciated not only by the general public but also by large segments of the military.

The flexibility of the chopper is amazing. Flying close to the
ground, or "nap of the earth," dodging trees, and slipping through
ravines, it can quickly adapt to the needs of the moment by flying
in formations permitting heavy support fire to the front and both
flanks while maneuvering for a landing. The landing site can be
selected at greater distances from the point of departure than is
the case with other kinds of troop transport; resupply is easy. Reserves can be quickly shifted, as shown by tests in which a two-
battalion force has been moved 100 miles in less than an hour.

Initial successes can be instantly exploited and the enemy kept
under observation without fear of outrunning supply lines. The
commander fights the enemy, or encircles him, without having to
consider terrain except in the sense of screening from hostile fire.

It seems too good to be true. All these capabilities add up to
what any lightning-war commander would consider ideal. But
there are, of course, limitations. The helicopter still requires an
inordinate amount of maintenance though the problem is a dimin-
ishing one. It is a reasonably safe aircraft as was shown by statistics
from Southeast Asia battle zones where there was an accident rate
of less than one in 10,000 sorties. At the same time, in spite of its
speed and maneuverability, the chopper is most vulnerable to
enemy fire at the most critical moments of operations, that is,
while in close proximity to the enemy. It cannot pretend to be an
assault weapon in the manner of a tank, or perhaps even a horse.

As to vulnerability, initial reports from Southeast Asia gave
figures that were misleading and which aroused critical comments
from politicians opposed to the American military and its commitments. Excerpts from a report by Major General Robert G.
Williams, former commander of the 1st Aviation Brigade in Vietnam, as quoted in the Army "Command Information Fact Sheet,"
Issue 132, dated June 19, 1969, are therefore most interesting.

The Army has been operating helicopters in Vietnam since December 1961. They were initially employed against a very primitive
enemy who was armed with obsolete rifles and few, if any, automatic

weapons. In this environment helicopters were operated without the protection of helicopter gunships and other supporting fires were very limited. Since 1961 there has been a steady increase in the enemy's firepower—automatic rifles, 50-caliber machine guns and other anti-aircraft weapons are in his arsenal. As the enemy's threat against our aircraft has increased, so has our capability to counter this threat. We have mounted machine guns on both sides of the troop-carrying helicopters which are escorted by COBRAS firing rockets and other improved munitions. We have improved our tactics. Helicopter formations avoid overflying concentrations of enemy troops; routes to and from objectives are carefully selected; and supporting fires are habitually used in the preparation of landing zones.

During 1962 the loss rate for helicopters in Vietnam was one to every 5,290 sorties. As result of our improved weaponry, tactics and techniques, in calendar year 1968 we lost only one helicopter in 12,716 sorties. The loss of one helicopter in Vietnam in 1962 would hardly make news; however, it represented one per cent of our inventory. Based on that rate and on our current aircraft inventory, we would have to lose in a single day 34 helicopters to be comparable to one in 1962. Such a loss would obviously receive much publicity.

Many people are of erroneous opinion that the helicopter by the very nature of its construction is a fragile piece of machinery. Actually, it is a pretty tough bird. Not only can it take considerable punishment and come home with many wounds, but it also has one major advantage over fixed wing aircraft. When it is shot down or comes down with mechanical difficulties, its flight characteristics are such that it can usually achieve a survivable landing for the aircraft and crew. For example, the first OH-6 CAYUSE helicopter to complete 1,000 hours of combat flying had, at the end of the 1,000 hours, been shot down five times and recovered, received fire on 57 occasions, and survived 150 bullet strikes. It was finally retrograded to the States for overhaul and is probably at this time back in Vietnam flying again.

We have been able to cope with the guerrillas and the organized enemy units by employing helicopters to make our forces highly mobile and to free ourselves, when necessary, from the tenuous land lines of communications which are so vulnerable to enemy interdiction. As General Westmoreland stated in a speech on the 1st of November 1968: "How many troops would have been needed without the helicopter? If we accept the ten to one ratio [The ratio stated by the French and

British authorities as necessary to overcome jungle guerrilla resistance.] we would need nearly two and one-half million troops to
counter the combined strength of the Viet Cong and North Vietnamese Army in South Vietnam—or one million more men than are
there now."

Be that as it may, mobile warfare waged against a numerically
superior enemy on terrain of his own choosing promises little in
the way of decisive victory and much in the line of stalemate or
defeat. Vietnam techniques cannot be employed advantageously
against an enemy possessing such sophisticated antiaircraft weapons
as hand-held, heat-seeking rockets. A truly modern antiaircraft
defense, similar to what might be expected in a major confrontation with Russia, could well prove disastrous to the attacking
forces.

General Williams' references to fire support make it apparent
that the same integration of fire and maneuver, so important in
any battle success, is even more vital where fast movement increases the difficulties of timing.

The promising future of airmobility was carefully looked into
through the medium of a board of qualified professionals headed
by General Hamilton H. Howze, former Chief of Army Aviation,
who was assisted by a large panel of scientists. General Howze,
then commanding the XVIII Airborne Corps, was a lifelong
cavalry and armor officer of unusual combat experience with a
forward-looking, analytical mind. Under his guidance on what
became known as the Howze Board, the foundation was laid for
the creation in 1963 of the 1st Cavalry Division (Airmobile).

The Airmobile Division totals just under 16,000 personnel,
generally divided into three brigades, an artillery group of 3-
105mm battalions and one aerial rocket battalion. A signal battalion and an engineer battalion are augmented by the usual
administrative and logistical services and by the all-important
helicopter-transport unit. Possibly one of the most important segments is the air cavalry squadron which consists of four troops;
one is a conventional mechanized reconnaissance unit; the other
three are broken into a scout section (6 light helicopters); a gun
section (rocket and machine gun firing) and a conventional pla-

toon. One troop is usually parcelled out to each of the three brigades of the airmobile division.

A future fire support platform, or "gunship," may be expected to have a computer-directed fire-control system, a direct sight for searching by the copilot, a 30-mm cannon, grenade launchers, antitank missiles to penetrate any current tank armor, about 100 wing rockets integrated with a computer, 250 knots speed and an ability to range over 2000 miles, with two to three hours on station.

The main combat elements are nine maneuver battalions which are assigned to the brigades on the task force principle, that is, as required. While some 450 helicopters are assigned to the division, the concept of operations provides for lifting only about one-third of the personnel at any one time, units being shuffled from one point of a battlefield to another.

Otherwise, the concept follows the conventional doctrine of finding the enemy, fixing him in place, and fighting him to a decision.

The method of employing airmobile troops can be illustrated by an account of a typical battle in Vietnam, based on factual reports from participants. The story concerns the action at Hoa Hoi in the autumn of 1966. The lack of front lines or other lines of demarcation used in conventional warfare makes the dispositions and the accent on mobility similar to that forecast for future nuclear war. The control system used parallels the principles set forth by the masters as applied to this kind of environment.

At this point in the chronicle of blitzkrieg, it may sound as if the blitz moved like a group of auto racers at the Indianapolis Speedway. Actually, while the movement *between* skirmishes or battles is fast, enemy contact usually develops an over-the-ground speed more suggestive of the conventional engagements which make up the great bulk of military history. There are always field fortifications to breach and streams to cross, all producing delays. Lost time is made up by the command celerity with which attacks are launched, by carefully integrating fire support, and by maintaining close command supervision to keep up constant pressure leading

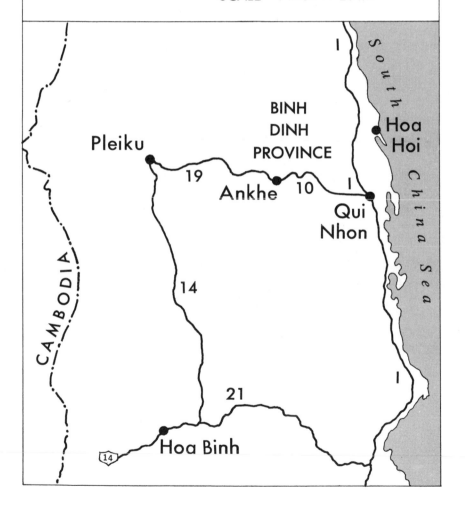

SKETCH
MAP...
SOUTH VIETNAM

SCALE   1 INCH = 20 MI.

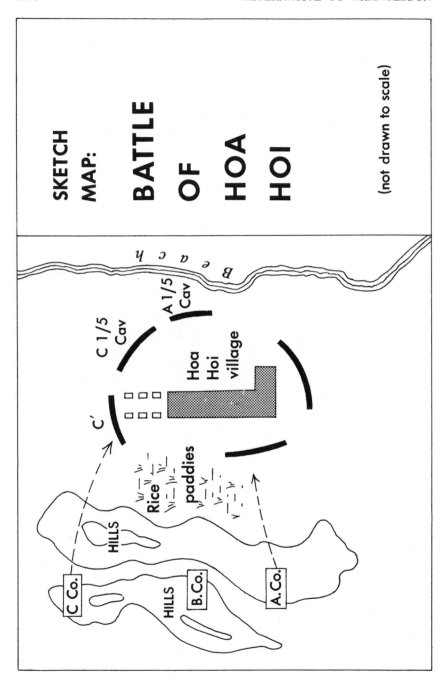

SKETCH MAP:

BATTLE OF HOA HOI

(not drawn to scale)

to pursuit. But an action reminiscent of an old-time siege is not untypical.

The Hoa Hoi fight was part of Operation IRVING, a "search and destroy" campaign in Binh Dinh Province on the east coast of Vietnam. It was a question of locating fanatical bands of Viet Cong or North Vietnamese units and driving them to the seashore. The small village of Hoa Hoi was built around a single main street, lined with the usual nipa, bamboo, and oil-tin shacks of the country. The ground leading to the beach is open, while to the west of the village are rice paddies and then hills.

On October 2, 1966, a force of pajama-clad guerrillas swept through the street, killing and mutilating the headmen and terrifying the villagers. One escaped and succeeded in getting word of the attack to the headquarters of the 1st Cavalry Division (Airmobile), where a relief expedition was sought in pursuance of the Operation IRVING objectives. The 1st Battalion, 12th Cavalry, was known to be airborne to positions in the hills west of the Hoa Hoi area.

Shortly after 0900 hours of October 2, Lieutenant Colonel James Root, now Colonel, commanding the First Battalion, was flying near Hoa Hoi westward bound in his helicopter. With him in the command ship were his operations officer (S-3), Major Leon Bieri, and the artillery liaison officer, Captain John Sutton. Each had specific control functions to perform. Root manned the command radios, one linking him to his company commanders and the other to the brigade commander. Bieri, operating the transport helicopter radio net, directed the movements of the twelve transport helicopters assigned to the battalion for the operation. Sutton, on the artillery net, indicated the positions to be taken for the supporting artillery battery and prepared to coordinate the artillery fire missions.

At 0945 Root got a radio message from the air cavalry troop of the brigade, reporting that its scout section had received heavy fire from the south end of Hoa Hoi; two choppers had been downed. The troop commander had called for his gunships and his infantry platoon was developing the situation.

Root turned his helicopter toward Hoa Hoi. He knew that his companies were readied for movement to planned positions in the hills west of the beach and village. A change in objectives would not complicate matters, for the situation at Hoa Hoi looked promising. As he neared the village, the cavalry troop commander radioed that his unit was now completely engaged and was receiving heavy fire from Cong elements entrenched in the hamlet, using 50-caliber machine guns, mortars, and grenade launchers. Root could see the two downed choppers and judged that they were now severely hit. Unfortunately the beach area gave very little cover.

Root was half-formulating a recommendation to brigade to put his unit into the battle at Hoa Hoi when a call from the brigade commander asked him if his battalion was conveniently disposed to perform that very task. Root lost no time in acknowledging affirmatively.

The weather was clear and hot, with the heaviness that comes with the approach of the monsoon. Little or no wind was stirring. Heat waves danced up from the sand on the beach and shimmered slowly across the village and the rice paddies to the west. Then the hills rose sharply, covered with the thick tropical vegetation common to the area. Root felt a wave of gladness that he did not have to fight the terrain.

A sequence of events, as familiar to the battalion as a repertoire of plays to a football team, then took place. First came the placing of the artillery. Acting on Root's stated plan of attack, Captain Sutton reached the artillery battery, directing them to emplace on the high ground behind the rice paddies. Using their own airlift, the battery presented quite a sight as it got into position. Each gun and its load of ammunition were picked up in the same sling, the ammunition dangling below. The chopper then flew to the designated spot, gently grounded the ammunition load, then moved off a few feet to set down the gun. All over in a few seconds. Sometimes, using color designations for guns, and spotting panels of the same color in the new position, a precise and rapid emplacement was guaranteed.

Colonel Root knew that his B (Bravo) Company was in the best state of readiness for a move. He at once called the commander, Captain Fred Mayer, rapidly outlined the situation, directed the company to prepare for immediate movement and informed Mayer that he would meet him and B Company in the air. Root's problem was to intercept Bravo Company and to point out the landing zone or objective. Mayer would do the rest. The meeting effected and radio information exchange continuing, Root's chopper swooped to the south end of the village dropping a smoke grenade on the proposed landing zone (LZ) to mark it beyond question.

Meanwhile Captain Sutton had insured that the artillery battery was registering on Hoa Hoi. Hence, Captain Mayer lost no time in bringing his platoons successively to their initial positions.

The original plan of moving the battalion into the hills for a possible flushing out of Viet Cong was now dead. Root therefore moved directly to the A (Alpha) Company position, where troops were being readied for the coming airlift. He picked up Captain Fields in his chopper. While the twelve transport choppers were emplacing Bravo Company, Root flew Fields over the area, outlined the situation, and gave the same instructions that had been given to Mayer, namely that Alpha would land on the southwest corner of Hoa Hoi, opposite Bravo, and later Charlie Company would move to the northern edge to make a three-pronged pincers movement that would squeeze out the defenders.

With Bravo in place, the transport choppers were now moving back to begin the lift of Alpha. In spite of the just-completed reconnaissance with Fields, Root had Fields change into the leading craft of the Alpha choppers and then guided the formation back to the village to make certain that there would be no error in landing zone. He had long since learned that there is only one chance when moving into a "hot" LZ.

As it did for Bravo Company, Root's chopper zoomed over the proposed Alpha LZ while Major Bieri again accurately dropped a smoke grenade on the selected spot. There was no mistake.

It was now learned that Bravo Company had met with stiff resistance. At the outset, moving across the open beach area, 82mm mortar rounds hit the company command post, wounding Captain Mayer in the face and arms. Blood streaming, the commander continued to direct the advance across the open beach area to the trench system that the VC had prepared on the perimeter of the village.

Two other heroic actions took place. When the 2nd Platoon

was stopped by heavy fire, it shook itself and stood up with rifles belching fire to move resolutely forward, surprising the Viet Cong. Private First Class Salazar led his squad through a booby-trapped trench system that the VC had prepared, clearing the way for others following, then fell mortally wounded.

In the 3rd Platoon, Private First Class Royal, carrying a wounded comrade over an open field, was himself killed after reaching cover. As often happens, these examples of bravery set the example the entire battalion was to follow in the next thirty hours.

When Alpha Company landed at the southwest corner of the village, it immediately came under fire from machine guns sweeping the open area. The 3rd Platoon, under Lieutenant Donald Grigg then met a problem common in this very curious war. A few bewildered men, women, and children were stumbling over the open fields, fire falling all around them. Grigg dashed through concentrated fire, picked up two children and carried them to safety while other civilians followed. He then led his platoon in a sharp attack against the Viet Cong outpost.

Root flew helicopters with loudspeakers over the village, directing civilians to evacuate the area. It is difficult to fight a war in which it is considered politically necessary to maintain the good will of the native population even though many of those saved may be close relatives of enemy troops in the vicinity. In this case such doubtful friendships had to be part of a calculated risk. So some of the lightning-war characteristics of the action had to be forsworn for humanitarian reasons, at least insofar as they related to the passage of time. Probably between 150 and 200 women and children obeyed the airborne loudspeakers and drifted out into the paddies and beach areas in three groups.

All firing by American troops ceased for the better part of an hour until it became apparent that no more refugees were about to appear. The villagers stayed with the airmobile cavalrymen through the entire period of action, taking advantage of rations and hot drinks, bearing uncomplainingly the dangers of the firing when it resumed and when it continued through the hours of darkness.

When the attack was resumed, Charlie Company, with Captain

Darrell Houston, was led by Colonel Root into position at the north end of the village. By 1250 hours, Charlie had begun its move southward.

At about the same time, Alpha Company's 2nd Platoon suffered five men wounded in an attempt to cross a stream bed. The company's senior aid man, Specialist 4th Class Benaitis, ran 300 yards over the rice paddies to treat the men and help bring them to safety. Other wounded men were saved by the strong actions of PFC Donaldson. Blasting with his M/16 on automatic fire, Donaldson waded into the stream, surprised two Cong squads and in two minutes had killed twelve of the enemy, driving the rest far enough to secure the safety of the group of wounded. Donaldson was awarded the Silver Star for his action.

Curiously, Charlie Company sustained no casualties during the entire battle. It had met only light resistance until about 1600 hours, when it ran into entrenched defenders. However, the teamwork of Sergeant Jackson and PFC Willis prevented serious losses. Jackson spotted an enemy ambush; outflanking it, he sprayed the area with automatic fire, assisted by Willis. Jackson then suffered a creasing head wound which knocked him out, but Willis pulled him to cover, then threw a grenade or two at the enemy position. In spite of the fact that Willis was also hit, he revived Jackson and the two men renewed the attack, killing all eight Cong manning the ambush.

By late afternoon the resistance in Hoa Hoi seemed as strong as ever in spite of the fact that by actual body count, ninety Cong had been killed and twenty captured; only three of Root's battalion were killed up to that point. But advances had been made all along the line. Bravo Company had moved up to occupy the trench system abandoned by the enemy, inspired by the actions of Specialists 4th Class Norman Jackson and Richard Schmidt. These men crawled through a fire-swept and booby-trapped area to get a clear field of fire which they utilized to pour more than 4000 rounds of ammunition into the village. With their help, the linkage between Alpha and Bravo Companies was effected; action was also taken to tighten the contact between Alpha and Charlie Companies to the north.

Through much of the action the brigade commander had been

aloft over the area, watching developments carefully, but not intervening in any way until nearly dark, when he saw that gaps existed in the attacking lines to the north and east; it appeared that if a siege was laid under present conditions, many Cong would escape the trap in the darkness. Accordingly, he offered two additional companies to Colonel Root, Alpha and Charlie of the 5th Cavalry 1st Battalion. Twenty-four helicopters were assigned to the lift, after Colonel Root had gladly fallen in with the idea, and within a half hour both companies were landing on the beach. Root personally supervised the positioning of the companies, then, landing again under fire, established his command post with Bravo Company for the night.

Root issued orders for a tight band around the village, the attackers "holding hands" until daylight permitted a resumption of the attack so that no Cong could escape. There were numerous attempts to break the cordon during the night but all were thrown back.

Captain Sutton, in his capacity as artillery liaison, was a big factor in the successful containment. With his two forward observers, he faced murderous fire in moving to positions from which they were later able to adjust 883 rounds of ammunition on pinpointed targets, round by round, through the night. This action was coupled with the direction of flare aircraft overhead, artillery flares, and flares from Navy craft offshore.

It made for an eerie scene. In the ghostly light of the flares, medical evacuation and ammunition-supply helicopters maneuvered to find a suitable landing area. The Charlie Company executive, Lieutenant John Rieke, then took a flashlight to a possible spot which then became the center of Cong fire. Lieutenant Rieke calmly directed the two ships, narrowly averting more than one collision, meanwhile organizing the evacuation and resupply operations.

Captain Harold Fields, sensing that the enemy were trying to break out of a gap in the company sector, rushed his headquarters personnel—cooks, bottlewashers, and administrative aides—into the breach. There was an interim fire fight in which Cong came within twenty feet of the emergency position, but the attempt was thrown back.

At dawn, Root's unaltered plan of attack was put into action.

While Alpha and Bravo held on at the southern exits, Charlie Company made a sweep from north to south. This pinched out Alpha Company of the 5th Cavalry, which then was ordered into reserve at the original position of Charlie-Twelfth.

Captain Houston's Charlie Company did not have an easy time. Heavy fire was met again and again, but the aggressive spirit of the men did not flag. Machine gunners and scouts teamed up, exposing themselves daringly while they poured steel-jacketed lead into the Cong bunkers.

When the sweep was complete, Major Robert Thomas, Root's executive officer, landed on the southern edge of the village. Using information gained from his flight, Thomas led Companies Bravo and Charlie on a return combing of the village, with A Company of the 5th Cavalry providing the cork at the north end. Finally this company made a second attack on the south, terminating the battle of Hoa Hoi.

A total of 259 Cong had been killed and forty captured; American casualties were only three dead and eighteen wounded, an astonishingly small number considering the amount of ammunition fired and the bold maneuvering under fire that had taken place.

Initially, approximately a battalion of Viet Cong had been estimated as in Hoa Hoi. Post-action facts showed that the defense had been conducted by the Seventh Battalion, 18th North Vietnam Army Regiment, together with some portions of the 8th Battalion, 18th NVA Regiment. This accounted in part for the brutal murder of the village headmen.

Awards in this action alone for the cavalrymen involved one Distinguished Service Cross, thirty-five Bronze Stars for Valor, six Commendation Medals and an Air Medal for Valor.

The Hoa Hoi battle has several aspects of special interest, not only as an example of the versatility of airmobile troops but also as one of outstanding leadership and teamwork throughout all ranks. Knowledge that any nation possessed an abundance of such commanders, together with the means of keeping up the supply through training, would unquestionably constitute the most effective deterrent to foreign aggression anywhere in the world.

As Hoa Hoi developed it became more of a siege than a blitz.

Nevertheless, great mobility was manifested in the approach and deployment of assault and fire-support troops. Colonel Root was in complete control at all times, he and his staff exemplifying the best in on-the-spot supervision. The presence of the brigade commander, intervening only to provide needed reinforcements, was also in the finest blitz tradition.

The sequence of commitment of Colonel Root's forces exemplifies the precise timing so vital in modern war: 1) Artillery was emplaced in ample time to obtain necessary firing data and support the approach and subsequent actions of the battalion; 2) about five to eight minutes fire preparation was deemed adequate; 3) aerial rockets followed in a 15–30-second sequence; 4) artillery projectile time of flight was considered by the artillery liaison officer who was told the time at which the lead helicopters would cross designated control points and who regulated the fire from the air; 5) the artillery fire was lifted to allow the immediate delivery of the aerial rockets fired from gunships, which in turn marked the arrival of the first troop-laden choppers.

The Hoa Hoi fight has been intentionally presented in detail at the company level in contrast to previous accounts of blitz action. The purpose has been to show that lightning war does not always sweep resistance before it like the tide. The Israeli had many such miniature sieges during the Sinai campaign, yet the blitz tempo was maintained overall. In this case, Colonel Root's command, at the end of the battle, was ready for further action a hundred miles away.

The engagement was, like most Vietnam fights involving airmobile units, a separate battalion affair which ended by using rapidly displaced reinforcements. In this sort of war battalions are scattered far and wide, while division and brigade commanders supervise the moving of a "least-committed battalion" to a new critical area as required.

# 15 The Confrontation Deterrent

The brush-fire war, or crisis, and the war of attrition have to date been waged in corners of the globe far from the United States. This circumstance should arouse no surprise, for it is obvious that Sino-Russian interest in keeping western powers off balance is best served by fomenting trouble in precisely these areas. Some advantage inevitably results for them, since either the West keeps hands off while aggressors move in, or, where vital interests are threatened, a debilitating and unpopular war of the Vietnam type ensues. And ever-present is the shadow of involvement of general nuclear war.

The U.S. Strike Command and the airmobile concept have been discussed in relation to their roles in so-called limited wars. But limited wars are not the cause of the gravest concern. That is the possibility of a confrontation between major powers, occurring in all probability in Europe or the Middle East.

Here totalitarian expansionism must one day lead to a chain of circumstances resembling the slow-burning fuse that finally touched off World War II, in spite of the painful concessions made by peace- and trade-oriented politicians to dampen it by appeasement.

The West is kept off balance by varying the location of probes to determine its will to resist. "Russia's new target—Asia" in the *U.S. News and World Report* of August 11, 1969, states that "in this point in history Russia is thrusting deep into Asia with a drive unmatched since the era of Czarist expansion across Siberia. . . . The U.S. is attempting to liquidate its costly war in Vietnam [while] the Soviet Union is moving to establish its . . . authority in the area from which the U.S. is expected to pull back." It also quotes the French editor René Dabernat in *Le Monde* as saying, "The Kremlin portrays itself as the only remaining bastion against the Chinese menace [to the Far Eastern nations] and as the last defenders of white civilization's Asian frontiers" (to the Europeans). Dabernat fails to ask who is left in charge if Mao and the Kremlin later shake hands.

In 1969 news reports have indicated that the most stupendous build-ups of Russian war materials since 1945 are appearing on the borders of satellite Europe, hard on the heels of the takeover of Czechoslovakia. How long before a new probe begins there? Or in Berlin? Or what will it take to arouse western war fervor if events indicate a critical and imminent danger?

Creation of an effective deterrent to a deteriorating world situation is increasingly dependent upon the ability of NATO forces to cope with the very fluid, "extremely dynamic and violent" conflict forecast by Comrade Prusanov. The NATO forces must employ superior mobility to offset the plans of an enemy which has the initiative and the numerical superiority. The Strike Command and general military airlift from continental America are an important part of filling the need for emergency reserves. But above all looms the need for effective leadership of the blitz kind at tactical levels, plus an understanding of this need at higher levels, if the most challenging military situation in all history is to be met. The severity of the challenge transcends the usual command problems and stems from the need to walk the fence between conventional mobile war and the awesome possibility of triggering the lock on Pandora's box of nuclear weapons. None of the lightning-war masters had to face such problems.

The gist of the nuclear dilemma at command levels is contained in several quotes, again the *U.S. News and World Report* in the October 19, 1964, issue in an article headed "More Light on Who Does Control the Bomb."

In 1953 a new class of nuclear weapons was born. They were smaller and they produced less fall-out than earlier weapons. They were called "tactical" or battlefield weapons to distinguish them from the bigger "strategic" devices.

In 1954 these smaller weapons were made a key part of the defense of Europe. US Allies in the North Atlantic Treaty Organization were given to understand that these "battlefield nukes" would be used immediately, if needed. Planes, missiles and artillery units bearing the new weapons began to flow across the Atlantic.

In 1961, under President Kennedy, a new policy for the control of nuclear weapons began.

In the same issue, under the title "The Atomic Trigger—What They're Really Talking About," quotes from a report by the Republican National Committee:

Secretary of Defense McNamara told the Democratic Platform Committee in August 1964 what our NATO Allies had known for more than two years. Secretary McNamara stated: "The awesome responsibility to release such force, I believe, can rest only on the highest elected official in this country, the President of the United States. . . . I believe the American people should know the steps we have taken to eliminate the danger of actual attack by our strategic forces. . . . The release of weapons could come by Presidential decision alone. Complex codes and devices prevent any unauthorized action . . . two or more men must act independently and must decide the order has been given. . . . The permissive action link places an electronic lock on nuclear weapons which renders them impotent until unlocked by the President, who holds the coded electronic key to the weapons in his sole possession."

In the same issue, under the title "Nixon—the Unanswered Questions," Richard Nixon was quoted:

The people of America, and particularly the 250,000 American fighting men stationed in Europe are entitled to have these questions answered by President Johnson immediately:

1. Has he revoked the Eisenhower procedure which gave the NATO commander authorization to use battlefield atomic weapons to respond to a Communist attack when a communications breakdown makes it impossible for the President to give this order?

2. If he has revoked the policy, what substitute procedure has he adopted, if any, to protect the security of American and other NATO forces in the event of such an attack?

3. Is it not true that the entire NATO defense concept is dependent upon the use of America's nuclear power to repel an attack?

4. Is it not true that this NATO defense system will be gutted if the NATO commander is forbidden to react to an attack with battlefield weapons (atomic) unless and until the President alone, whether or not he is available at the time, authorizes their use?

5. Is it not true that the whole grandiose electronic-nuclear control machine that President Johnson referred to on September 16 in Seattle will collapse completely if the indispensable communications system should fail?

6. It is not true that any aggressor against the U.S. would strike at communications, coincident with his nuclear attack which, if successful, would consign our whole retaliatory strike into the trash heap . . . ?

A footnote to both articles stated that the information had been compiled exclusively from information in the public domain.

So far as is known the President of the United States has the only authority for the release of any nuclear weapon held in the U.S. arsenal. Political winds are variable and future administrations may have differing views. In any event, the question of delayed release is perhaps academic. Even if independent authority was given to the Supreme Allied Commander, Europe (SACEUR) to answer a request from some hard-pressed battalion commander to use nuclear weapons to save his unit from extinction, the request must inevitably be processed through the following headquarters after the concurrence of NATO:

Regiment or Brigade
Division
Army Corps
Field Army
Headquarters (Central, Northern, etc.), Army Group (CENTAG)
Allied Forces Central Europe (AFCENT)
Supreme Headquarters, Allied Powers, Europe (SHAPE)

Consideration in succession by these headquarters presents a formidable and time-consuming processing problem. 1) Is the request justifiable in view of the consequences? 2) What objections exist? 3) Should nonconcurrence by a lower headquarters be overruled? There may be valid objections in each case. And it is diffi-

cult to visualize circumstances in which any one of the headquarters could be bypassed. There have been many proposals
aimed to expedite matters but none has been practical and
effective.

The dilemma of the tactical commander must be acknowledged.
He is caught between the possibility of seeing his unit destroyed
by a superior enemy and of starting a world atomic holocaust. An
idea of the complexity of the general problem may be gained from
Morton Halperin's *Limited War in the Nuclear Age;* the anno-
tated bibliography lists 343 books and articles on the subject. But
the discussions are in general philosophical and not concerned
with the all-important impact on the military commander.

Command problems in the European environment differ somewhat from those in the series of combat incidents described in the
history of blitzkrieg. The strategic posture of NATO powers is one
of defense, whereas the blitz battles have uniformly treated of
attack. "Defense" in this sense, however, is the "offensive-defense" which depends primarily on counterattacks, pocketing,
encircling, and destroying the attacking enemy on a fluid battlefield where no conventional lines exist. While the blitz is scarcely
adaptable to the conventional defense of a locality from a fixed
position, it is an integral part of the kind of defense visualized for
a major confrontation in Germany.

Dependence in this situation is placed primarily upon armored
and mechanized divisions of American, British, German, and
possibly French troops to conduct a series of lightning-war battles
against an equally mobile enemy horde racing into the German
heartland. The great plains of northern Germany pose little more
than parade-ground problems for a powerful attacker. However,
as the Ruhr and central Germany are reached, a different picture
develops.

This is the area once described by Tacitus as an enormous
jungle, with a solid and terrifying forest. It appalled him with its
vastness, its impenetrable marshes, its brutal winters, and its clinging and freezing fogs. Today it is dotted with clean German towns
and cities, yet the rugged ground that so frightened Tacitus remains to confound an invader.

This heartland is the basis of the defense mission of the U.S.

Seventh Army. Normally housed in barracks, troops have practiced ad nauseam the emergency dispersal techniques which place them quickly into a planned defense position from which many different options may be exercised depending on the nature and location of the incursions.

There is a corridor leading to the heartland from the great northern plains—the valley of the Fulda, known as the Fulda Gap. Consensus has it that any invasion of Germany by mobile columns must gravitate to the Fulda Gap. Otherwise the invader must accept the risk of advancing over the rugged hills and through the dark forests where deployment off roads and trails presents real problems to motorized troops.

Command difficulties in the offensive-defense are ideally illustrated by the use of mobile elements in the initial stages of repelling an advance through the Fulda Gap. If an airmobile division is chosen for the leading role, the need for maximum mobility and the necessity to adopt blitz control methods are apparent. In considering the risks inherent in using a large-sized airmobile force as a unit, it is assumed that the invading enemy columns are composed of first-class troops equipped with sophisticated anti-aircraft weapons. This is a far cry from the battalion-sized actions in Vietnam (as at Hoa Hoi) where the enemy had neither tactical air support nor heat-seeking antiaircraft rockets.

The airmobile division in a delaying action role will be performing a mission typical of mobile troops throughout history. As such, it becomes a member of a closely coordinated field army combat team; fortunately it is a role for which the division seems particularly well fitted.

To date there has been no deployment of an airmobile division as a unit and, fortunately, no wars conducted under immediate nuclear threat. So an account of the action of the division showing the problems of its leaders must be presented in a generalized narrative form. But the defense of the Fulda Gap has been war-gamed on countless occasions and war games have a habit of repeating themselves in subsequent actual conflict, whether on land or sea.

Major General Tip McFadic was in his command helicopter en route to a series of visits to his brigade commanders in the murky predawn of a spring day in 1971. His Seventh Airmobile Division, alerted some forty-eight hours earlier in response to a warning that a Russo-Satellite blitz against Germany was imminent, was now in widely scattered bivouacs with their helicopters concealed in the heavy woodlands. Occupation of the assembly areas, and displacement to others at frequent intervals to avoid detection, had been practiced over and over again.

As his command chopper sped over the somber treetops McFadic was glad that he had succeeded in having the airlift capabilities of the division beefed up during his recent tour of duty in the Pentagon. Now, when casualties occurred, a reserve would be available to carry out minimum requirements. At that time he had had no idea that he was soon to command this airmobile division.

He had scarcely settled himself and glanced around at his companions, the division artillery officer, Colonel Tompion, and the Communications-Electronics officer, Major Radon, when the semidarkness was obliterated by a single blinding flash from far to the north. Within a few seconds a noise like a dozen speeding freight trains was heard even through radio headsets and a shock wave shook the chopper.

"A high altitude megaton or more burst near the Baltic," guessed Tompion. "Here we go for broke! Let's see if the radio works."

McFadic and Tompion tried the command and artillery nets. There was no response.

"It was intended as a warning that they mean business, I think," said Major Radon. "It will knock out radio communications and maybe some land lines in the North. But our new super-high-frequency satellite system for divisions and higher units should remain operative and our local radio may not be out for more than an hour or so."

"The important conclusion is that an invasion has begun," said McFadic, "and the important question is whether we shall be authorized to release nuclear weapons. Are you sure that our assigned loads and the issue system are in readiness, Tompion?"

"Oh, yes, we're okay," replied the artilleryman.

"Then let's pour the gas to this crate and hurry our visits to the brigades," urged McFadic.

All units proved to be in readiness. McFadic felt that a wise policy had decreed the use of many small-lift choppers rather than lesser numbers of large craft. The smaller choppers were well hidden in the woods, and he had had a hard time locating his own units.

At the last brigade headquarters a helicopter courier from Mc-Fadic's division headquarters was waiting with a directive for the General to fly at once to Field Army headquarters and confirmed the fact that the satellite radio system was operative. Invading mobile divisions were streaming across the northern plains, seemingly unstoppable in their thrust to the German industrial areas near Essen.

The Army Commander came straight to the point. "Our plans for this emergency still stand, McFadic," he said. "We can expect our screen of armored cavalry and other units to hold any immediate push from the northeast. It is up to us to plug the Fulda Gap. The 20th Armored and the 36th Mechanized Divisions are ready to take the brunt of an attack from that direction, but they are going to be delayed by the crush of refugee traffic that we have expected all along. Your 7th Airmobile Division will move out at once to the maximum distance northwest of Fulda and Kassel needed to delay the advance of hostile troops short of Kassel until at least noon the day after tomorrow. By then the 20th Armored can take over."

"Are there any NUDETS [Nuclear Detonation Reports] or any indications that our side can release nuclear weapons, General?" asked McFadic. "And what can I expect from Air Force Tactical Air?"

"There has been only that one high burst, Tip," answered the Army Commander. "Several airfields have been hit by conventional weapons, but with only minor damage. Our warning system worked well," he added. "As to our release, I understand that SHAPE [Supreme Headquarters Allied Powers, Europe] has queried Washington without getting an answer. But don't worry about your support. Part of the air staff from Wiesbaden will be here in a moment to coordinate air strikes with you, and you can count on at least three squadrons of fighters, maybe more. Your action will be the critical point of the Army effort for the next thirty-six

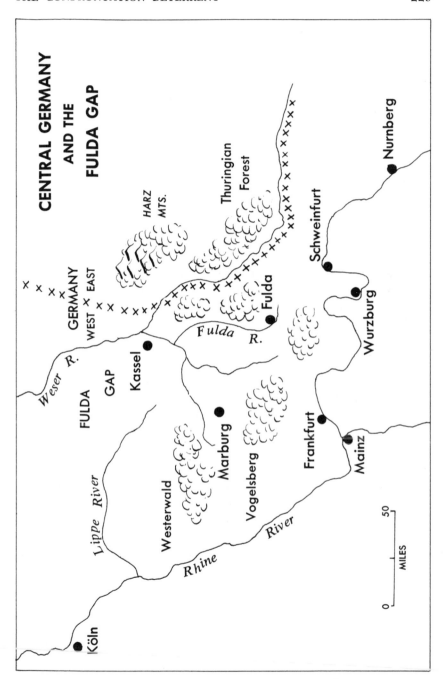

CENTRAL GERMANY AND THE FULDA GAP

hours. And besides the tac-air we can provide Pershing missile strikes for you on call."

McFadic's watch showed that it was nearly noon. Minutes were pressing. Fortunately, communications in the area had returned sufficiently close to normal for him to call his own command post. His assistant division commander, Brigadier General Bitts, the air cavalry squadron commander, the air liaison officer and the artillery executive officer were directed to take to the air to meet him over Kassel at 1300 hours, land, and discuss tentative plans. Voice radio codes were put into effect.

When his subordinates arrived they made a short reconnaissance of an area all had been over many times and landed on a high hill overlooking the rolling ground of the Fulda Gap, stretching far to the northwest.

McFadic turned to Lieutenant Colonel Fargo, the commander of the air cavalry squadron." The initial action is yours, Pete," he said, "you will have the new heavy gunship company attached to you to give added fire support. Then you will have air cover from at least two tac-air squadrons. Move straight through the Gap until you establish contact with main enemy forces, as far out as Paderborn if possible. Delay them to the maximum without getting heavily engaged yourself. It is purely a hit and run deal."

As Fargo got on the radio to start his already alerted troops moving, McFadic outlined his plan of action. The 1st and 2nd Brigades were to be airlifted successively to occupy and defend "Jackknife Ridge," a terrain feature extending partly across the Gap and as far to the northwest as McFadic thought time would permit preparation of the defensive ground. When Jackknife became untenable, the Second Brigade would move overland, withdrawing to Baldur Ridge, three to five miles to the southeast, and conduct a new defense from that position, covered by the First Brigade. This latter unit would then withdraw overland, pass through Baldur Ridge and the 2nd Brigade, and occupy an assembly position in division reserve.

The 3rd Brigade was to be airlifted after dark to positions from which a counterattack could be launched, ideally this would take place just after the 1st Brigade began its withdrawal. McFadic and Colonel Sideband, commanding the 3rd Brigade, planned to fly over possible assembly areas at once, while the other commanders and Colonel Tompion's artillery started their moves.

But it was all a matter of conjecture—a question of whether the 1st and 2nd Brigades could in fact hold Jackknife Ridge until approximately noon the next day.

By late afternoon McFadic's command post had been flown to a point between Kassel and Fulda and was in operation. The Chief of Staff had readied a computer readout of the updated positions of the 20th Armored and 36th Mechanized Divisions. There was cause for concern. The units were essentially stalled, trying to buck a flood of refugees fleeing south and choking the roads. German civil agencies organized to cope with just this sort of emergency had had little success. McFadic could not believe the figures; perhaps the automation system was running behind. He therefore dispatched General Bitts to fly to the 20th and the 36th, hasten the exchange of liaison officers and get the facts; he was beset with worry over risking helicopters in mass in this sophisticated and nuclear-charged environment, especially since there had been no word on authorization to release his own nuclear weapons in case of impending disaster. And of course it took an appreciable time to get weapons out of storage and unlock them.

The afternoon news from the cavalry squadron and its powerful supporting gunships had been more reassuring. Their ability to pick up distant targets quickly, engage two simultaneously, and produce target coordinates on a display panel for relay to McFadic's computerized headquarters was proving highly effective. Clearly the enemy had nothing like it. Two of their columns, speeding down the roads that converged just north of Kassel, had been stopped and forced to deploy nearly ten miles short of that town. Ten light aircraft and a dozen tanks had fallen prey to the gunships with, incredibly, no losses sustained by the air cavalrymen.

Far overhead the Air Force fighters had apparently established at least local control of the air. Three Mig 23s had been knocked down while the remainder of the group fled. Strange, thought McFadic, to provide such limited air resources to support an important strategic thrust!

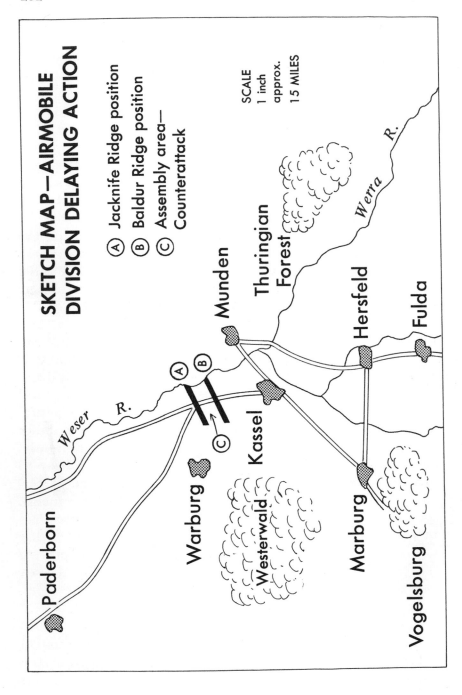

SKETCH MAP—AIRMOBILE
DIVISION DELAYING ACTION

Ⓐ Jacknife Ridge position
Ⓑ Baldur Ridge position
Ⓒ Assembly area—
   Counterattack

SCALE
1 inch
approx.
15 MILES

Lift for advance parties of the First and Second Brigades had been completed. Estimates indicated that both units would be in position by dark. It did not seem possible to McFadic that at their present rate of advance enemy armor could reach Jackknife Ridge before dark. With the coming of night the Third Brigade would begin its lift to the counterattack assembly area. Colonel Tompion's division artillery, already in position behind Jackknife Ridge, had been able to execute a few long range missions called for by the cavalry; these would increase hour by hour. So far, so good.

Better yet, McFadic received approval for the firing of a Pershing missile into the stalled enemy concentrations in front of the air cavalry. The latter reported timely and accurate delivery with devastating results. More much needed delay.

The General was nearly exhausted, but he had the knack, shared by many of the great leaders, of catnapping when the opportunity offered. He snatched a half hour after a hasty meal of packaged rations and, refreshed, flew to check on the progress of the 1st and 2nd Brigades. He would establish an advance command post near that of the former unit. The ability of the 1st Brigade to hold would largely determine the timing of the entire operation.

Lieutenant Colonel Bohrsite, the Division G-3, was directed to fly to the counterattack assembly area and to advise McFadic of developments. He had scarcely arrived in the early darkness before transmitting in the simple voice code some extraordinarily good news. Advance parties of the 3rd Brigade had surprised an enemy reconnaissance unit on high ground and had overpowered the personnel during a radio transmission by the parent headquarters. The 3rd Brigade intelligence officer, fluent in Russian, was satisfied that the takeover was unreported and stated that "arrangements" had been made to keep the radio operative for an hour or two at least. McFadic grinned. Sideband's intelligence officer was known to be as skillful in karate as he was fluent in Russian.

Near midnight a motorized enemy force struck hard at the 1st Brigade. Though it was a ferocious assault, made under flares, it became evident that the force was small and that the Brigade could easily hold. What daylight would bring was another matter.

On a hunch McFadic framed a message to Army requesting that an 80 KT nuclear weapon be placed on a contingent mission and describing the massed Soviet forces within the Fulda Gap and in front of Jackknife Ridge as an ideal target. At 0800 hours of the new day General Bitts, who had returned from his visits to the 20th Armored and 36th Mechanized Divisions, reported that the nuclear request had been acknowledged but that no action had resulted. He was in touch with the refugee situation, he said, but offered little hope that help would arrive before the next noon.

The staff prepared a situation map and transmitted it by facsimile through the computer chain. McFadic again checked the computer system for facts that he himself already knew and determined that it was running from thirty to sixty minutes late. Not too bad. He doubted that it would ever get much better as long as machines were run by people.

The Chief of Staff found the data processing a gold mine. Higher headquarters, instead of pestering McFadic in these critical hours, had simply pushed the buttons to get SITREPS and other routine reports automatically. With the time saved he had been able to go over the logistical situation and among other things to establish POL dumps to refuel the helicopters near the defensive positions. What the Chief did not know was that the Army Commander had made a flight over the area and had determined for himself that matters were going as well as could be expected.

A predawn mist was beginning to clear. Whether this would benefit the attackers or the defenders was hard to assess.

The 3rd Brigade was now well situated in the counterattack assembly area, along with radar surveillance equipment. Radar had disclosed flanking Soviet movement guarded by light aircraft south of Warburg. Air cavalry gunships of the 7th Airmobile had shot them down; the enemy still had no answer to the gunships, especially the new, heavy types.

The country was thick and the ridges selected for the assembly of the 3rd Brigade and the launching of the counterattack seemed ideal. But by midmorning the weight of the enemy attack had smashed hard against Jackknife Ridge. The valiant cavalry was still striking at the flanks but was now taking moderate to severe losses. Four heavy gunships had perhaps become too bold and had succumbed to enemy ground gunners. Two air cavalry troops were down to 50 percent effectiveness.

It was apparent that Jackknife Ridge could not be completely held through the noon hour. The 2nd Brigade was taking severe losses. Although the 1st Brigade had not been hit so hard, it would not be possible to extend the frontage to cover adequately the withdrawal of the 2nd Brigade to Baldur Ridge.

At this juncture the Army Commander arrived by chopper at McFadic's advance command post. He approved another Pershing strike on call about 1130, an hour and a half away, to aid the beleaguered 2nd Brigade. Air Force fighters were directed to concentrate support just before withdrawal, while Tompion's artillery massed its fires. But it was going to be a near thing.

"Tip, I know about your request for the 80KT nuclear mission," the Army Commander had said, "but we haven't heard a damned thing. We've even phoned CENTAG and SHAPE as to possible policy but without success. We understand that there have been urgent requests from the British in the north, as well, yet not a word. On the whole, I had expected more air and rocket action here. It seems peculiar. It may be that they do not expect to press this attack, or to inflict any serious damage in the rear, but to concentrate on the capture of the industrial Essen area. Then they might propose to negotiate—draw back from here and keep Essen —much as they did in Cuba. But of course, we can't bank on that."

When the Army Commander left McFadic directed the withdrawal of the 2nd Brigade and the phased withdrawal of the artillery. Lieutenant Colonel Nugent, the G-2, was directed to observe the 1st Brigade, compare personal observation with intelligence reports and keep McFadic informed. General Bitts came on the phone to recommend no displacement of the main command post. This was concurred in. Then McFadic flew to the 3rd Brigade and Colonel Sideband.

Here all was in order and there was an excellent view of the action on Jackknife. Gunships and Tompion's artillery continued to break up enemy formations, but the flood poured down.

On radio McFadic and Nugent agreed that the 1st Brigade could not hold beyond 1330 hours. They were in fact in grave danger on the right flank where attackers had rushed in behind the retiring Second Brigade. The brigade executive came on the radio net to confirm this for his commander and further gave the disturbing report that the 1st had taken nearly 25 percent casualties. A small counterattack to cover the withdrawal was planned for 1330.

McFadic authorized the 1st Brigade to carry out their plans and directed his energies to setting up support for the 3rd Brigade counterattack, estimated for about 1400, or when enemy dispositions and formations seemed suitable. He repeated his orders that all remaining artillery and gunships and all available Air Force fighters were to mass in support.

McFadic began to worry that in some manner the 80KT nuclear request might be granted and be fired at the wrong place at the wrong time. This had happened in maneuvers and war games and if the 80KT hit his own troops the results would be catastrophic. So he asked General Bitts to cover on the subject with Field Army. At 1330, as the brigade withdrew, he wished that he had the nuclear support after all. Thousands of enemy vehicles were piled up just short of Jackknife Ridge preparing for a pursuit of the 1st Brigade.

One vital problem, replete with risk, stood out. The counterattack would soon be marked by utter confusion in the objective area as Sideband's men swept into the enemy columns from the flank. If a protracted melee ensued, the 3rd Brigade would be in a most dangerous situation, perhaps itself counterattacked by the onrushing Soviets. Accordingly Colonel Sideband and General McFadic coordinated the movement of all available division airlift set to the task of extricating the 3rd Brigade elements. It would have to be a "thumb-a-ride" proposition. No time to assign choppers to specific units; it would be difficult enough to tell friend from foe.

McFadic decided just after 1400 that the hostile troops moving into the areas between Jackknife and Baldur Ridges were present in sufficient numbers and were sufficiently subject to surprise to justify his launching the counterattack. By 1530 it was evident that it had been signally successful. Pershing missile, artillery, and fighter plane missions had been well timed. Enemy columns were demoralized. Units advancing from the rear were piling up and adding to the suitability of the nuclear target once the 3rd Brigade was out of the way. McFadic could not resist calling to the Army Commander with a request for a small yield weapon on the grounds that his division was taking heavy losses and might take still more. A nuke might well end it. There was no concurrence nor any indication that any troops on the European continent had been granted nuclear authority.

By 1900 the 2nd Brigade was well established on Baldur Ridge, ready for a new enemy onslaught. Because of the high casualty rates, it was necessary to change plans. The Baldur Ridge defense had to be bolstered by taking the 1st Brigade from reserve. The 3rd Brigade formed a new reserve after reorganizing from the counterattack.

McFadic was close to complete exhaustion. But he revived when General Bitts called from the command post to say that the refugee situation was clearing rapidly. The leading units of the 20th Armored should arrive by daylight. McFadic felt certain that Baldur Ridge could be held through the hours of darkness, assuming that air superiority continued to rest with the U.S. Air Force. On this score he had succeeded in his mission against great odds. The question was at what cost.

Times change. With passing years, experience here and there will probably demonstrate that, given enough closely integrated fire power, helicopter-borne units can operate in the most complex environments. Critics once said that the lowly jeep could not be used in battle; it has become indispensable. On the other hand, it may develop that airmobile units can be better used as support forces for armored or mechanized divisions. Even in World War II, armored divisions generally fought by combat command (brigade) and these commands were not often integrated into action against a single objective.

The crystal gazers are probably right in forecasting highly fluid warfare under the threat of atomics. It seems reasonably accurate to say that mobility and risk increase along the same curve. In this narrative example, which reflects most European thinking, the entire tempo has been stepped up. What would have happened if General McFadic had holed up in a cave with a host of electronic gadgetry to direct the action from the rear? How could Air Force, missile and artillery action, and the timing of the withdrawals have been executed?

# 16  Attainment of the Blitz
##      Capability

Throughout this discussion of battles, actual and theoretical, of personalities, of principle and method, and of technical developments to aid the command and control process, there has run the theme of skilled leadership. Without the presence of a forceful and knowledgable commander the blitz is inconceivable. There were generals who met the challenge of mobile war during the forties and during the Israeli campaigns. The description of a new breed of leader in the analysis of airmobile combat in Vietnam provides some assurance that a degree of skill will be present if the possibility of nuclear war, supported by electronic gadgetry, one day unhappily presents itself. The skills of the masters were for the most part acquired through study and practical experience. Few were born to the baton of a field marshal.

Lack of the skills they learned has been historically disastrous. Manpower is a nation's most precious resource. The decline of the British Empire can be laid squarely to the deaths of so many young Englishmen at the Somme and other similar World War I battles of attrition, fought by methods so deplored by Liddell Hart; World War II exacted only the final payment. The blows were foretold by the "Charge of the Light Brigade," where "someone had blundered." In much the same way, the French never really recovered from Verdun, either spiritually or physically.

Today's great concern over cost analyses in the development of weapons systems means little if it is not recognized that inept battalion and division commanders can lose not only the systems but also the irreplaceable manpower that uses them.

The need for leadership on a broad base and in every echelon of command is incontrovertible. Following General Eisenhower's reasoning that a special type of leadership is required, it is only natural to ask where the new leaders are to come from.

The question will raise some eyebrows. Does not the United States now have the most able group of military command personalities in its history? Definitely, yes; but the senior members of the ground forces are veterans of an age when there were opportunities for relatively independent command in a small army. They had experience in handling men and in decision-making in lower echelons, going on to battle commands in the mobile phases of World War II.

Since their day, one and possibly two generations of professionals have come into being. Korea and Southeast Asia have offered little independence to these tyros, except for the small percentage of them involved in airmobile battle and in certain unusual tank actions. So the "old order changeth" and the new is deficient in the kind of experience afforded by service under Patton or Rommel.

Even if national policy were today oriented toward the development of blitz commanders, some formidable obstacles would remain, many well-nigh insoluble. It is more than unfortunate that in the cases where corrective action does seem practicable, there is no apparent disposition to seek it or, worst of all, even to acknowledge that the problem exists.

The attitude of the public, shaped in part by the news media, is in general antiwar. It results in the playing down of military values and in less respect for the career soldier. This is the first obstacle to leadership development. The public attitude toward the professional military today is far from conducive to the recruitment of potential commanders. It is a condition that is not within the power of the services to remedy.

True, there are faint protests. Secretary of Defense Melvin Laird was quoted as saying (press releases dated August 15, 1969) that "people in uniform are overly criticized, underpaid and prone to be forgotten once they have served their country." *The*

*National Observer* commented editorially in its issue of April 20, 1969, that "once the search for scapegoats and devil theories [is] ended, the country can get down to a sober assessment of the kind of defense posture it really needs. For this the generals and the admirals will have to be listened to and their advice weighed. It cannot be the final word, but it cannot be disregarded, either, in the erroneous belief that it is they who must shoulder all the blame for America's recent troubles abroad."

Still, these are hardly words to persuade a wavering patriot to shoulder a rifle or to seek a commission.

There are other obstacles that *do* fall within the purview of the military and in some degree are subject to military control. These include:

Lack of command opportunity
Training area constraints
Personnel instability
The slighting of training in combat leadership techniques (high
    level staff training at expense of "command")
Doctrinal rigidity

If a young man should decide in favor of a professional military career, what would his chances be of getting the kind of practical leadership training that would keep him from killing hundreds or thousands of his fellow Americans through a series of battle-field blunders? The answers may surprise the average citizen and to some extent the semiprofessional military enrolled in the Reserve or National Guard.

Take the matter of actual tactical training ground available as against the numerous forts and posts located in out-of-the-way areas. A proposal to train a professional football team in a gymnasium or on a tennis court would be ridiculous, but no more so, in reality, than the attempt to train battalions and brigades in integrated exercises within the confines of so-called military reservations. Emphasis on the training of the individual soldier, especially in acquiring skills with long-range weapons takes up thousands of acres. The remaining ground that is safe for tactical drills is insufficient. On maneuvers, restrictions on the movement of heavy vehicles over roads and through private property destroy all semblance of realism. As a result, the captain or the colonel is placed in the same position as the football quarterback who must get all his experience from reading books and conducting chalk talks.

Worse, the personnel demands for both the leaders and the led to fill specialist requirements around the globe, as well as the policy of planning career job rotation, often prevent the formation of any team whatever. The number of command slots compared to the number of officers in staff and administrative posts is so small that only by frequent rotation of commanders can any command opportunity be offered. The result is that the leader scarcely gets the feel of an organization before he is off; the unit itself suffers from a mishmash of command policies.

Even within a training garrison, demands for personnel for various work details, the usual absentee lists for leaves, sick leave, and special schooling, seriously deplete tactical units. The leader of a platoon or company then faces a situation, again comparable to the football quarterback, this time to one who must hold signal practice with only three linemen and a back. Tactical plays are impossible. While various panaceas are proposed year after year, conditions, especially in wartime, continue to be difficult.

Emphasis in the service schools is primarily on staff training. This is understandable, since the lack of training ground precludes extensive field work, and the art of field command does not, at the moment, lend itself to the classroom. Instruction that does deal with command functions centers on methods of inspiring subordinates to follow a leader and not on the techniques of controlling combat action.

In spite of forward-looking agencies such as the Combat Developments Command Experimentation Center (Fort Ord, Calif., and Hunter Liggett Reservation, Calif.), doctrine is largely shaped by the static battle and jungle experiences of Korea and Vietnam. To a considerable extent emphasis is on the Green Beret concept of guerrilla warfare, a type that has its place but is based on conditions that the geopolitical and military policies of the western world must seek to avoid. Not only has it been unproductive in the larger sense but also it detracts from efforts to build a real deterrent to major confrontations.

Comments of Major General Kenneth Strong, formerly Chief of Intelligence for Eisenhower's Allied Command in Europe, in *Recollections of a British Intelligence Officer,* are as pertinent today as when comparing French and German doctrines at the outbreak of World War II:

> German students had been practicing . . . rapid deployments from a marching column . . . on the orders of the leading battalion commander. The instructor said, "Gentlemen, please note that in the French Army, similar orders [can] be given by no one below the rank of commander of an army corps."
>
> I do not believe that you can teach individuals something that is contrary to the general strategic doctrine. The strategic doctrine of Germany at that time was to advance with spearheads of [armor], supported by air, to ignore the dangers on the flanks and to back up their columns with infantry. The ordinary soldier was taught to advance whatever the circumstances . . . to be at all costs a leader. As a result the German Army had become an army of leaders and of individuals; both officers and men . . . had developed a strong and rewarding sense of trust and comradeship.

It would not be accurate to say that American doctrine in any way resembles that of the French in 1939, yet it is all a matter of emphasis. It takes doing, not talking, to emphasize. General Strong's quotation speaks of Germans, but the spirit is quite in keeping with the American character, however much Americans may be preoccupied today with jungle fighting.

From a national defense standpoint, all these inhibitions to the development of a corps of adepts in lightning-war techniques make depressing reading. Without doubt a critic unfamiliar with the entire spectrum of combat training both in Europe and the United States would quarrel with them. The facts are there, however, if one will but dig for them.

Fortunately, all is not lost unless these inhibiting factors are ignored or discounted. Within the past generation, American ingenuity in the field of simulation techniques has advanced to the point where the development of tactical leaders needs only the signal to go ahead, as with the inauguration of the NASA moon programs.

The initial step in a program of instruction in tactical leadership techniques is to recognize the fact that the list of training obstacles and inhibitions is not only formidable, but also that there is very little that the military or even the civil government can do about it. The public attitude and that of the news media will probably not change; only under a dictatorship is it unwise to bait the brass. More land for blitz training is simply not available. Many fruitless efforts have been made to rectify a personnel situation that seems insoluble. The worldwide whirligig of job rotation and replacement is incomprehensible both to Congress and the military. Possibly early aptitudes for mobile command might be noted on fitness reports and officers allowed to settle either in a combat command or staff "discipline," or in an administrative field, leaving them there except for periods of academic instruction. Possibly training programs may one day place major emphasis on unit or team training. But there are valid objections to these and other proposals and changes seem unlikely. So an effective substitute must be found, one that appeals to taste and interest and that produces results at low cost.

Tactical instruction at the higher levels has in past years centered in map exercises which provide excellent training in tactical and organizational principles, staff duties, and procedures; broad decision-making is included. Complex data can be kept track of in mechanized war games by electronic data processing.

In some respects, however, these methods do more harm than good to the budding mobile commander. They teach him to think, which is good, but they encourage him to think deliberately, which in later actual tight situations can be disastrous. Missing are the ingredients that trip many a map problem virtuoso when he at last enters combat. (The *Washington Post* of Nov. 10, 1968 quotes editorially from a two-year study made by the civilian-run Systems Analysis Office of the Pentagon which showed that casualty rates in battalions commanded by tyros are 20 per cent higher than in those headed by experienced men.)

In the map problem he is given a rundown on the enemy situation; in combat he will rarely have more than a very sketchy picture. In combat time presses constantly: incoming shells, interrupted communications, harassment from higher headquarters and the pressure of the imponderables of weather, terrain, and mechanical and physical breakdowns all rudely intrude on decision-making.

Basically, effective leadership training is only a matter of subjecting a student to problems in tactics at all levels, with added elements of dynamic command and control in an environment vividly simulating battlefield conditions of stress.

Simulation is by now a time-tested art. The Link Trainer and its successive improvements for training aircraft pilots is fairly well known outside the aircraft industry. Here the trainee has knowledge of the aircraft systems and procedures gained from books and observation. In the trainer he must demonstrate his knowledge physically under different stress configurations (engines out, fires, hydraulic failures and the like) that can be simulated realistically while the pilot is under increasing pressure to make a safe landing. The trainee frequently "crashes" during the initial phases, but as the instruction proceeds it becomes more difficult to make him so lose control that he crashes.

The world was thrilled when Neil Armstrong was finally forced to take manual control of the Lunar Module to change the computer-predicted landing spot on the moon. Could he have done this without the simulation training afforded him by eight flights in an LLTV (Lunar Landing Training Vehicle)? Armstrong was quoted as saying earlier that the trainer did an excellent job of capturing the handling characteristics of the lunar module, unlike any aircraft he had ever flown, and giving him a high level of confidence in his ability to pick out a spot satisfactory for the LM landing. The remarks were prophetic.

The point is that the exercise of mobile command, as illustrated in the historical examples of the blitz, is as much if not more a matter of doing, rather than of thinking. And if the latter statement seems strange it is because much of the need for intensive thinking is minimized by reason of working within established doctrine.

Effective ground force training for lower levels of mobile command is already in progress at the Armor School, Fort Knox, Kentucky. It shows what can be done to couple mobile-minded thinking and the physical activity with which it must be associated. Dr. R. A. Baker, formerly of the Human Resources Research Organization (HUMRRO), devised an electronically operated terrain board for each of two activities—the Miniature Armor Battlefield (MAB) for tank combat instruction, and the Armored Cavalry Trainer (ACT) for training in reconnaissance functions. These simulate realistically the problems faced by tank and reconnaissance platoon leaders. The results of this training have been gratifying in the extreme. After only one week's experience, young trainees were taken into the field and tested in comparison with first lieutenants and captains who had had some recent practical experience in Europe. The trainees proved superior, though only slightly.

Follow-up studies showed that overseas commanders rated the simulation-trained officers as uniformly superior or outstanding; only one or two officers who had not had the training received this rating. Commanders said that they were astounded that the trainees were so tactically proficient.

This is of course a fine start, but the great need is for oncoming commanders proficient at the battalion level and higher. Simulation at these levels is obviously more complex and therefore more difficult to stage. Nevertheless, a technology that produces digital computers and simulates moon landings cannot fail to develop testing machinery with realistic environments, loaded with imponderables, for tactical problem-solving by aspiring commanders. The machinery will involve a dynamic presentation of a tactical map, with live, moving units and enemy thrusts, adjusted to scale, and accompanied by live mock-ups of the communications and computerized networks. The basic layout must of course be supported by suitable scripts, display panels (mounted perhaps in command-van mock-ups) and movies or TV clips showing battlefield maneuvering, command and staff visits and the like. With the pressures of time entering into the action, an ideal method is offered for circumventing the training obstacles of unsuitable terrain, personnel instability, and lack of actual command opportunity.

Devices to fill the needs are not easily created. An effort was made to construct a model of a battalion- and brigade-sized operation at a cost of about $250,000. Because of faulty simulation techniques, employed over the protests of experienced technicians, the effort collapsed. Nevertheless, the principles are there. They must be applied if leaders suitable for mobile command are to be developed. There seems to be no other choice.

The cost of Dr. Baker's boards run about $20,000 each and at this rate could be profitably distributed throughout the chain of military garrisons and National Guard armories. One absolute requirement is that the training personnel must be permanently assigned. A common complaint about Pentagon war-gaming is that game administrators' "teams" are forever being subjected to personnel shifts just as they become productive. The lack of extensive recorded documentation means that replacements are unable to acquire skills without a long learning period.

Simulation training should therefore be administered by civilians and behavioral scientists, reinforced by retired officers with extensive experience with mobile divisions in combat. What caused Berthier to use civilians in Napoleon's supreme headquarters applies equally here—no rotation.

When industry is charged with creating the hardware for a simulation system, costs may skyrocket unless controlled by knowledgable designers. As one scientist said, "Building a $50,000 device in six months can rapidly change to 18 years and $35 million, with 35 registered engineers, if you let the XYZ Corporation have free rein with it."

If the cost of training leaders were placed at a hundred million, how does it compare to the cost of the weapons systems that trainees may one day lose through battlefield ineptitude? Compare that cost with the cost of a hundred thousand lives, including enemy lives, that could be saved by competent blitz command skills exerted from division down to platoon. In simulation training machinery is substituted for the hundreds of personnel involved in field training who waste time and money when the trainee makes a mistake. There is also a burning requirement for "training trainers" to train others in practical fieldwork; simulation is ideal for that purpose.

The answer is plain. Command training by simulation is the cheapest and most effective national security investment. Through its use, the sought-for corps of capable tactical commanders will insure the viability of a lightning-war capability, with its consequent effective deterrent influence.

A review of the methodology of the masters can be translated into a summary of principles and techniques that could be useful as a sample list of study subjects, suitable for inclusion in courses in practical leadership.

If the aspiring leader is born with, or has acquired, the force, moral courage, and other attributes shared by the great commanders and wishes to imitate their ways he will base his command attitude on courtesy and understanding throughout all ranks and will insist on observance of these traits. His directives to his staff will be positive and comprehensive, representing his own concept of operations.

He will adopt an attitude of reasoned audacity towards the logistical and intelligence functions, depending upon a highly controllable command to overcome the deficiencies in information and supply. He will strive for perfection, but will not allow shortages to prevent a decisive strike at the opportune moment.

He will organize his headquarters so as to speed the flow of information, especially of decision-making information. His staff will be a working and harmonious team, able to separate routine from the essential and to handle both with judgment.

He will shun the methods of General Dare, never attempting to take command prerogatives from a subordinate. On the other hand, he will patiently advise inexperienced leaders, particularly when it is necessary to coordinate various elements of the command.

He will operate—and observe in person—from advance positions, using the most suitable ground or air transport, and will secure his headquarters by posting it near that of the principal effort of the operation.

He will not hesitate to employ his staff during actual operations as his eyes and ears. He will insure that the staff efforts are tactfully carried out and are primarily aimed at providing additional resources where they are needed.

He will insure that all tactical movement in the presence of the enemy is covered by adequate and timely supporting fires of artillery, by aircraft, and by other suppressing agencies.

He will tirelessly demand the highest standards of communications effectiveness by taking a close personal interest in the communications function. Where this includes ADPS he will insure that the system is organized to support the command methods and not permit the reverse.

He will see to it that key forces likely to be utilized in making initial contact with the enemy are trained by battle drills aimed at rapid and violent commitment.

Nearly all these items concern acquired skills rather than personality characteristics and therefore can be taught. One may say, "But all commanders should do that, lightning war or no." Possibly true. But with blitz techniques it is the speed of execution that is the payoff. The student trained by simulation devices where each of the principles is brought home by some need of action on his part and is coupled with a real sense of the pressure of time will be adequately imbued with blitz techniques.

Skeptics will in all probability deride the idea that a corps of mobile command adepts will in fact constitute the principal element of a deterrent to aggression, or that an overall national blitz capability will prove a deterrent, but the evidence of history supports it.

The reputation of the German generals unfortunately deterred Britain and France from intervening to check the start of World War II. Patton was the fear of the Oberkommando Wehrmacht when the Ardennes offensive was planned. "That Devil Forrest" had an influence out of proportion to the size of his command in the American Civil War. Napoleon held Europe in thrall for nearly two decades.

It could be argued that some of these men engineered the ruin of their own nations. Actually they got into trouble only when sound military advice was ignored by politicians or when there were no effective governmental curbs on the military. Had Hitler stopped with the Battle of France, what would have been the fate of Europe? Only the Little Corporal's insatiable lust for more conquest kept him from consolidating an empire.

The blitz capability must be regarded as a tool of national defense and not an instrument of aggression. It is important to remember that to be effective it is not necessary for a deterrent to intimidate the people or even the politicians of another nation. It is only necessary to give pause to its professional soldiers who advise politicians, who in turn base aggressive policies on the probability of winning. They will not risk war with a nation they know is able to respond quickly with strategic air forces and with tactical forces able to mass weaponry under experienced and skilled commanders.

An Associated Press dispatch from Taipeh, by Leonard Pratt, on January 17, 1970, states that U.S. military advisors propose to abolish several divisions of the Nationalist Chinese Army and to provide the remainder with up-to-date arms and equipment. "We're teaching them the lessons of Vietnam and Israel," says U.S. Major General R. C. Ciccolella, "and those are the lessons of firepower and mobility, not of numbers."

They are getting the idea, for a lightning-war capability is quiet and unobtrusive. It does not brandish nuclear rockets; it is comparatively inexpensive. As a national defense posture in the United States and NATO it should meet with public acceptance, if not strong support.

All in all, it is the only Alternative to Armageddon in today's feral world.

# Index